It has been widely recognized that British culture in the 1880s and 1890s was marked by a sense of irretrievable decline. *Fictions of loss in the Victorian fin de siècle* explores the ways in which that perception of loss was cast into narrative, into archetypal stories which sought to account for the culture's troubles and perhaps assuage its anxieties. Stephen Arata pays close attention to fin-de-siècle representations of three forms of decline – national, biological, and aesthetic – and reveals how late-Victorian degeneration theory was used to "explain" such decline. By examining a wide range of writers – from Kipling to Wilde, from Symonds to Conan Doyle and Stoker – Arata shows how the nation's twin obsessions with decadence and imperialism became intertwined in the thought of the period. His account offers new insights for students and scholars of the fin de siècle.

FICTIONS OF LOSS IN THE VICTORIAN FIN DE SIECLE

FICTIONS OF LOSS IN THE VICTORIAN FIN DE SIECLE

STEPHEN ARATA

University of Virginia

CAMBRIDGE
UNIVERSITY PRESS

CAMBRIDGE
UNIVERSITY PRESS

University Printing House, Cambridge CB2 8BS, United Kingdom

One Liberty Plaza, 20th Floor, New York, NY 10006, USA

477 Williamstown Road, Port Melbourne, VIC 3207, Australia

314-321, 3rd Floor, Plot 3, Splendor Forum, Jasola District Centre, New Delhi - 110025, India

79 Anson Road, #06-04/06, Singapore 079906

Cambridge University Press is part of the University of Cambridge.

It furthers the University's mission by disseminating knowledge in the pursuit of education, learning and research at the highest international levels of excellence.

www.cambridge.org
Information on this title: www.cambridge.org/9780521101271

First published 1996

A catalogue record for this publication is available from the British Library

Library of Congress Cataloging in Publication data
Arata, Stephen.
Fictions of loss in the Victorian fin de siècle / Stephen Arata.
p. cm.
Includes bibliographical references.
ISBN 0 521 56352 6
1. English fiction – 19th century – History and criticism. 2. Degeneration in literature. 3. Literature and society – Great Britain – History – 19th century. 4. Politics and literature – Great Britain – History – 19th century. 5. Regression (Civilization) in literature. 6. Loss (Psychology) in literature. 7. Social change in literature. 8. Social problems in literature. 9. Culture in literature. I. Title.
PR8978.D373A73 1996
823′.809353 – dc20 96-3489 CIP

ISBN 978-0-521-56352-9 Hardback
ISBN 978-0-521-10127-1 Paperback

For Lisa

"Happiness is this, he thought. It is this."

Contents

Acknowledgements *page* xi

Introduction Decline and fall 1

PART ONE STRANGE CASES, COMMON FATES

1 Strange cases, common fates: degeneration and fiction in the Victorian fin de siècle 11

2 The sedulous ape: atavism, professionalism, and Stevenson's *Jekyll and Hyde* 33

3 Wilde's trials: reading erotics and the erotics of reading 54

PART TWO BETWEEN THE BODY AND HISTORY

4 Men at work: from heroic friendship to male romance 79

PART THREE THE SINS OF EMPIRE

5 The Occidental tourist: Stoker and reverse colonization 107

6 Strange events and extraordinary combinations: Sherlock Holmes and the pathology of everyday life 133

7 A universal foreignness: Kipling, race, and the great tradition 151

Conclusion Modernist empires and the rise of English 178

Notes 185

Index 229

Acknowledgements

Many good people have left their marks on these pages. William Veeder has been teacher, mentor, friend since well before this project took shape; I remain blessed by his conscientiousness and his tough-mindedness. When I began writing Lawrence Rothfield asked all the right, hard questions. When I was nearly finished Herbert Tucker and Paul Cantor offered sage counsel and practical advice in equal measure. Andrea Atkin read more drafts of more chapters than anyone; through it all her good sense and critical acumen never faltered. Over the past five years I have learned much, not all of it literary, from my conversations with Jerome McGann, who seldom failed to startle me into thought. Many others took time from busy lives to read and to help me in my usually great need: Beth Sharon Ash, Sara Blair, Alison Booth, Janet Bowen, James Chandler, Marianne Conroy, Stephen Cushman, Marianne Eismann, Ellen Feldman, Jessica Feldman, Susan Fraiman, Nancy Jacobson, Michael Levenson, Eric Lott, John Morillo, Jahan Ramazani, Lisa Ruddick, Michael Sittenfeld, Sheila Sullivan, Ronald Thomas, Lynn Voskuil, Orrin N.C. Wang, and Anthony Winner.

Time to write, that most precious of commodities, was given me by way of a fellowship from the American Council of Learned Societies and a Sesquicentennial Faculty Associateship from the Center for Advanced Studies at the University of Virginia. For this generous bounty, much thanks.

An earlier version of Chapter 1 appeared in *Centuries' Ends, Narrative Means*, ed. Robert Newman (Stanford University Press, 1996). Versions of Chapters 2 and 7 first appeared in *Criticism* (1995) and *English Literature in Transition 1880–1920* (1993) (hereafter *ELT*), respectively. Portions of Chapter 5 originally appeared in *Victorian Studies* (1990). Permission to reprint is gratefully acknowledged.

It seems almost impertinent to thank my wife, Lisa Goff, for bearing with such patience and good humor this sometimes unwelcome lodger in our home. My sense of what I owe her is as deeply felt as it is impossible to express. This book may be about loss, but my life with her has been only gain.

INTRODUCTION

Decline and fall

This is a book about loss and the stories it generates. In the last years of the nineteenth century English writing was especially rich in such stories. Across disciplines and genres are heard the same anxieties concerning the collapse of culture, the weakening of national might, the possibly fatal decay – physical, moral, spiritual, creative – of the Anglo-Saxon "race" as a whole. A sense of abiding loss is familiar enough in many periods (our own included), but the idioms used to express that sense will always be historically specific. So too will be the ways in which such perceptions are cast into narrative, into stories a culture tells itself in order to account for its troubles and perhaps assuage its anxieties.

Though I do not hesitate to draw in works from other disciplines, my primary texts in this study are widely read fictional narratives of the 1880s and 90s. A nation, or any imagined community, is held together in part by the stories it generates about itself. We are perhaps more familiar with fictions that tell of a people's origins, cast in the form of epic or myth: Aeneas founding Rome, or Brutus Albion. Heroic narratives like these are instrumental in the creation and maintenance of collective identities – and one thinks of their proliferation throughout the nineteenth century – but nations also sustain themselves in literally more prosaic ways. We need not unreservedly assent to Georg Lukács's claim that novels are epics for a fallen age in order to maintain, along with Lukács, that fictional prose narrative is the preeminent aesthetic form through which modern communities in the West make and remake themselves.[1] This being the case, we need to account for the decidedly eschatological impulse pervading so much late-Victorian fiction. Heroic narratives of foundation give way to stories of the end time. It may be, as contemporary commentators seldom tired of iterating, that the ends of centuries inevitably breed such dark fantasies. To paraphrase Oscar Wilde, fin de siècle always feels like fin du globe. It may also be, as Frank Kermode has shown, that the Victorian fin de siècle reenacts patterns of apocalyptic yearning that reach back many centuries.[2] Yet it is undeniably the case that the late Victorians enact their own peculiar patterns, speak their own dialect.

This study focusses on fin-de-siècle representations of three forms of decline: national, biological, aesthetic. As I argue throughout, in late-Victorian thought these terms often entailed one another, so that a discussion of any one of them led to consideration of the other two. Nation, body, art: it seemed to many that their respective declines were mutually implicated. Under these broad headings were arrayed a variety of more specific (though still unwieldy) anxieties, including but not limited to the retrenchment of empire, the spread of urban slums, the growth of "criminal" classes, the proliferation of "deviant" sexualities, the rise of decadent art, and even the demise of the three-decker novel. As John Stokes points out, "lumping things together" is a habit of mind characteristic of the Victorian fin de siècle.[3] Indeed, the conviction that a wide variety of seemingly disparate phenomena were, on some deep level, connected was one of the energizing fictions of the period.

Of the social vocabularies available to fin-de-siècle writers to articulate their sense of decline, this book attends most closely to those generated by the pseudo-science of degeneration theory. Like its better-documented counterpart, "progress," "degeneration" was a term no late-Victorian thinker could do without. As a critical tool, its value coincided with its reach. Recent works by Daniel Pick, William Greenslade, and Sander Gilman have shown how degeneration theory enabled middle-class commentators to forge functional links among manifestly unlike phenomena.[4] (An 1894 study, for instance, gathered under this one critical paradigm discussions of financial institutions, the development of landed property, dinosaurs, crayfish, rudimentary organs in mammals, and the decline of empires.[5]) Even in less extreme usages, degeneration theory permitted writers to move easily through a wide range of topics.

Invariably, the topics addressed were ones that from a middle-class perspective gave most cause for alarm. The class allegiances of degeneration theory are always highly visible: as Greenslade puts it, degenerationism was "an enabling strategy by which the conventional and respectable classes could justify and articulate their hostility to the deviant, the diseased and the subversive."[6] From its modern beginnings in the 1850s in the work of Benedict-Augustin Morel, the study of degeneration was at once a branch of biology and a form of cultural criticism undertaken by a beleaguered bourgoisie. Morel, a clinical psychiatrist specializing in the study of cretinism, wanted to develop criteria by which to identify the degenerate subject, but he placed this endeavor within a wider concern for the fate of the nation. Degeneracy afflicted the individual, but its supposed causes (poverty, malnutrition, prostitution, crime, alcoholism, pollution) and effects (sterility, madness, imbecility, suicide, revolution) reached deep into the collective life of the people. At every point the biological model of the degenerate provided ways to theorize social decay.

This protean quality brings its own problems, of course. Like the great totalizing vocabularies associated with the names of Hegel, Darwin, Marx, and Freud, the vocabulary of degeneration so saturated Western consciousness in the fin de siècle that tracking it can be difficult.[7] "Knowledge" about degeneracy quickly achieved the status of popular wisdom, available for use by a wide variety of non-specialists. One need not have studied, or even have read, the works of pathologists or clinicians in order to "know" what degeneracy looked like or what it entailed. This assimilation into the vernacular of a technical discourse was aided by the ease with which degeneration mapped onto older paradigms of decline and fall from the Old Testament onward. Even within scientific communities, moreover, significant conceptual slippages occurred, with little agreement as to proper methods or objects of study. This was especially the case in Great Britain, where the study of degeneration was not organized around commanding figures like Morel in France or Cesare Lombroso in Italy. The relative absence of sharply defined schools of thought in Britain was a further reason that degeneration "theory" there was less a coherent system than a form of common sense.

It is as a form of common sense that I approach the various invocations of degeneration in the period. Nothing like scientific or methodological rigor can be said to structure them. As Antonio Gramsci reminds us, one strength of common sense is that it "cannot be reduced to unity and coherence" and thus can accommodate conceptual contradictions that might otherwise prove disabling.[8] Sometimes degenerative paradigms were brought forward consciously and clearly, as when London newspapers used Max Nordau's *Degeneration* (1895) to help "explain" the accusations brought against Oscar Wilde. Other times those paradigms pervade the background, giving texture and lending resonance to critical lamentations over perceived losses of various kinds. My object has not been to bring these and other instances into some kind of ultimate coherence – impossible in any case – but rather to indicate the differing ways in which a small cluster of basic tropes could be articulated and deployed.

Unsystematic and commonsensical as it was, knowledge about degeneration was nevertheless considered to be the purlieu of the trained specialist. The Victorian fin de siècle is the moment of full emergence for a figure I call the "professional reader," the man (and it is invariably a man) whose training allows him to extract "useful" meaning from a welter of often confusing signs. A vigorous interest in hermeneutic method – specifically, in the value of close reading – links together practitioners from a variety of disciplines: medicine, psychiatry, criminology, sociology, anthropology, and literary criticism among others. These are fields whose status as professional disciplines was being consolidated during this period, so perhaps it is not surprising that they share a desire for methodological rigor. As the example of Freud and psychoanalysis shows clearly, this interest in close reading grows in part from a faith in interpretation as a form of therapy, a way of mastering troubles by coaxing meaningful pattern out of unruly experience. The classic detective story, as exemplified by Doyle's Sherlock Holmes stories, also relies heavily on this faith. As the following chapters will show, the professional man is a recurring figure of authority in late-Victorian fiction. The losses felt at century's end are finally inseparable from the interpretive paradigms used to name them, while those paradigms in turn cannot be understood apart from the professional critics who developed and deployed them.

As I mentioned, the key coordinates of my study are works of popular fiction. I have thus omitted from consideration several writers – Hardy, Gissing, Butler, Conrad come most quickly to mind – who frequently figure in discussions of late-Victorian loss and angst. If in the modern world literature is invested, as Fredric Jameson argues, with "the function of inventing imaginary or formal 'solutions' to unresolvable social contradictions," much more of that kind of cultural work goes on in popular fiction than is generally acknowledged.[9] As I argue, such texts were important disseminators of "knowledge" about degeneracy. A form of popular wisdom, degeneration theory received many of its most compelling articulations in the highly commonsensical modes of popular fiction. Indeed, to a greater extent than on the Continent, public discussion in Britain about social problems was carried on through the medium of mass market texts. That their strivings to achieve satisfying solutions never wholly succeed constitutes their interest and much of their value. *Dracula* for instance addresses, in displaced form, the issue of British imperial decline while also charting a variety of paths by which, in fantasy, that decline may be reversed or transcended. That the "solutions" Stoker's novel offers are finally implausible, self-contradictory, or mutually inconsistent only sharpens our sense of the (perhaps) irresolvable social problems evoked.

In giving extended attention to popular texts, I take issue with at least one tenet of our own popular wisdom, namely that, even at its best, such fiction does no more than cheerfully reproduce dominant ideologies. As the citations throughout the following chapters abundantly indicate, the last decade has seen fin-de-siècle popular fiction become the object of extended and fruitful critical inquiry. Yet in most accounts the value of such texts is still said to lie in their "transparency," the way they offer "direct access to a bedrock of ideology or myth."[10] While this claim is doubtless true of many popular texts (as well as of many works of high culture), as a general rule it needs qualifying. Indeed, the narratives I examine are notable for the sophistication with which they give shape and voice to contemporary problems, as well as for the ways in which they attempt to resist dominant ideological structures.

A few final words about the form and scope of this book. Its tripartite structure was suggested by a line in Holbrook Jackson's groundbreaking study of the fin de siècle, *The Eighteen Nineties* (1913). Looking back at the period, Jackson argued that the 1890s split into halves, divided neatly at mid-decade by Oscar Wilde's trial and conviction. The first half, Jackson wrote, was "remarkable for a literary and artistic renaissance, degenerating into decadence; the second for a new sense of patriotism degenerating into jingoism."[11] As a rough indication of the way the period felt to contemporaries, this seems accurate enough. Jackson was a smart and sympathetic critic of the fin de siècle, and in his work we can already sense scare quotes surrounding his use of terms like "degeneracy." Indeed, Jackson everywhere prompts us to question the comfortable symmetry of his formulation, with its familiar rhythms of alternating renaissance and decay.

Just as important, though, he also invites us to consider the *relation* between the halves of his formula, to ask whether "decadence" and "jingoism" are mutually implicated rather than simply opposing terms. For the most part, though, subsequent critics have declined his invitation. As Stokes rightly notes, where Jackson "looked for synchronic interaction" among the period's many facets, later readers have usually "isolated the discrete thread, the significant 'tendency'," and thus explained the whole by the part.[12] The fin de siècle may have enjoyed lumping things together, but twentieth-century criticism has, for good or ill, tended to separate things out.

While the present study cannot pretend to anything like Jackson's scope, it does work to bring seemingly unlike thinkers into productive conversation. Indeed, this book was originally motivated by a desire to bring within the same critical frame such disparate writers as Wilde and Kipling, Nordau and Stevenson, Symonds and Haggard, Doyle and Stoker. In the most general sense, I wanted to see what connections could be forged between fin-de-siècle "decadence" and "jingoism." One link was immediately apparent: both terms were used by medical specialists and cultural critics alike to designate forms of degeneracy. Yet it also became clear that, from the perspective of contemporary observers, jingoist imperialism seemed to have been called into existence by decadence, as a counterweight to aesthetic excess. In other words, there is compelling reason to read, say, Kipling alongside Wilde, since the former's ethos of masculinist imperial adventure was in large part a response to the perceived dangers of Wildean aestheticism. At the same time, as works like *The Light that Failed* and Haggard's *She* reveal, masculinist adventure was itself thoroughly "infected" by decadent (and therefore "degenerative") paradigms.

Since this study examines tropes of degeneration, and since late-Victorian degenerationism was obsessed with the decay of organisms both individual and collective, "body" and "nation" finally seemed more appropriate and more flexible terms to use than Jackson's "decadence" and "jingoism." Loosely speaking, Chapters 1, 2, and 3 attend more closely to questions of the body, Chapters 5, 6, and 7 to the nation, with Chapter 4 serving as a pivot between the two sets of three chapters. Yet, as the following pages will amply show, anxieties about the decay of the individual body were inseparable from anxieties about the decay of the collective "body" figured in national or racial terms.

Finally, I should stress that this book does not attempt to determine whether British society was declining "in fact" during this period, nor does it offer criteria by which such a determination could be made.[13] While the works I examine address real and pressing historical problems, my interest is finally in the varying ways in which "history" becomes textually encoded. I approach these texts as forms of "symbolic action" in Kenneth Burke's sense. According to Burke, literary works are "answers to questions posed by the situation in which they arose." Yet they are never "merely answers, they are *strategic* answers, *stylized* answers."[14] Imaginative works are not timeless accounts of universal human concerns, nor as artifacts are they wholly self-consuming or self-reflexive. In however displaced or attenuated a manner, they are human responses to specific human situations, responses necessarily articulated in the materials and idioms of the moment. Yet in their "adopting of...strategies for the encompassing of situations," works of imagination remake those situations. Their relation to history is always asymptotic. "The situations are real," Burke writes, just as "the strategies for handling them have public content," yet the literary work (fiction or nonfiction) is unavoidably "false" in so far as it constitutes a "stylized" response.[15] In the end this is no less true of a professedly factual work like J. A. Froude's treatise on empire, *Oceana*, than it is of Bram Stoker's delirious recasting of imperial history as Gothic fantasy in *Dracula*. Each is, in Burke's happy phrase, the "dancing of an attitude."[16]

PART ONE

Strange cases, common fates

CHAPTER I

Strange cases, common fates: degeneration and fiction in the Victorian fin de siècle

HOOLIGANS AND FLESHLY POETS

To begin, consider two essays written by the Scottish literary journalist Robert Buchanan. Both invoke degeneration in order to condemn a popular author, though the authors condemned could hardly be less alike. In December 1899 Buchanan attacked Rudyard Kipling in "The Voice of the Hooligan," inaugurating a by now familiar line of Kipling criticism. "The Voice of the Hooligan" linked Kipling's literary ascendancy with the rise of militant jingoism and lamented the barbarizing effects of both on British culture. Kipling's "exaltation to a position of almost unexampled popularity," Buchanan argued, could be accounted for only by the fact that "in his single person [he] adumbrates...all that is most deplorable, all that is most retrograde and savage, in the restless and uninstructed Hooliganism of the time."[1] Late-Victorian fears of the "hooligan" drew heavily on middle-class portrayals of the urban poor as a degenerate race whose physical and psychological health had been irreparably damaged by modern city life.[2] Buchanan extends this category to include those portions of the bourgeoisie whose appetites had likewise been brutalized by contemporary conditions. For Buchanan, the hooligan was the type of the modern degenerate, Kipling its most dangerous spokesman. His fiction pandered to "whatever is basest and most brutal" in modern man, quickening the decline of a once-great English people.[3]

Buchanan, when he is remembered, is sometimes remembered for this essay, though his name is more often linked with a piece published twenty-eight years previous to it. In 1871, under the pseudonym Thomas Maitland, he attacked Dante Gabriel Rossetti in "The Fleshly School of Poetry," thereby earning himself some notoriety among readers of Victorian verse. Where Kipling offended with his violence and vulgarity, Rossetti alarmed with his sensualism and "intellectual hermaphroditism." The vocabulary of degeneration again comes into play, this time in connection with what Buchanan thinks of as Rossetti's perverse addiction to the senses and his confounding of gender categories. Fleshly poets are unnatural men, the critic argues. To support this contention, he reads Rossetti's artistic productions as symptoms which betray the pathological deviations of the artist's diseased body. In Rossetti's painting and poetry there is visible

> the same thinness and transparence of design, the same combination of the simple and the grotesque, the same morbid deviation from healthy forms of life, the same sense of weary, wasting, yet exquisite sensuality; nothing virile, nothing tender, nothing completely sane; a superfluity of extreme sensibility, of delight in beautiful forms, hues, and tints, and a deep-seated indifference to...all the thunderous stress of life, and all the straining storm of speculation.[4]

This is diagnosis rather than analysis, and so it is meant to be. In such critical discourse the question, as Barbara Spackman suggests, becomes "not *who* produced a text but *what* – what disease, what atavistic deformity, what hereditary fault."[5] The disease of the fleshly poet finds its counterpart in the disease of the fleshly poem, with body and text each displaying the same telltale "symptoms." Turn where we will in his poetry, Buchanan says, we find only Rossetti and his "sickness." No one of his poems is "quite separable from the displeasing identity of its composer," who cannot help but put "the most secret mysteries" of his being on display in "shameless nakedness."[6] In Kipling too Buchanan finds the same impulse to self-exposure, the same aversion to "anything that demands a moment's thought or a moment's attention," the same uncontrollable desire for sensual gratification, in this case the gratification associated with inflicting punishment, exerting mastery, or indulging brutal instincts.[7]

Despite their differences – and it is difficult to imagine figures more unlike than Rossetti and Kipling – these two writers are in Buchanan's view indicative of larger troubling trends in the culture. While, as forms of "deviance," fleshliness and hooliganism appear to have little in common, they represent for him the two end points at which a debased modernity has arrived. A similar claim is made by Arthur Waugh in his alarmist *Yellow Book* essay of 1894, "Reticence in Literature," where the "two excesses" into which modern English writing has fallen are further coded by gender: "on the one hand, the excess prompted by effeminacy – that is to say, by the want of restraint which starts from enervated sensation; and, on the other, the excess which results from a certain brutal virility, which proceeds from coarse familiarity with indulgence."[8]

This yoking together of seemingly distinct forms of "excess" was common practice among social critics. The title of Hugh E. M. Stutfield's 1895 essay, "Tommyrotics," economically combines the condemnatory terms "neurotic" and "erotic" (both referring to an effeminized sensualism) with Kipling's hooligan soldier Tommy Atkins to create a single figure of modern degeneracy.[9] What is usually occluded in such diatribes, though, are the specific social conditions that encouraged this yoking together. If fleshly poets and hooligans inevitably sprang to mind together, that was in part because the former seemed to have created the latter. The hooligan's masculine assertiveness was widely seen as a conscious reaction against the perceived effeminacy of contemporary life. Writing in 1888, William Watson suggested that the very existence of Rider Haggard could be blamed on the "enervated" writers preceding him.[10] But in reacting against one form of degeneracy, the hooligan simply fell into another. Avoiding effeminacy, he became barbarous instead. As William Greenslade points out, bourgeois "ambivalence towards the hooligan reflected the subtle ideological role he had come to perform."[11] A stick to beat decadents with, he was himself cause for anxiety among middle-class social critics. Indeed, the class allegiances of writers like Buchanan, Waugh, Stutfield, and Watson are always plainly in view. For them, the "want of restraint" shown by hooligans and sensualists alike finally indicated a fatal falling away (though in different directions) from bourgeois norms of proper behavior.

Falling away; swerving; deviating; declining: that these metaphors so thoroughly saturate late-Victorian criticism is one indication of the influence exerted by degenerative models. In "The Fleshly School of Poetry" Buchanan invokes modern degeneration theory's founding text, Benedict-Augustin Morel's *Traité des dégénérences* (1857), when he calls Rossetti's writerly excesses "morbid deviation[s] from healthy forms of life." Whether Buchanan actually read Morel is irrelevant; he probably did not. Nor did he need to, since by the 1870s Morel's definition of degeneration as "a morbid deviation from an original type" had long since passed into public usage on both sides of the Channel.[12] The word "morbid" was itself among the most highly charged and loosely defined critical terms of the final quarter of the century.[13] Indeed, the most striking feature of Buchanan's essays is the unself-conscious and "untheoretical" way they appropriate vocabularies of degeneration to make their points. Buchanan gives no indication that he might be working with anything other than widely understood paradigms, unneedful of further explication or justification. Much of the condemnatory power of the essays arises precisely from Buchanan's belief that he is merely speaking the language of common sense.

For Buchanan, as for Waugh and Stutfield, bad writing has become a matter of biology. The degenerate artwork becomes the symptom and sign of its author's pathology. Public danger also lurks in such texts. According to Buchanan, degenerate art is itself an instrument of contagion, "diligently spreading the seeds of disease broadcast wherever [it is] read and understood."[14] Or is it rather, Buchanan worries, that the seeds of degeneration, already sown in the culture, simply await a fertilizing influence? Does the deviant artwork call forth an answering echo, awaken a degeneracy lying dormant in the public body? If so, then Rossetti and Kipling are less the causes of degeneracy's spread than its catalysts. Rossetti's hypersensualism, Kipling's libidinous Hooliganism, Buchanan suggests with unease, find their counterparts within society at large. The problem of degeneration moves from the spasms of single bodies to the decay of the body politic and back again, and in attempting to negotiate these exchanges Buchanan's essays generate much frantic energy. What begin as excoriations of deviant individuals quickly become laments for the decline of civilization as a whole. The degenerate artist, by definition one who has fallen away from the common level of men, is paradoxically also Representative Man, the type of the modern age. In between artist and culture stands the degenerate text, at once symptomatic, infectious, and disturbingly mimetic.

DEGENERATION AND COMMON SENSE

Buchanan's two essays help map out our terrain. He identifies three kinds of "morbid deviation," which are to his mind mutually implicated. The deviations are biological: both Rossetti and Kipling are victims of unspecified nervous disorders that make them write as they do. They are social: fleshliness and hooliganism name larger trends within the culture which depart from healthy forms of public life. And they are aesthetic: Rossetti's poetry perverts Romantic sensibility while Kipling's fiction perverts the standards of classical realism. Also running through both essays is a largely inchoate critique of modernity itself as a kind of degeneracy.

I have situated Buchanan's essays alongside a body of knowledge I am calling "degeneration theory," but it is important to be clear about what is involved here. Beginning at mid-century the study of degeneration occupied researchers across a number of scientific and humanistic disciplines. Much "technical" literature was produced on the subject, most notably in the fields of cellular biology, clinical psychiatry, and criminology. As the distances separating those three fields suggest, however, "degeneration" had no single fixed meaning or material referent. Indeed, meaning and referent notoriously changed according to the type of research being done. Even within disciplines there were disagreements about what the term meant and how it ought to be studied.[15]

At the most general level, nearly everyone accepted Morel's definition of degeneration as a morbid deviation from an original and thus normative type. This formulation begged a number of questions (How did one define a type? What constituted deviation? How were morbid changes distinguished from healthy?), but it also proved highly portable. As a critical designation, degeneration moved with often disconcerting fluidity through a broad range of nineteenth-century intellectual disciplines. With it, theorists could trace the vicissitudes of single-celled organisms, map the genealogies of outworn families, or reveal the fate of nations. They could account for deviations in literary form or explain the behavior of crowds. The term became a component of debates over the growth of cities, the expansion of empire, the rise of criminal classes, the growth of mass culture, and the development of socialist and anarchist philosophies, not to mention the blossoming of decadent art. It also provided ways to make connections among these disparate phenomena. As Robert Nye notes, by the 1880s degeneration theory "served to provide a continuum between biological and social thought that makes nonsense of the usual efforts to distinguish between them, and was so culturally useful that it could explain persuasively all the pathologies from which the nation suffered."[16] Indeed, the power of the degenerative model rested largely in the way it linked the private with the collective, the individual life with the life of the people. Tying physical maladies, psychological disorders, and social disturbances together in a vast analogical universe, degeneration became, in Daniel Pick's apt phrasing, "the condition of conditions, the ultimate signifier of pathology."[17]

As such diversity implies, while allusions to degeneration abound in the latter half of the century, at no point did its "theory" possess anything resembling a coherent terminology or rational methodology. Such incoherence nevertheless did not inhibit – indeed probably spurred – the avalanche of treatises that appeared between 1850 and the turn of the century. That same incoherence also made it easier for "knowledge" about degeneration to be assimilated into the vocabularies of everyday life. As a model for the movements across time of individuals or groups, degeneration could also be mapped onto a variety of familiar narrative models of decline and fall.[18] Tropes of degeneration were easily appropriated for use by non-specialists. As Buchanan's example suggests, one need not have studied the subject in order to cash in on the insights it appeared to offer.

Knowledge about degeneration thus became a form of "common sense" as Antonio Gramsci defines it. In Gramsci's formulation, common sense is "the 'folklore' of philosophy," or that "conception of the world which is uncritically absorbed by the various social and cultural environments in which the moral individuality of the average man is developed."[19] Like folklore, common sense is the repository of a "wisdom" which, though powerful and in many ways enabling, is "not critical and coherent but disjointed and episodic" (325). As a "generic form of thought common to a particular period," common sense is "diffuse, unco-ordinated," lacking the rigor and coherence associated with true philosophical or scientific inquiry (331–32). (As Gramsci notes, and as the "scientific" study of degeneration bears out, science too can be a locus of common sense.) In uses such as Buchanan's, knowledge about degeneration is indeed deployed "disjointedly," though it is no less functional for all that.

For common sense is never simply a form of blindness. Inhering in its inchoate formulations is what Gramsci calls "good sense." The perceptions and responses that together make up a common sense "conception of the world" may be fragmented, diffuse, and therefore uncritical, but that does not necessarily make them false (327–28, 346). In other words, common sense may point toward pressing historical circumstances without being able accurately to name or even to recognize them. For Gramsci, the "spontaneous philosophy" of a given social group always involves a misrecognition of historical phenomena, yet it also serves to make those phenomena visible for more critical scrutiny. The contemporary problems that critics tried to address were real enough, even as the attempts themselves were reductive, misleading, and often regrettable. A charitable reading of Buchanan's essay on Kipling, for example, would see in it a sincere though muddled attempt to elucidate the connections between domestic class conflict and imperial ideology, a project taken up more coherently by Lenin a generation later. For many late-Victorian writers, degeneration helped to name a plethora of disturbances characteristic of modernity in the West. If their namings were finally misnamings, they still help us identify the disturbances.

Degeneration theory was one of many forms that bourgeois common sense took in Britain in the last half of the nineteenth century. Like other forms of common sense, it readily betrays its class allegiances. As all historians of the subject point out, the study of degeneration was invariably put in the service of an empowered middle class. It was an effective means of "othering" large groups of people by marking them as deviant, criminal, psychotic, defective, simple, hysterical, diseased, primitive, regressive, or just dangerous. As Greenslade correctly points out, degenerationism effectively "naturalises…class fear into a biological fact."[20] Yet we should be wary of the urge to identify a "politics" of degeneration. While it is true that the study of degeneration buttressed a wide range of repressive practices, it also provided support for various kinds of social activism. Everyone agreed, for instance, that degeneration was intimately linked to poverty and urban blight, but that knowledge did not entail any particular political program. In testimony given before the British Parliament's Interdepartmental Committee on Physical Deterioration (1904), reformists and reactionaries cited the work of pathologists with equal fervor. The committee, charged with investigating "the causes and indications of degeneracy in certain classes of the community, and the means by which it may be arrested," concluded that degeneration resulted not from moral turpitude or an unfortunate gene pool but from poor housing, bad food, polluted air, and inadequate hygiene.[21] Campaigns to sterilize the poor invoked the specter of the degenerate subject; so did movements for better housing, more humane labor laws, and improved medical care. These polarized responses do not negate the claim that degeneration is a class-specific discourse, since the kinds of philanthropy and reform suggested are themselves grounded in middle-class ideology. Nevertheless, we should resist the temptation to posit a monolithic patriarchy which subjugates all others (also monolithically conceived) by means of oppressive discourses. As the recent work of Nye, Pick, Spackman, and Greenslade has shown most convincingly, the many and disparate situations in which such discourses could be invoked indicate just how numerous were the "positions" from which middle-class critics could speak. The uses of degeneration theory provide a striking instance of Foucault's power/knowledge nexus, but (as Foucault's work everywhere makes clear) the potential political deployments of knowledge are many and varied. If "knowledge is not made for understanding" but "for cutting," as he claims, it can nonetheless cut in several directions.[22]

Such fractures and discontinuities become most evident as we move away from technical discussions of degeneration and toward its myriad invocations in the popular realm. Popular usage could on occasion be highly informed – the works of Morel, Lombroso, Nordau, Maudsley, and others were widely known and often cited – yet they were more often disjointed. Nevertheless, a relatively small cluster of issues was continually worried over by nearly everyone who invoked degeneration and its paradigms. As Buchanan's essays suggest, fears about the breakdown of individual identities were imbricated on fears about an ongoing and perhaps irreversible social decline. Cutting across both sets of anxieties were concerns about the proper functions of art in a well-ordered and healthy society.

That last issue – the proper social functions of art – turns out to be central to nearly all late-Victorian invocations of degeneration. Recent studies of degenerationist discourses have with good reason tended to stress how they were used to shape public discussion of disruptive social issues, from urban poverty to gender relations to agricultural decay to foreign trade deficits to Home Rule. Yet it is also striking how eagerly degenerationists allowed themselves to become entangled in what have to be considered as forms of literary criticism. There are several reasons for this. On one level, literary works were often brought forward as evidence of this or that type of degenerative illness (as Buchanan brings forward Rossetti and Kipling), though literature as a whole was, paradoxically, praised for its potentially therapeutic effects. The idea that artistic genius was closely allied to both criminality and to forms of mental illness was given wide currency by Lombroso's 1888 *L'uomo di genio* (translated as *The Man of Genius* by Havelock Ellis in 1891), J. F. Nisbet's *The Insanity of Genius* (1891), and the second edition of Francis Galton's *Hereditary Genius* (1892).[23] Degeneration theorists from Morel through Maudsley, Lombroso, and Nordau (himself a novelist) tended to view imaginative writing as the preeminent human activity while also considering it essentially pathological in nature.

To yoke imagination to disease is of course to invoke a model of literary activity with a long and complex history. Yet in many cases that model gains a new biological specificity in the last half of the nineteenth century. A brief comparison clarifies the difference. When in "The Decadent Movement in Literature" (1893) Arthur Symons notes that the "representative literature of to-day, interesting, beautiful, novel as it is, is really a new and beautiful and interesting disease," he is, despite his emphasis on novelty, in fact pointing out the continuities between his own historical moment and earlier epochs of "decadence." Contemporary literature "has all the qualities that mark the end of great periods, the qualities that we find in the Greek, the Latin, decadence."[24] By contrast, when in *Degeneration* (1895) Nordau argues that Pre-Raphaelite poets suffer from retinal irregularities that prevent them from seeing the world as it really is, and that such malformations are due to nervous exhaustion brought on by the stress of modern life, he is making a new kind of argument – one grounded, as Symons's is not, in a (mis)understanding of biology and genetics – about the novelty of modern literature.

Degenerationists became enmeshed in aesthetics in another way. Works of literature offered models of interpretative procedure that theorists were quick to appropriate in their attempts to decipher degeneration's complex signs. Because degenerative illness presented itself to the interested observer as a series of marks and symptoms to be interpreted, certain aggressive forms of reading were required to make sense of the evidence. The text to be read took many shapes – bodies, cells, cultures, nations, races, historical periods, as well as works of literature. Yet all were open to interpretation in similar ways and according to similar protocols. In any case, such texts had to be properly read, had in fact to be vigorously *over*-read, before their damaging or therapeutic effects were revealed. From its beginnings, degeneration theory identified such vigorous overreading as the *sine qua non* of the discipline. As Greenslade puts it, pathologists "fostered a sense that what might really be happening...lay somehow hidden, buried from sight, yet somehow graspable through patient observation of the contours of the surface."[25] This insistence on hermeneutic method – a method, moreover, associated with a specific emerging professional class, in this case physicians – links degeneration theory to other manifestations of the same impulse in the period, most notably Freudian psychoanalysis as well as nascent forms of professional literary criticism. The commitment to overreading in turn is the ground for what Allon White calls "symptomatic reading," which is so prevalent a feature of nearly all fin-de-siècle interpretative discourses.[26] If imaginative writing was often figured as a product of disease, that disease was made visible through the hermeneutic expertise of the professional critic, whose own writing was untainted by the various pathologies afflicting the artist.

The remainder of this chapter considers more closely the nature of that hermeneutic expertise, since the diagnoses of biological, cultural, and aesthetic deviance offered by degenerationists were inseparable from the interpretive paradigms in which they were couched.

STIGMATA AND "STRONG REPRESENTATION"

According to Morel, the degenerate subject was himself a text to be read, since he displayed the signs of his condition written unmistakably on his body. The droop of a lip, the curve of an ear, the twitchings of a hand all seemed to signify univocally, attesting to pathology. Morel labelled these marks "stigmata," another of his lasting contributions to the lexicon of the later nineteenth century. His successors developed increasingly elaborate taxonomies designed to classify and collate all possible combinations of these signs. The last half of Eugene Talbot's widely read handbook, *Degeneracy: Its Causes, Signs, and Results* (1898), for example, is taken up with detailed instructions on how to identify "The Degenerate Cranium," "The Degenerate Face and Nose," "Degeneracy of the Lip, Palate, Eye, and Ear," "The Degenerate Teeth and Jaw," and so on.[27] The psychiatrist Henry Maudsley, the most important English theorist of degeneration, firmly and succinctly tied sign to essence. "Without doubt," he wrote, "the character of every mind is written in the features, gestures, gait, and carriage of the body, and will be read there when, if ever, the extremely fine and difficult language is fully and accurately learnt."[28] As scientific methods became ever more sophisticated, the author of a popular handbook on degeneration confidently asserted, the body of the criminal deviant would be recognized for what it was, a mere "sign-board denoting the rottenness within."[29]

In postulating this correspondence between outer sign and inner being, degenerationists revealed their debt to older semiotic systems like physiognomy and phrenology. Yet to a greater extent than these earlier "sciences," degeneration theory made apparent, often unwittingly, the troubling multivalence of bodily signs. Indeed, in practice the difficulty and not the ease of accurate interpretation was more likely to be apparent. "Hitherto I had noticed the backs of his hands as they lay on his knees in the firelight, and...I could not help but notice that they were rather coarse – broad, with squat fingers. Strange to say, there were hairs in the centre of the palm."[30] Jonathan Harker's initial description of Count Dracula – rank breath, protruding teeth and brow, scanty hair, pointed ears, abnormally thick eyebrows, pale skin, in addition to the squat fingers and hairy palms – would have placed him for Bram Stoker's first readers within degeneracy's purlieu. Indeed, the Count's outward appearance does correspond to a "rottenness within." Yet it is a rottenness that long goes undetected, despite the vampire's penchant for walking openly "through the crowded streets of your mighty London." Even to eyes as practiced as Professor Van Helsing's in the novel, Dracula is not immediately recognizable as a public threat, and much narrative energy is expended in determining where exactly on the spectrum of deviance "Nordau and Lombroso" – those two prominent theorists of degeneration – "would... classify him."[31]

As Van Helsing's experience suggests, despite claims that the body's stigmata spoke univocally, degeneracy's signifiers could in fact be notoriously hard to interpret. Only the trained professional observer could make sure distinctions between the truly healthy man and what Robert Reid

Rentoul labelled the "faker." The faker had learned to mask the outward signs of his condition, to dissemble with his very body. To all appearance unmarked, at times "crafty and cunning enough to avoid breaking the law," the faker "act[ed] the part of the normal man or woman" even while harboring degeneracy's seeds within. The "ill-defined case of degeneracy" – telling adjective, that – was "by far the most dangerous," Rentoul claims, because it made policing difficult and because it blurred the distinction between health and sickness. "The schoolmaster, the tailor, the parent" all might be diseased without anyone – even, sometimes, the victim – recognizing the fact.[32]

Morel had acknowledged the impossibility of reducing degeneracy to its physical signs. What he called "internal differences" also came prominently into play. These encompassed not just abnormalities of the body's interior – tissues, organs, nerves, skeleton – but also breakdowns in one's emotional or intellectual or moral being.[33] Such "mental stigmata" were by definition inaccessible to outside observers, locked away in the body's interior or in the even more remote processes of the psyche. Indeed, in the last analysis degeneracy was not reducible to any combination of its signs, whether they were outward and visible or inward and hidden. It was no accident that Morel lighted on the word "stigmata" to describe these phenomena, nor that the term enjoyed such wide currency among his successors. Like the marks left on the religious believer, degeneracy's stigmata were manifestations of an essence which was beyond human sense perception. Degeneration touched the body, saturated and transfigured it, but the thing itself could be located nowhere. It was never equivalent to any one of its symptoms, but was always located just beyond whatever mark was being interrogated. Degenerative insanity was "a fixed fact...more potent than all theories," according to W. W. Godding, yet "it will elude your most careful scrutiny with scalpel and microscope."[34] The body was a text inscribed with degeneracy's runes, a text which, in its separate parts or as a whole, might be deceptive, overdetermined, or even illegible, a text that would give up its truths only under the pressure of a professional scrutiny.

If the study of degeneration encouraged certain aggressive forms of reading, it also associated itself with equally aggressive modes of writing. As a rule, degenerationists traded in what Alexander Welsh has called "strong representations": a making visible through narrative of what cannot be directly perceived.[35] Like professionals in other disciplines – the geologist who excavates the story of creation from the fossil record, or the barrister who persuades a jury that his account of a crime is accurate – the clinical psychiatrist worked to construct a compelling and "truthful" portrayal from an array of mute and often ambiguous facts.

Like the barrister, too, degenerationists were centrally concerned with revealing "character." In one sense, their representations made character and disease synonymous. Because degeneration inevitably manifested itself in even the smallest gesture, no aspect of one's being could be considered apart from the disease. Degenerationists thus continually found themselves trying to untangle thickets of motive, intention, will, and desire as they related to a self conditioned by countless social forces. This is territory traditionally occupied by the realist novel, which has almost always taken its most vital task to be the examination of individual character within a specific cultural milieu. (Welsh lists the High Victorian novel among the influential purveyors of strong representations.) Sounding uncommonly like George Eliot, Eugene Talbot warned his fellow scientists that the ultimate significance of a characterological trait could be determined only after a series of complex evaluations of the entire organism within its physical environment.[36]

Given such strictures, it comes as no surprise that degenerationists availed themselves of novelistic techniques associated with High Victorian realism.[37] Indeed, for many the realist novel became the normative "type" against which later literary "morbid deviations" were measured. In appropriating the discursive strategies of realist novelists, critics – and here Nordau is the best example – implicitly set their own critical discourse in opposition to the various "diseases" of much fin-de-siècle literature.

At the center of these narrative strategies was a radical historicizing of character. Because degenerative disease revealed itself not simply as a state of being but also as a narrative, one that knitted together the stages of a single life as well as the lives of different generations, its study required an acute historical sense. Each individual carried not only the residues of all the acts of his own life but also those of the lives of his ancestors. "To search adequately into the unillumined region of a person's character," Maudsley argued, "in order to find out the motives of his conduct...would manifestly necessitate the complete unravelling of his mental development, if it did not compel us to undertake, in historical retrospect, an analytic disintegration of the mental development of the race from its beginning."[38] Like the earth itself in Victorian paleontology, the self could no longer be imagined as immutable. Instead it was riven by history, sedimented by innumerable strata of earlier lives and fates, molded into its present shape by an ineluctable and almost unimaginably distended past. Individuals were palimpsests, written over with the marks of ancestors near and remote. (We recall the popularity of Francis Galton's composite photographs in the 1870s and 80s.) The scientist who would understand character, Walter Bagehot contended in 1871, must adopt the methods of the geologist, since "man himself has...become 'an antiquity'." An attentive eye could read "in the frame of each man the result of a whole history of all his life, of what he is and what makes him so; of all his forefathers, of what they were and of what made them so."[39]

Though Bagehot does not draw directly on degenerationist tropes, he stands as an important transitional figure between mid- and late-Victorian uses of biological paradigms for cultural study. His conception of individual identity as multiply determined by heredity and environment stands firmly in a British tradition of neo-Lamarckian thought that includes Herbert Spencer and T. H. Huxley. But he also anticipates some of the concerns of critics like Maudsley and Nordau who invoke degeneration as a dominant paradigm in their thinking. In this context Bagehot's *Physics and Politics* (1871) is worth pausing over for the proleptic light it throws on Nordau's book. Two concerns link Bagehot to Nordau: their shared interest in the possibility of theorizing national character, and their belief that literary language is central to the formation of collective identities. For both Bagehot and Nordau, the key words are "style" and "imitation."

In *Physics and Politics* Bagehot takes a traditionally neo-Lamarckian view of character. He argues that human beings, like all successful organisms, thrive by continually accommodating themselves to their environments, thus preserving an ever-changing equilibrium with ever-changing milieux. At first these adaptations result from acts of volition, but by frequent repetition they become what Huxley termed "artificial reflex actions." Such reflexes, having been imprinted on the nervous system, are transmitted biologically to future generations. Thus "by born nervous organization," Bagehot writes, descendants possess what their forebears acquired only through the long process of habituation (8). In a memorable phrase that yokes Lamarckian biology to Aristotelian ethics, Bagehot claims that the wholly civilized man is literally "charged with stored virtue" (6).

Bagehot then extrapolates from this argument to posit the existence of national character. The transmission of acquired traits is "'the connective tissue' of civilization" (8) since it allows for continuity across generations, but this diachronic explanation does not account for a community's synchronous existence. In other words, Lamarckian biology explains why individuals are like their ancestors but not necessarily why they are like each other. Bagehot's response is to argue for the primacy of what he calls the "imitative instinct" in mankind. The "innate tendency of the human mind to become like what is around it" is one of the strongest parts of its nature (36). What binds us into communities, he contends, is ultimately our instinctual desire to be like one another.

The audacity of this argument is that Bagehot uses it to derive the existence of nations solely from physiological processes. He insists that imitation is instinctual, a response of the body that is not directed by rational reflection or choice. Unlike Ernest Renan, who claimed that communities are built on "consent, the desire to live together, the will to perpetuate the value of the heritage one has received in an undivided form,"[40] Bagehot dismisses all conscious activities (consent, will, rational desire) from the process of nation-making. "We must not think that this imitation is voluntary, or even conscious," he warns. "On the contrary, it has its seat mainly in very obscure parts of the mind, whose notions, so far from having been consciously produced, are hardly felt to exist" (92–93). According to Bagehot, a nation's "character" – its ideology, history, customs, institutions – are written on the nerve tissues of its citizens, who are bound through their bodies to each other and to their collective past. In effect, Bagehot rewrites in biological terms Edmund Burke's argument that society is constituted by an unbreakable contract between the dead, the living, and the unborn. But where both Burke and Renan speak of a cultural heritage, Bagehot talks of a biological inheritance.

What is the medium through which imitation proceeds? The magic word for Bagehot is "style," and he has in mind the power of literary language to construct subjectivities and form character. Individuals are unconsciously moved to imitate whatever style has come to dominate their age. They do not think independently but rather "catch the words that are in the air, and the rhythm which comes to them they do not know from whence; an unconscious imitation determines their words, and makes them say what of themselves they would never have thought of saying" (33). Those airy words and rhythms must nevertheless originate somewhere, and so Bagehot looks to the poets, who for him become legislators of the nation in ways that Shelley did not dream.[41] "Some writer...not necessarily a very excellent writer or a remembered one," hits on a manner which all others feel compelled to imitate. This dominant style, which gives "a curious and indefinable unity" to an historical period, seems to appear entirely at random. "Of course there [is] always some reason" for its emergence, yet it lurks in so murky a region of the collective psyche as to be effectively inaccessible (88–89). For Bagehot, "style" is the Platonic essence which differently informs the various manifestations of the national character: political institution, law, philosophical system, religion, domestic arrangement, taste, dress, and the arts. Since they originate in physiological processes, none of these systems can be ultimately defended on the grounds either of its cultural usefulness or of its rationality. In the latter claim Bagehot again echoes Burke, though in the former he turns Burke on his head.

Regarding these conclusions, we can certainly agree with Christopher Herbert that Bagehot "carries out...about as systematic and lethal a deconstructing of Victorian habits of thought as one could well imagine" in the early 1870s.[42] Yet it is also true that within a brief time such modes of thought became the norm. Sociological investigations like Gustave Le Bon's *The Crowd* (1896), for instance, stress both the irrational nature of "group psychology" and the importance of rhetoric on the formation of collective identities; political theorists like Benjamin Kidd and Arnold White take for granted that politics is biology; psychiatrists like Maudsley begin from the assumption that character is physiologically determined; and cultural critics like Nordau wrestle with the suspicion that literary language exerts undue influence on a nation's psychic health.

As these examples suggest, however, a significant gap separates Bagehot from his successors. Bagehot explicitly offers his argument as evidence that civilization inevitably advances. Progress is made a function of biological law. Like the early Herbert Spencer, Bagehot sees Western Man moving ever upward as he continues to adapt successfully to changing social environments. This commitment to the ideology of Progress marks him as eminently Victorian. Yet as Sander Gilman and J. E. Chamberlin note, progress had its "dark side": the same "laws" which provide the ground of Bagehot's optimism could as easily be cited to support bleaker conclusions. In 1880 the zoologist Edwin Ray Lankester ridiculed equating change with progress, claiming that modern social conditions in fact made degeneration ever more probable. "It is well to remember that we are subject to general laws of evolution, and are as likely to degenerate as to progress."[43] Like Bagehot, Lankester argued that organisms adapt to their environments, but unlike him he believed that under the pressures of industrialization contemporary society had itself become pathological. Individuals and nations alike could adapt only by disfiguring themselves. Lankester, in an analogy that would be endlessly cited in the fin de siècle, pointed to the nauplius, a species of ship's barnacle that had become steadily less complex over time in response to "less varied and less complex conditions of life."[44] The moral was irresistible: as civilization progresses, Lankester wrote, "possibly we are all drifting, tending to the condition of intellectual Barnacles."[45] It is but a short step from Lankester's barnacles to the overdeveloped, vampiric Martians of H. G. Wells's *The War of the Worlds* (1898).

Maudsley further developed Lankester's argument, warning that a new and degenerate "species" of humanity – the "savages of a decomposing civilisation" – would eventually usurp the land. Given the rapid spread of degenerative traits among the populace, Maudsley asks rhetorically, "what will be the end thereof?" He then offers a Wellsian nightmare vision of the future:

> Once the dissolution of things has got full start and way, it will be vastly quicker than the evolution has been; for the degenerate products of social disintegration will not fail, like morbid elements in the physiological organism or like the poisonous products of its own putrefaction, to act as powerful disintegrants, and to hasten by their anti-social energies the downward course. Not that humanity will retrograde quickly through the exact stages of its former slow and tedious progress...it will not in fact reproduce savages with the simple mental qualities of children, but new and degenerate varieties with special repulsive characters – savages of a decomposing civilisation...who will be ten times more vicious and noxious, and infinitely less capable of improvement.... [They will be] social disintegrants of the worst kind, because bred of the corruption of the best organic developments.[46]

This is degeneracy as a byproduct of modernity. We might again think of Wells, this time in relation to *The Time Machine* (1895) and its depiction of the two paths open to an irreversibly decaying civilization: Morlockian barbarism and Eloiesque decadence. Indeed, Wells told Huxley that the novel's theme was "degeneration following security."[47]

Significantly, among the "forewarning intimations" of Britain's "inevitable decline and death," Maudsley foregrounds the spread of degenerate language and writing. He divides such writing into three categories: "elaborate introspective self-analyses; thin and shrieking sentimentalities; emasculated sensualities."[48] Though his focus is on the clinical aspects of degenerative disease, Maudsley does not hesitate to cite certain forms of literary production as exemplum, symptom, and carrier of pathology.

Such sudden leaps from biology to politics to aesthetics might be disconcerting were they not so frequent in the writings of fin-de-siècle social critics. The notion that social decay was inextricably entwined with the decline of language and literature was a commonplace of the period.[49] The immediate impetus for Robert Buchanan's attack on Kiplingesque hooliganism, for instance, was his ire over the vulgarization of language in public schools. Hugh Stutfield's "Tommyrotics" tirade was prompted by fear that "the pathological novel" and "the mental disease [of]...civilised mankind" might endlessly feed each other.[50]

Elsewhere in his essay Stutfield invokes contagion as his model for the way that degenerative tendencies pass between text and audience. In the same vein, James Ashcroft Noble warned that "an epidemic of such perverted emotion as is displayed in certain notorious recent books...would be a more appalling public calamity than the worst outbreak of influenza."[51] Janet Hogarth likewise makes the connection between writing and disease explicit when she argues that literary "style" has become the primary vehicle for the spread of degenerative practices. The diseased artist, she warns, often "contrives to shroud the corpse of sensuality in the fair, white linen garment of a beautiful style." Such language seduces the unwary and "disarms [even] the hostile critic." In the modern world literature and disease have become synonymous, though Hogarth acknowledges that "it is a little depressing that the ravings of lunacy should on the surface bear such a strong likeness to what has hitherto been accepted as literature."[52]

NORDAU AND THE USES OF PROFESSIONAL READING

Not coincidentally, in their essays Stutfield, Noble, and Hogarth all take notice of Nordau's recently translated *Degeneration*. The signal popularity of this massive work – the first English edition went through seven printings in 1895 – attests to the period's fascination with the topic of degeneracy, but also to Nordau's dexterity at translating the discourses of clinical pathology into a pop vernacular.[53] Nordau's canniest move is to situate his discussion squarely within the realm of everyday culture, with examples drawn not from the prison or madhouse but from the lecture hall and coffeehouse. More specifically, throughout most of its great length *Degeneration* presents itself as a work of *literary* criticism. To be sure, Nordau labors to appropriate the authority of science for his argument, but the argument itself consists almost exclusively of extended analyses of literary texts. The late-Victorian obsession with the effects of "diseased" writing on cultural health is given its most extended airing in the pages of *Degeneration*. Literature in fact comprises nearly the only data the book offers, yet Nordau nevertheless is able to find cases of degenerative illness everywhere he looks. Tolstoy, Ibsen, Zola, Swinburne, Baudelaire, Nietzsche, and Verlaine provide the leading coordinates of the investigation, but *Degeneration* ranges encyclopedically across every literary style and movement of the day.

Nordau defends his hermeneutic procedures by arguing that no distinction need be made between reading bodily stigmata and reading texts. One "sure means of proving that the application of the term 'degenerates' to the originators of all the *fin de siècle* movements in art and literature is...no baseless conceit, but a fact," he writes, "would be a careful physical examination of the persons concerned, and an inquiry into their pedigree."[54] Crania would be measured, features classified according to well-established criteria. Yet such intrusive procedures (which Nordau ruefully admits would not be tolerated) are not the critic's only option. He also has recourse to other "vital manifestations" of disease – works of art, which "betoken degeneracy quite as clearly" as physical stigmata (17). The same organic defects which produce malformed earlobes also produce "the disorderly tumult" (21) of degenerative art. Nordau works tirelessly to establish the organic basis of all artistic activity, to trace idiosyncrasies of style back to their sources in the chemical vagaries of nerve cells or the misfirings of synapses. The degenerative writer cannot help but reveal himself in his every word, since his words reproduce his sickness. Thus whereas the healthy man tells us what he thinks, the sick man can only tell us what he is. The very desire to write becomes entangled with degenerative impulses of varyingly exotic nature: echolalia, logorrhoea, graphomania, impulsivism, rabachage, onomatomania.

Like many others, Nordau blames the spread of degeneracy ultimately on "the vertigo and whirl of our frenzied life" (42). The human organism was not built to bear the frantic pace of the modern world. To live now involves "an effort of the nervous system and a wearing of tissue" (39) unparalleled in history. The pandemic fatigue of the Western nations is one sure indication, Nordau argues, that humanity's Lamarckian adaptations have swung in the direction of pathology. "Under any kind of noxious influences an organism becomes debilitated" (16). Because artists tend to be most sensitive to external stimuli, they exhibit degenerative pathologies most clearly. In a critique of *Degeneration* Bernard Shaw summed up this part of Nordau's argument with his customary lucidity. Mr. Nordau's "message to the world," Shaw wrote, "is that all our characteristically modern works of art are symptoms of a disease in the artist, and that these diseased artists are themselves symptoms of the nervous exhaustion of the race by overwork."[55]

Yet Nordau's message is at once more textured and more insidious than Shaw was willing to credit. Nordau is concerned not simply with excoriating degenerate works of art, but also with showing how art in general operates to construct collective identities. Here two key terms – imitation and style – recur, though Nordau puts them to different uses than did Bagehot. For the later writer, the imitative instinct comes into play only when organic exhaustion has reduced individuals to a state of hysteria. In Nordau's lexicon, "hysteria" is the last station on the road to degeneracy, afflicting more men (since they are more likely to be immersed in the vertigo and whirl of life) than women. The hysteric is characterized by an utter inability to resist suggestion, especially when it comes to him via the strong rhetorical patternings of literary language. One "result of the susceptibility of the hysterical subject to suggestion is his irresistible passion for imitation, and the eagerness with which he yields to all the suggestions of writers and artists" (26). In the modern world, the relation between writer and public exactly reproduces that between degenerate and hysteric. The former, organically disoriented by the frenzy of modernity, produces chaotic and "insane" (though still rhetorically effective) visions which the latter, weak and abulic, takes as model and guide. For Nordau the "complete coincidence of [the] clinical picture of hysteria with the description of the peculiarities of the *fin de sècle* public" (26) marks the age as nothing else does.[56]

Nordau possesses a profound reverence for the power of literary language, even (or especially) when that language is "diseased."[57] Like Bagehot, Nordau designates "style" – a particularly resonant word for a fin-de-siècle public familiar with the work of Ruskin, Pater, and Wilde – as the medium in which collective character is formed. What constitutes a degenerate literary style? For Nordau, degenerate works in all their varied forms – and there are many – share one overriding feature. They signify promiscuously. Nothing induces more anxiety in Nordau than the suspicion that language is not, as it ought to be, "clear, homogenous, and free from internal contradictions" (91). The healthy mind recognizes innate bonds between words and things, since "every word, even the most abstract, connotes a concrete presentation or a concept" (57). The degenerate writer refuses to respect such firm correspondences, and his texts as a result generate meanings with scandalous abandon. Every detail is overdetermined – "mystified" is Nordau's preferred term – and thus capable of leading an hysteric public into unforeseeable realms. Attention is focussed on the signifying power of language itself, not on what is signified. For "anyone who demands that words should be the media of definite thoughts" (136), such a situation is close to intolerable. Extreme cases of degenerative prose involve "the stringing together of wholly disconnected words" (94), a procedure which overthrows the logic of grammar, dissociates terms from their natural referents, and disrupts accustomed connections between ideas. "All is discrepant, indiscriminate jumble" (11).

In his own paranoid fashion, Nordau is groping toward a description of a kind of post-realist writing that Nietzsche defined more succinctly. With consummate irony (for he is in part describing himself) Nietzsche also claimed that the decadent modern imagination manifests itself as "style," a style that foregrounds a vitality of the word at the expense of organic form. Here is Nietzsche in *The Case of Wagner* (1888):

> For the present I merely dwell on the question of *style*. – What is the sign of every *literary decadence*? That life no longer dwells in the whole. The word becomes sovereign and leaps out of the sentence, the sentence reaches out and obscures the meaning of the page, the page gains life at the expense of the whole – the whole is no longer a whole.[58]

What Nietzsche calls "the *lie* of the great style" occurs when an "anarchy of atoms" pretends to an artistic wholeness it does not possess. (Thus Nietzsche can make the perverse claim that Richard Wagner is "our greatest *miniaturist* in music.")

Pace Nietzsche, and despite the bleak picture painted in *Degeneration*, Nordau retains an Enlightenment faith in the saving power of reason. Significantly, he invests this power in the critic, who stands apart from the unhealthy symbiosis of degenerate writer and hysteric public. Confronted with the "lisps and stammers" (557) of "stylized" writing, the critic's task becomes, if not to halt meaning's proliferation or unity's demise, then to identify these conditions accurately. It becomes a diagnostic task, in other words. In Nordau's view the physician and the literary critic perform identical interpretive operations, operations whose ultimate goal is to unearth truths hidden by a welter of confusing signs. Criticism "is the sacred duty of all healthy and moral men" (556) because it possesses enormous therapeutic value. (In the same vein, Stutfield argues that "what we lack nowadays is a school of sound, fearless, and vigorous criticism."[59]) Effective criticism reclaims lost souls. In present conditions, Nordau cautions, "the police cannot aid us" in "the work of protecting and saving those who are not already too deeply diseased" (557).

This Arnoldian belief in the efficacy of criticism requires Nordau to distinguish firmly between the imaginative works he cites and his own critical practices. Perhaps not surprisingly the distinction refuses to remain properly distinct. Indeed, Nordau's text manages to suggest that the degenerative artist finds a shadowy double in the figure of the critic himself. Shaw was by no means the only reviewer to point out that Nordau's prose exhibited many of the same "pathologies" he identified in others. Graphomania and logorrhoea came most readily to mind.[60] Beyond these superficial correspondences, the pathologist-critic shared with his putative subject a sense of the world as a vast semiological field which could only be understood in the interrelations of all its elements. Both kinds of men were addicted, to lift Henry James's phrasing, to seeing one thing through another, and other things through that. This insight Nordau understandably represses, though its presence is felt whenever he stresses the innate "mysticism" of the deviant imagination. According to him, "the simplest word uttered" appears to the degenerate as "an allusion to something mysteriously occult."

> In the most commonplace and natural movements he sees hidden signs. All things have for him deep backgrounds; far-reaching shadows are thrown by them over adjacent tracts; they send out wide-spreading roots into remote substrata. Every image that rises up in his mind points with mysterious silence, though with significant look and finger, to other images distinct or shadowy, and induces him to set up relations between ideas, where other people recognize no connection. (46)

A more succinct account of the procedures of degeneration theorists could not easily be imagined. From Morel onward, the study of degeneration constantly threatened to teeter into "occult" practices as the hidden signs and mysterious silences of the body were compelled to yield up their secrets.

Yet, by moving out to a larger context, we can also say that Nordau is here describing the practices of professional readers across a number of disciplines nascent in the period. A commitment to aggressive interpretation, to reading strongly against the grain in the service of hidden and ostensibly enabling truths, is common not only to the study of pathology but also to such recently consolidated hermeneutic practices as psychology, sociology, anthropology, criminology, and – as Nordau himself continually demonstrates – literary criticism.[61] What links together these and other like disciplines is their status, newly won in this period, as professional discourses. The late-Victorian doctor of pathology differs from the phrenologist or physiognomist of mid-century primarily in the institutionally conferred authority he enjoys. Thus, despite the highly visible connections between phrenology and degeneration theory, the two practices can be distinguished on the grounds of the latter's status as a professional discourse. Nordau himself trades heavily on such professional authority by calling attention to the way his literary readings are embedded within larger discourses of medicine and criminology. His interpretations strive to be "professional," and thus authoritative, in a way wholly distinct from the belletristic tradition associated with more conventional critics of the period like George Saintsbury or Edmund Gosse.

The rise of "professional man" in turn coincides with the final consolidation of power during the nineteenth century in the hands of a capitalist bourgeoisie.[62] By definition professionals are middle class (and in this period male); their discourses are among the means by which middle-class life elaborates and extends itself. Certainly, degeneration theory provides an at times startlingly clear instance of this process. Nordau reveals the theory's class-bias when he asserts that, despite degeneracy's rapid spread, "the *bourgeoisie* are sound" (2), an assertion his evidence seems everywhere to contradict. He theoretically locates the problem instead within an exhausted aristocracy and certain sections of a depraved working class. In practice, however, the degenerate label is attached to any aesthetic or political program that Nordau considers disruptive of middle-class ideals: degenerative practices "mean the end of an established order, which for thousands of years has satisfied logic, fettered depravity, and in every art matured something of beauty" (3). Nordau, like many of his brethren, designates all progressive political programs as ideologies of the pathological. Indeed, he suggests, given a certain level of intelligence, degenerate individuals are invariably driven to become either mystical poets or else socialists. Severe cases lead to anarchism or – it comes to the same thing for Nordau – a love for the poetry of Swinburne.

We can easily dismiss or ridicule Nordau, though such responses fail to account for the status his book enjoyed. Despite his desire for that book to be considered a work of science, *Degeneration* is instead an unusually clear articulation of the "common sense" view of degeneration and of its relation to such diverse topics as sexual deviance, national character, class, literary style, interpretation, professionalism, and modernity. The book also reveals how thoroughly entwined degeneration theory was with the collective anxieties of the bourgeoisie in this period. Nordau's arguments were in most cases simply extensions and elaborations of highly "respectable" habits of thought; as Stokes correctly notes, he "seemed at the time to be interestingly extreme rather than woefully eccentric."[63] Nordau is mean-spirited, his conclusions nasty and narrow, but that very nastiness often serves to foreground the fears he tries to ward off. Invocations of degenerative paradigms are invariably tied up with concerns about the decline and fall of the bourgeoisie. Indeed, though degeneration theory is overtly concerned with the Other, it covertly expresses the anxieties of a middle class worried about its own present status and future prospects.

CHAPTER 2

The sedulous ape: atavism, professionalism, and Stevenson's Jekyll and Hyde

In an early review of *The Strange Case of Dr. Jekyll and Mr. Hyde* (1886), Andrew Lang noted the most striking feature of Robert Louis Stevenson's tale. "His heroes (surely *this* is original) are all successful middle-aged professional men."[1] Indeed, one could hardly miss the novel's foregrounding of the stature enjoyed by "Henry Jekyll, M.D., D.C.L., LL.D., F.R.S., etc."[2] In Lang's view this interest in professional men defined Stevenson's novel at least as much as its portrayal of the grotesque Edward Hyde. If *Jekyll and Hyde* articulates in Gothic fiction's exaggerated tones late-Victorian anxieties concerning degeneration, atavism, and what Cesare Lombroso called "criminal man," it invariably situates those concerns in relation to the practices and discourses of lawyers like Gabriel Utterson, doctors like Henry Jekyll and Hastie Lanyon, or even "well-known men about town" (29) like Richard Enfield. The novel in fact asks us to do more than simply register the all too apparent marks of Edward Hyde's "degeneracy." It compels us also to examine how those marks come to signify in the first place. As Stevenson understood, one thing professional men tend to be good at is close reading. Another is seeing to it that their interpretations have consequences in the real world. *Jekyll and Hyde* proves to be an uncannily self-conscious exploration of the relation between professional interpretation and the construction of criminal deviance. The novel is also a displaced meditation on what Stevenson considered the decline of authorship itself into "professionalism."

THE ATAVIST AND THE PROFESSIONAL

In Edward Hyde, Stevenson's first readers could easily discern the lineaments of Lombroso's atavistic criminal. In one of degeneration theory's defining moments, Lombroso had "discovered" that criminals were throwbacks to humanity's savage past. While contemplating the skull of the notorious Italian bandit Vilella, Lombroso suddenly saw history open up before him, illumined as if by lightning.

This was not merely an idea [he wrote many years later], but a revelation. At the sight of that skull, I seemed to see all of a sudden, lighted up as a vast plain under a flaming sky, the problem of the nature of the criminal – an atavistic being who reproduces in his person the ferocious instincts of primitive humanity and the inferior animals.[3]

"Thus were explained anatomically," Lombroso continues, such diverse attributes as the "enormous jaws, high cheek bones, prominent superciliary arches, solitary lines in the palms, extreme size of the orbits, [and] handle-shaped ears" of the criminal, as well as various moral deformities like the propensity for "excessive idleness, love of orgies, and the irresponsible craving of evil for its own sake." These features were all signs of a form of primitive existence which normal men and women had transcended but which the criminal was condemned to relive. In his physiognomy as in his psyche, the atavistic criminal bore the traces of humanity's history and development.[4]

From the first publication of Stevenson's novel, readers have noted the similarities between Lombroso's criminal and the atavistic Mr. Hyde.[5] Lombroso's descriptions of criminal deviance fit snugly with longstanding discourses of class in Great Britain. Lombroso's work first reached a wide audience in England thanks to Havelock Ellis's *The Criminal* (1891); the combined influence of Ellis and Lombroso was in part due to the ease with which the new "scientific" categories mapped onto older, more familiar accounts of the urban poor from Mayhew onward. As we saw in Chapter 1, much of the "legitimacy" of degeneration theory derived from the way it reproduced the class ideologies of the bourgeoisie. Equating the criminal with atavism, and both with the lower classes, was a familiar gesture by the 1880s, as was the claim that deviance expressed itself most markedly through physical deformity.[6] Stevenson's middle-class readers would have had as little trouble deciphering the features of the "abnormal and misbegotten" Hyde, his "body an imprint of deformity and decay," as Stevenson's middle-class characters do (78, 84). "God bless me," exclaims Utterson, "the man seems hardly human. Something troglodytic, shall we say?...or is it the mere radiance of a foul soul that thus transpires through, and transfigures, its clay continent?" (40). Utterson's remark, moreover, nicely demonstrates how old and new paradigms can overlap. He at once draws on familiar Christian imagery – Hyde's foul soul transfiguring its clay continent – and a Lombrosan vocabulary of atavism, with Hyde-as-troglodyte reproducing in his person the infancy of the human species.

In considering degenerationism as a class discourse, however, we need to look up as well as down. Both Lombroso and Nordau argue that degeneration was as endemic to a decadent aristocracy as to a troglodytic proletariat. And, indeed, Hyde can be read as a figure of leisured dissipation. While his impulsiveness and savagery, his violent temper, and his appearance all mark Hyde as lower class and atavistic, his vices are clearly those of a monied gentleman. This aspect of Hyde's portrayal has gone largely unnoticed, but for Stevenson's contemporaries the conflation of upper and lower classes into a single figure of degeneracy would not have seemed unusual. Lombroso's criminal may have been primitive in appearance, but his moral shortcomings – "excessive idleness, love of orgies, the irresponsible craving of evil" – make him a companion of Jean Floressas des Esseintes and Dorian Gray, not Vilella. Nordau took pains to insist that the degenerate population "consists chiefly of rich educated people" who, with too much time and means at their disposal, succumb to decadence and depravity.[7]

Lombroso and Nordau have in mind not only the titled aristocracy but also a stratum of cultured aesthetes considered dangerously subversive of conventional morality. That Stevenson meant us to place Hyde among their number is suggested by the description of his surprisingly well-appointed Soho rooms, "furnished with luxury and good taste" (49). Hyde's palate for wine is discriminating, his plate is of silver, his "napery elegant." Art adorns his walls, while carpets "of many plies and agreeable in colour" cover his floors. This is not a savage's den but the retreat of a cultivated gentleman. Utterson supposes that Jekyll bought the art for Hyde (49), but Stevenson in a letter went out of his way to say that the lawyer is mistaken. The purchases were Hyde's alone.[8]

In Edward Hyde, then, Stevenson created a figure who embodies a bourgeois readership's worst fears about both a marauding and immoral underclass and a dissipated and immoral leisure class.[9] Yet Stevenson also shows how such figures are not so much "recognized" as created by middle-class discourse. He does this by foregrounding the interpretive acts through which his characters situate and define Hyde. Despite the confident assertions of the novel's professional men that Hyde is "degenerate," his "stigmata" turn out to be troublingly difficult to specify. In fact, no one can accurately describe him. "He must be deformed somewhere," asserts Enfield. "He gives a strong feeling of deformity, though I couldn't specify the point. He's an extraordinary-looking man, and yet I really can name nothing out of the way. No, sir...I can't describe him" (34). Enfield's puzzled response finds its counterparts in the nearly identical statements of Utterson (40), Poole (68), and Lanyon (77–78). In Utterson's dream Hyde "had no face, or one that baffled him and melted before his eyes" (36–37). "The few who could describe him differed widely," agreeing only that some "unexpressed deformity" lurked in his countenance (50). That last, nearly oxymoronic formulation – "unexpressed deformity" – nicely captures the troubled relation between the "text" of Hyde's body and the interpretive practices used to decipher it. Hyde's stigmata are everywhere asserted and nowhere named. The novel continually turns the question of Hyde back on his interlocutors so that their interpretive procedures become the object of our attention. "There is my explanation," Utterson claims. "It is plain and natural, hangs well together and delivers us from all exorbitant alarms" (66). It is also, we are immediately given to understand, wrong, though its delusions differ only in degree from other "plain and natural" explanations brought forward in the tale.[10]

Indeed, what makes *Jekyll and Hyde* compelling is the way it turns the class discourses of atavism and criminality back on the bourgeoisie itself. As Lang recognized, Stevenson's novel is finally more concerned with its middle-class professional "heroes" than it is with the figure of Edward Hyde. Among the story's first readers, F. W. H. Myers felt this aspect acutely, and it prompted him to protest in a remarkable series of letters which suggest that he interpreted Hyde as a figure not of degenerate depravity but of bourgeois "virtue."[11]

Shortly after its publication Myers wrote to Stevenson, whom he did not know, enthusiastically praising *Jekyll and Hyde* but suggesting that certain minor revisions would improve the novel. After noting some infelicities of phrasing and gaps in plotting, Myers came to what he considered the story's "weakest point," the murder of Sir Danvers Carew. Hyde's mauling of Carew's "unresisting body" offended the decorous Myers ("no, not an elderly MP's!"), but his primary objection was that such an act was untrue to Hyde's nature. Because "Jekyll was thoroughly civilized...his degeneration must needs take certain lines only." Hyde should be portrayed as "not a generalized but a specialized fiend," whose cruelty would never take the form Stevenson gave it. At most "Hyde would, I think, have brushed the baronet aside with a curse."

Stevenson's reply was polite, passing over the bulk of Myers's suggestions in silence. He did pause to correct him on one subject, though, that of a painting in Hyde's lodgings. Myers had questioned whether the doctor would have acquired artwork for his alter ego. Stevenson answered that Hyde purchased the painting, not Jekyll. Myers's response was disproportionately vehement. "Would Hyde have bought a picture? I think – and friends of weight support my view – that such an act would have been altogether unworthy of him." Unworthy? Myers and his weighty friends appear to feel that Hyde's character is being impugned, that his good name must be defended against some implied insult. Asking "what are the motives which would prompt a person in [Hyde's] situation" to buy artwork, Myers suggests three, none of which, he argues, applies to Hyde's case.

> 1. There are jaded voluptuaries who seek in a special class of art a substitute or reinforcement for the default of primary stimuli. Mr. Hyde's whole career forbids us to insult him by classing him with these men.
>
> 2. There are those who wish for elegant surroundings to allure or overawe the minds of certain persons unaccustomed to luxury or splendour. But does not all we know of Hyde teach us that he disdained those modes of adventitious attractions?...
>
> 3. There are those, again, who surround their more concentrated enjoyments with a halo of mixed estheticism...Such, no doubt, was Dr. Jekyll; such, no doubt, he *expected* that Mr. Hyde would be. But was he not deceived? Was there not something unlooked for, something Napoleonic, in Hyde's way of pushing aside the aesthetic as well as the moral superfluities of life?...We do not imagine the young Napoleon as going to concerts or taking a walk in a garden....I cannot fancy Hyde looking in at picture shops. I cannot think he ever left his rooms, except on business. (17 March 1886)

This is a most unfamiliar Hyde! On the evidence of Myers's letter we would have to pronounce him an upstanding citizen. Myers clearly perceives how easily Stevenson's Hyde could be taken not for a brute but for a dandy. At no point is Myers worried that Hyde might be considered atavistic. Instead, he is concerned that Hyde's reputation not be smeared by association with "jaded voluptuaries" and aesthetes. In attempting to clear him of such charges, Myers presents Jekyll's alter ego as the very image of sobriety and industry, manfully disdainful of the shop window, the art gallery, the concert hall – of anything that might savor of the aesthetic or the frivolous. Myers praises Hyde's simplicity of dress: he is not a fop but a "man aiming only at simple convenience, direct sufficiency." Unconcerned with personal adornment, he is "not anxious to present himself as personally attractive, but [relies] frankly on the cash nexus, and on that decision of character that would startle" those less forceful than himself.

We might dismiss Myers's reading as eccentric, especially given the absence of any irony in his references to Hyde's "business," freedom from personal vanity, or reliance on the cash nexus (blackmail and prostitution appear to be the primary drags on his resources). Yet Myers's admittedly exaggerated response illuminates an important aspect of Stevenson's novel. Edward Hyde may not be an image of the *upright* bourgeois male, but he is decidedly an image of the bourgeois male. While Hyde can be read as the embodiment of the degenerate prole, the decadent aristocrat, or the dissipated aesthete, it is also the case that his violence is largely directed *at* those same classes. Of the three acts of violence we see Hyde commit, two – his trampling of the little girl and his striking of the prostitute – involve lower-class women. Hyde's third victim is the novel's only titled character, Sir Danvers Carew. That Hyde shares Myers's disdain for aesthetes is made plainer in Stevenson's manuscript draft of the novel. There, Hyde murders not Sir Danvers but a character who appears to be a caricature of the aesthetic stereotype, the "anoemically pale" Mr. Lemsome. Constantly "shielding a pair of suffering eyes under blue spectacles," Lemsome is considered by the respectable Utterson as both "a bad fellow" and "an incurable cad."[12] The substitution of Carew for Lemsome suggests that the two characters were connected in Stevenson's mind, just as for Nordau aesthetes like Oscar Wilde are grouped with troubling aristocrats like Lord Byron as disruptive of middle-class mores.

Mr. Hyde thus acts not just as a magnet for middle-class fears of various "Others" but also as an agent of vengeance. He is the scourge of (a bourgeois) God, punishing those who threaten patriarchal code and custom. Indeed, the noun used most often in the story to describe Hyde is not "monster" or "villain" but – "gentleman." This novel portrays a world peopled almost exclusively by middle-class professional men, yet instead of attacking Hyde, these gentlemen more often close ranks around him.[13] Enfield's "Story of the Door," though it begins with Hyde trampling a little girl until she is left "screaming on the ground" (31), concludes with Enfield, the doctor, and the girl's father breakfasting with Hyde in his chambers (32). Recognizing him as one of their own, the men literally encircle Hyde to protect him from harm. "And all the time...we were keeping the women off him as best we could, for they were as wild as harpies. I never saw a circle of such hateful faces; and there was the man in the middle,...frightened too, I could see that" (32). The homosocial bonding that occurs in this scene is only intensified by its overt misogyny. Though both he and the doctor profess to feel a profound loathing for Hyde, Enfield refers to him with the politeness due a social equal, consistently calling him "my gentleman" or "my man." Indeed, Enfield derives vicarious pleasure from watching Hyde maul the girl.[14] Though he could easily have prevented their collision, Enfield allows them to run into one another "naturally enough" (31). Neglecting to intervene until Hyde has finished his assault, Enfield describes the incident with some relish, nonchalantly admitting to Utterson that the beating "sounds nothing to hear" (31). (Though he goes on to say that it "was hellish to see," that does not unring the bell.) That Hyde acts out the aggressions of timid bourgeois gentlemen is emphasized once again in the beating of Sir Danvers. That gesture of "insensate cruelty" is performed with a cane "of some rare and very tough and heavy wood" (47), which was originally in the possession of Gabriel Utterson. The stick breaks in two, and Stevenson takes care to let us know that both halves make their way back into the lawyer's hands after the murder (47, 49).

It is Edward Hyde's covert affinities with professional men that prompted Myers to describe him as a kind of bourgeois Napoleon. Myers recognized that Stevenson had created a figure whose rage is the rage of a threatened patriarchy. It is only a seeming paradox to say that Hyde is most like himself when he behaves like a gentleman. Yet to leave matters here would do an injustice to the complexity of Stevenson's vision, an injustice Myers himself is guilty of. While *Jekyll and Hyde* is a compelling expression of middle-class anger directed at various forms of the Other, the novel also turns that anger back on the burgesses themselves, Stevenson included.

It does this in part by taking as one of its themes the education of a gentleman, in this case Mr. Hyde. Most critical accounts of the novel have with good reason focussed on the social and psychological pressures that lead Jekyll to become Hyde. Yet Stevenson is also concerned with the reverse transformation. That is, the novel details the pressures which move Hyde closer to Jekyll.[15] It is one thing to say that Hyde acts out the aggressive fantasies of repressed Victorian men, another altogether to say that he comes eventually to embody the very repressions Jekyll struggles to throw off. Yet this is in fact a prime source of horror in the tale: not that the professional man is transformed into an atavistic criminal, but that the atavist learns to pass as a gentleman. Hyde unquestionably develops over the course of the novel, which is to say he becomes more like the "respectable" Jekyll, which in turn is to say he "degenerates." Degeneration becomes a function not of lower-class depravity or aristocratic dissipation but of middle-class "virtue."

Needless to say, Mr. Hyde's education into gentlemanliness exacts a considerable cost. The Hyde who ends his life weeping and crying for mercy (69) is not the same man whose original "raging energies" and "love of life" Jekyll found "wonderful" (95–96). By the time he is confined to the doctor's laboratory, Hyde is no longer Jekyll's opposite but his mirror image. Where earlier the transitions between Jekyll and Hyde were clean and sharp (and painful), later the two personalities develop a mutual fluidity. By the end the doctor's body metamorphoses continually from Jekyll to Hyde and back again, as if to indicate that we need no longer distinguish between them.

How does one become a gentleman? If born into a good family, by imitating one's father. That Jekyll and Hyde stand in a father–son relationship is suggested by Jekyll himself (89) as well as by Utterson (37, 41–42), who suspects that Hyde is the doctor's illegitimate offspring. After "gentleman," the words used most often to describe Hyde are "little" and "young."[16] The idea that Hyde is being groomed, as Utterson says, "to step into the said Henry Jekyll's shoes" (35), is reinforced by the doctor's will naming him sole heir, as well as by the lawyer's description of this "small gentleman" (46) as Jekyll's "*protégé*" (37). Indeed, when Jekyll assures Utterson that "I do sincerely take a great, a very great interest in that young man" (44) he sounds like a mentor sheltering a promising disciple.

If Hyde is to assume his mentor–father's position, he must be indoctrinated in the codes of his class. As Jekyll repeatedly insists, Hyde indulges no vices that Jekyll himself did not enjoy. What differs is the manner in which they enjoy them: Hyde openly and vulgarly, Jekyll discretely and with an eye to maintaining his good name. As Hyde learns from his encounter with Enfield, gentlemen may sin so long as appearances are preserved. Having collared Hyde after his trampling of the little girl, Enfield and the doctor are "sick...with the desire to kill him" (thus replicating Hyde's own homicidal rage), but "killing being out of the question" they do "the next best": they threaten to "make such a scandal...as should make his name stink" (31–32). They extort money as the price of their silence, in the process teaching Hyde the value of a good reputation. "No gentleman but wishes to avoid a scene," Hyde acknowledges. "Name your figure" (32). When Enfield winds up his narration of this incident by telling Utterson that "my man was a fellow that nobody could have to do with" (33) he seems to be describing not a violent criminal but a man who cannot be trusted to respect club rules.

A commitment to protecting the good names of oneself and one's colleagues binds professional men together. Utterson, remarkably unconcerned with the fates of Hyde's victims, directs all his energies toward shielding Jekyll from "the cancer of some concealed disgrace" (41). Sir Danvers' death awakens fears that the doctor's "good name...[will] be sucked down in the eddy of the scandal" (53). After the murder Jekyll himself admits, "I was thinking of my own character, which this hateful business has rather exposed" (52). As Enfield's actions indicate, blackmail is an acceptable way to prevent such exposure. Utterson mistakenly believes that Hyde is blackmailing Jekyll, but rather than going to the police he hits on the happier and more gentlemanly idea of blackmailing Hyde in turn (42). By far the most potent weapon these men possess, however, is silence. Closing ranks, they protect their own by stifling the spread not of crime or sin but of indecorous talk.[17] In turn, the commitment to silence ultimately extends to self-censorship, a pledge not to know. Utterson's motto – "I let my brother go to the devil in his own way" (29) – finds its counterpart in Enfield's unvarying rule of thumb: "The more it looks like Queer Street, the less I ask" (33). ("A very good rule, too," Utterson agrees.) Enfield explicitly equates knowledge with scandal when he says that asking a question is like rolling a stone down a hill: "presently some bland old bird...is knocked on the head...and the family have to change their name" (33). Knowledge's harm is suffered most acutely by Dr. Lanyon, whose Christian name of Hastie nicely indicates his fatal character flaw. Warned by Hyde that it is always wiser not to know, Lanyon nevertheless succumbs to that "greed of curiosity" (79) which leads directly deathward.

By means of Mr. Hyde, Jekyll seeks of course to slough off these same burdens of respectability, reticence, decorum, self-censorship – of gentlemanliness – and "spring headlong into the sea of liberty" (86). In tracing the arc of Hyde's brief career, however, Stevenson shows how quickly he becomes simply one of the boys. Over the last half of the novel Stevenson links Hyde, through a series of verbal echoes and structural rhymes, to various bourgeois "virtues" and practices. Not only do we discover Hyde beginning to exercise remarkable self-control – that most middle-class of virtues and seemingly the furthest from his nature – but we hear him speaking confidently in Jekyll's tones to Lanyon concerning the benefits of science and the sanctity of "the seal of *our* profession" (80; my emphasis).[18]

The kind of structural rhyming I refer to is most noticeable during Hyde's death-scene, when Utterson and Poole, having violently burst in the door of the rooms above Jekyll's laboratory, are startled by what they find.

> The besiegers, appalled by their own riot and the stillness that had succeeded, stood back a little and peered in. There lay the cabinet before their eyes in the quiet lamplight, a good fire glowing and chattering on the hearth, the kettle singing its strain, a drawer or two open, papers neatly set forth on the business table, and nearer the fire, the things laid out for tea; the quietest room, you would have said, and except for the glazed presses full of chemicals, the most commonplace that night in London. (69–70)

We are apt to share their bewilderment at first, since this is the last tableau we might expect Stevenson to offer us at this juncture in the story.[19] Yet it has been carefully prepared for. The novel is full of similar domestic tableaux, invariably occupied by solitary gentlemen. When they are not walking or dining, it seems, these men sit at their hearths, usually alone. It is Utterson's "custom of a Sunday...to sit close by the fire, a volume of some dry divinity on his reading-desk" (35). When the lawyer visits Lanyon, he finds the doctor sitting alone over his wine after dinner (36). Later he finds Jekyll in nearly the same position (51). Utterson shares a friendly fireside bottle of wine with Mr. Guest, though their conversation leaves him singularly unhappy (54–55). It is one of Stevenson's triumphs that he transforms the hearth – that too-familiar image of cozy Victorian domesticity – into a symbol of these men's isolation and repression. In turn, the most notable thing about the scene Utterson and Poole stumble upon is that it is empty of life. The lamplight soothes, the kettle sings, the chairs beckon – but no one is home. Recognizing this, we recognize too the subtle irony of calling it "the most commonplace" sight to be seen in London.

We next discover that the lifeless Hyde's "contorted and still twitching" body lay "right in the midst" of this scene (70). On the one hand, it is a fit setting for Hyde's last agony and suicide. The terrors suffered by Hyde during his final days arise in part from his surroundings: the very symbols of bourgeois respectability that he exists to repudiate do him in. On the other hand, he seems to feel bizarrely at home in these surroundings. If for instance we ask who set the table for tea on this final night, the answer has to be Hyde and not Jekyll, since Utterson and Poole, prior to breaking in the door, agree that they have heard only Hyde's voice and Hyde's "patient" footsteps from within the room that evening (69). (Poole insists that his master "was made away with eight days ago" [65].) Beside the tea things is "a copy of a pious work for which Jekyll had...expressed a great esteem, annotated, in his own hand, with startling blasphemies" (71). We may be tempted to think that Hyde is responsible for those annotations, but that is not what the sentence says.[20] These are not fussy or pedantic quibbles, but rather indicate how carefully Stevenson has blurred the boundary between the two identities. It is Jekyll who is now blasphemous and who violently berates the man at Maw's (66), Hyde who sets a quiet tea table and cries to heaven for mercy.[21] On adjacent tables Utterson and Poole discover two cups, one containing the white salt used in Jekyll's potion, the other containing the white sugar used in Hyde's tea (71). Both are magic elixirs: the first transforms a gentleman into a savage while the second performs the reverse operation. Having found his place by the hearth, Mr. Hyde knows what posture to assume: "Thenceforward, he sat all day over the fire in the private room, gnawing his nails; there he dined, sitting alone with his fears" (94). If this sounds more like Utterson or Lanyon than the Hyde we first met, it is meant to. Bitter, lonely, frightened, nervous, chewing his nails (we recall that Utterson bites his finger when agitated [65]), and contemplating violence: Edward Hyde is now a gentleman.

THE SEDULOUS APE

The Strange Case of Dr. Jekyll and Mr. Hyde is an angry book, its venom directed against what Stevenson contemptuously referred to as that "fatuous rabble of burgesses called the public."[22] The novel turns the discourses centering on degeneration, atavism, and criminality back on the professional classes that produced them, linking gentlemanliness and bourgeois virtue to various forms of depravity. At the same time the novel plumbs deep pools of patriarchal anxiety about its continued viability. Indeed, *Jekyll and Hyde* can be read as a meditation on the pathology of late-Victorian masculinity. Jekyll's case is "strange," Stevenson suggests, only in the sense that it is so common among men of the doctor's standing and beliefs.

Yet if *Jekyll and Hyde* is a consummate critique of the professional men who formed the bulk of its readership, the novel was also self-consciously written to please, which it did. In no respect is Stevenson more of his age than in the tortuous acts of self-definition and self-positioning that allowed him at once to dismiss and to court the fatuous rabble.[23] Ironically, the publication of *Jekyll and Hyde* marked the emergence of Robert Louis Stevenson as a "professional" author in the narrow sense of being able, for the first time, to support himself solely by means of his trade. No longer a coterie writer relying on his father for financial help, Stevenson now enjoyed a popular acclaim that would last until his death. He professed to find such acclaim distressing, a mark of artistic failure and an indication that he had become, in his stepson's words, "the 'burgess' of his former jeers."[24] "I am now a salaried party," Stevenson wrote to William Archer after the success of *Jekyll and Hyde* led to a lucrative commission from an American magazine. "I am a *bourgeois* now; I am to write a weekly paper for *Scribners'*, at a scale of payment which makes my teeth ache for shame and diffidence...I am like to be...publicly hanged at the social revolution."[25] "There must be something wrong in me," he confided to Edmund Gosse, "or I would not be popular."[26]

Stevenson's critique of professional discourses in *Jekyll and Hyde* turns out also to be a displaced critique of his own profession. The 1880s and 90s, like the 1830s and 40s, constitute a key moment in the professionalization of authorship over the course of the nineteenth century. The founding of The Society of Authors, the revision of international copyright laws, the widespread adoption of the full royalty system, and the appearance of full-time professional literary agents like A. P. Watt and William Morris Colles were only the most visible among many signs of this process.[27] In the early stages of his career Stevenson took little interest in (and little care of) his finances. Like many writers, he usually sold his copyrights for a lump payment instead of negotiating for royalties. Moreover, as Peter Keating points out, even when Stevenson did not sell his books outright, as in the case of *Treasure Island*, he *thought* he had.[28]

After 1884, following the founding of The Society of Authors and the vigorous consciousness-raising campaign led by its first president, Walter Besant, such financial naiveté was no longer possible. Yet Stevenson still ambivalently resisted the idea that imaginative writing constituted a professional discourse. His resistance was based on two factors. First, he saw professionalism as inseparable from the middle classes, that fatuous rabble he preferred to jest at rather than join. Second, he associated professional writing with a functionalist "realism" which he in theory opposed. As we saw in Chapter 1, it was precisely this kind of realist prose that was invariably held up as the norm against which "deviant" writing was measured. Nordau linked traditional notions of mimesis – "every word...connotes a concrete presentation or a concept" – both with "healthy" art and with his own critical writing. This linkage was made not just by pathologists but also by many of those who, like Besant, were most interested in professionalizing the author's trade. With realism designated as the language of professionals, Stevenson in opposition turned to what he (often vaguely) called "style" as the mark of the truly imaginative writer.

Thus, for Stevenson, to be professional was to be bourgeois, and to be bourgeois was to embrace the very blindnesses, evasions, and immoralities delineated in *Jekyll and Hyde*. Indeed, the salient biographical fact to recall here is that the novel was composed during Stevenson's three-year "imprisonment" at Skerryvore, the Bournemouth house purchased by Thomas Stevenson for his son and daughter-in-law.[29] This was a period of personal crisis and transition for the writer. Prior to it were years of self-styled bohemianism, fashionable dabblings in socialism, and occasionally self-indulgent nose-thumbings at "the fathers," his own included. Until he took possession of Skerryvore, Stevenson had never had a permanent address. In his letters he repeatedly refers to his occupancy of the house as a capitulation to bourgeois convention, a "revolt into respectability."[30] To Gosse he complained: "I am now a beastly householder," and when Archer came to visit he found his friend ensconced in the heart of "British Philistinism."[31] Stevenson's always-fragile health was never worse than during these years, nor were his always-difficult relations with Thomas ever pricklier. When Thomas died in mid-1887 Stevenson immediately fled house and country, not returning to England during the seven remaining years of his life.

The biographical context throws some light on the motivations underlying *Jekyll and Hyde*. Writing it was in part an expression of self-loathing for what Stevenson perceived as his betrayal of former ideals.[32] Yet, as his letters and essays indicate, Stevenson was also intensely engaged at this time with the question of what it meant to be a professional author. For him, the normative definition of professionalism came, as it did for most writers of the period, from Besant, whose lecture "The Art of Fiction," delivered in April 1884 to the Royal Institution, prompted lengthy replies first from Henry James and then from Stevenson. Besant, having recently helped organize The Society of Authors, was explicitly interested in redefining fiction-writing as a profession analogous to the law, medicine, certain sciences, and other of the arts. If the "fine arts" like painting or sculpture enjoy a status denied to writers, he contends in the lecture, that is because they are organized into culturally sanctioned professional institutions. Besant correctly perceived that the painter who was permitted to append "R.A." to his name was accorded a respect no novelist could win.[33]

Throughout the essay, however, Besant's implicit model for the fiction-writer is not the painter or sculptor but the professional scientist.[34] Wedded to the twin gods of positivism and empiricism, the Besantian novelist recognizes that fiction is "of this world, wholly of this world" and therefore seeks to reproduce the surfaces of life exactly as he finds them. Like the scientist too, the novelist reports his findings in a "transparent" prose, one that refuses to call attention to itself as writing. For Besant such transparency is the mark of professional writing in all disciplines. It at once vouches for the truth of the information conveyed while also ensuring that the professional's "products" will find the widest possible market. In the view of his detractors, however, Besant had succeeded primarily in degrading fiction-writing from a sacrament into a trade. He urges novelists to look after their self-interest by considering their products first as marketable commodities and only secondarily as art. For many writers Besant's position was scandalous, akin to the mercenary views confessed by Anthony Trollope in his recently published autobiography (1882).[35] James eloquently objected to Besant's rules for successful novel-writing, rules which Besant offered as analogs to the procedural protocols that governed professional activity in other disciplines but which James considered as forming a risible do-it-yourself manual.[36]

In their replies James and Stevenson self-consciously distance themselves from Besant's professional author. They reject his implicit claim that the novel's function is to reproduce middle-class ideology by means of a facile mimesis. Both men were uncomfortable with the idea that the interests of the professional author ought to be at one with what Stevenson refers to elsewhere as "that well-known character, the general reader."[37] Of the two men, Stevenson took the more radical position by embracing a non-functionalist "style" as a kind of anti-mimesis. He argues that literature has nothing to do with reproducing reality but "pursues instead an independent and creative aim." Fiction, "like arithmetic and geometry" (two sciences, significantly, whose practitioners were not considered professionals in the nineteenth century), looks away from "the gross, coloured, and mobile nature at our feet, and regard[s] instead a certain figmentary abstraction." The novel in particular lives "by its immeasurable difference from life."[38] That difference is achieved only through a painstaking attention to what Stevenson terms the "technical elements of style." According to him, this craft so long to learn, unlike Besant's easily mastered rules, is precisely what separates true writers from the general public, making the former unpopular with all but the blessed few who cultivate "the gift of reading."[39] Affirming that "the subject makes but a trifling part of any piece of literature" and that "the motive and end of any art whatever is to make a pattern" and not to reproduce "life," Stevenson situates himself in opposition to dominant notions of realism, and thus also in opposition to the model of professional authorship proposed by Besant.[40]

It can be argued that, in rejecting Besant, Stevenson simply embraces a different model of professionalism, one that would become increasingly familiar in the modernist period. Certainly, in his hauteur regarding the reading public, as well as in his commitment to the values of craft, of style, of culture and taste, Stevenson participates in that reshaping of authorial self-presentation that Jonathan Freedman has identified most notably in James, Pater, and Wilde. As Freedman suggests, rejecting the middle-class marketplace could be a highly marketable strategy, just as distancing oneself from both the Besantian professional and the general reader could be a way of asserting one's own more authentic professionalism.[41]

Yet while James, Pater, and Wilde – all consummate modernist professionals by Freedman's standards – have been assimilated into the modernist canon, Stevenson has not. There are doubtless many reasons for this exclusion, but one has to do with Stevenson's conspicuously split allegiances, his dual commitment to aestheticism and "style" on the one hand and to what George Saintsbury called "the pure romance of adventure" on the other.[42] A feuilletonist who wrote pirate stories, Stevenson combined a Paterian attention to the intricacies of style and form with blood-and-thunder celebrations of male adventure. While aestheticism in turn became a key component of much Modernist writing, adventure did not. Stevenson's champions in the twentieth century have almost always been those who, like Proust and Nabokov, recognize in him a fellow dandy. Critical considerations of his adventure stories have, by contrast, tended to thrust him firmly back into the nineteenth century. I will take up the late-Victorian "male romance" more fully in Chapter 4; here I note only that the male romance was itself a rejection of both realism and professionalism. Unlike aestheticism, however, it rejected them in the name of a reimagined male bourgeois identity. It was thus a form of critique – occluded, self-interested, contradictory – arising from within the patriarchy itself. Stevenson's simultaneous embrace of aestheticism and adventure thus possesses a certain coherence, yet it was also the source of significant incoherences. Like Oscar Wilde, Stevenson cultivated a style both aesthetic and personal that carried within it an implicit critique of conventional middle-class mores. Yet like Andrew Lang, Rider Haggard, Arthur Conan Doyle, and other votaries of the male romance, Stevenson used the conventions of "adventure" (and again, those conventions could be said to structure both his work and, especially after the move to Vailima, his life) in an attempt to reshape his male middle-class readership and ultimately to affirm his ties to them.

That Stevenson felt this split in his allegiances with special acuteness while writing *Jekyll and Hyde* is suggested by his account of the story's genesis offered in "A Chapter on Dreams" (1892). In this essay Stevenson writes that *Jekyll and Hyde*, like many of his tales, originated in a dream which he simply transcribed and elaborated. Indeed "I am sometimes tempted to suppose...[that] the whole of my published fiction...[is] the single-handed product of some Brownie, some Familiar, some unseen collaborator, whom I keep locked in a back garret" of the mind "while I get all the praise."[43] Stevenson's conscious self – "what I call I, my conscience ego, the denizen of the pineal gland" – is left merely to bring some order to the Brownies' ideas and then to "dress the whole in the best words and sentences that I can find and make" (XVI, 187). For post-Freudian readers this account of creativity's sources in the unconscious will sound familiar. Like Freud, Stevenson is deeply indebted to Romantic paradigms of the artist: "A Chapter on Dreams" in effect reimagines Shelley's Cave of Prometheus in proto-psychoanalytic language. Like Freud, too, Stevenson distinguishes between dream and waking world in terms of a series of productive contrasts: energy and order, licentiousness and morality ("my Brownies have not a rudiment of what we call a conscience" [xvi, 188]), spontaneity and craft, and so on. It seems especially appropriate that Edward Hyde should spring from a dream, since like the Brownies he is so easily identified with the raging energies of the id.

Yet Stevenson's unconscious is distinctly un-Freudian in one respect, for it has developed what can only be called a business sense. Over the years, Stevenson writes, he has come to dream only *marketable* stories, for the denizen of the pineal gland has no use for any other. Where once the Brownies told tales that, though powerful, were "almost formless" (xvi, 178), now "they have plainly learned...to build the scheme of a considerate story and to arrange emotion in progressive order" (xvi, 186–87). They now "dream in sequence" and "tell...a story piece by piece, like a serial" (xvi, 187). This new-found restraint arises not from any intrinsic love of aesthetic form but because the Brownies "have an eye to the bankbook" and "share in [Stevenson's] financial worries" (xvi, 186). "When the bank begins to send letters and the butcher to linger at the back gate...at once the little people begin to stir themselves" (xvi, 183).[44]

Despite its comic tone, the essay's point is a radical one: in what Stevenson called "the days of professional literature"[45] even the ostensibly unbridled play of the unconscious has come to be determined by the exigencies of the pocketbook. Stevenson has become a professional author whether he would or no. In "A Chapter on Dreams" the creative unconscious is not, as it sometimes was for the Romantics or for Freud, a place elsewhere, freed from the disabling pressures of history. Instead it is decisively shaped by those pressures. To survive, an author must not only write to order but also dream to order. So well trained have the Brownies become, the essay ironically concludes, that they have begun to fantasize potentially marketable stories in styles entirely unlike Stevenson's own. "Who would have supposed that a Brownie of mine should invent a tale for Mr. Howells?" (xvi, 189). In learning to write like William Dean Howells, that champion of sturdy realist prose, the Brownies demonstrate that they know better than Stevenson himself what goes down best with the reading public. Increasingly dissevered from any individual ego, the Brownies place themselves in willing bondage to the demands of the marketplace.

Stevenson, thought by the world to be the "author" of his tales, is only an amanuensis – "I hold the pen...and I do the sitting at the table...and when all is done, I make up the manuscript and pay for the registration" (XVI, 187–88) – transcribing tales he can claim no credit for, since they come not from some deep authentic self but from the culture itself. If Stevenson succeeds in giving his middle-class readers what they want, the essay concludes, that is because they have manufactured his stories for him.[46] "A Chapter on Dreams" is in essence an elegy for Romantic paradigms of creativity. The Romantic visionary genius has become the Besantian purveyor of goods, a kind of literary shopkeeper.

"A Chapter on Dreams" also gives further weight to the claim that *Jekyll and Hyde* traces the gradual taming of Edward Hyde into a parody of bourgeois respectability. Like Hyde, the Brownies find that lawlessness and licentiousness simply do not pay, and that they must adjust accordingly. As in the novel, Stevenson concludes that there is no place elsewhere, no human activity not already saturated with ideology. The creative unconscious is shown to be wholly acculturated: not in opposition to bourgeois morality but unavoidably pledging fealty to it.[47] In a striking and bitter letter to Gosse, Stevenson called this servicing of the public a form of prostitution. "We are whores," he wrote, "some of us pretty whores, some of us not: whores of the mind, selling to the public the amusements of our fireside as the whore sells the pleasures of her bed."[48] His further point is that under modern conditions whoredom is the writer's only option. In another letter he returned to this same metaphor: "like prostitutes" professional authors "live by a pleasure. We should be paid if we give the pleasure we pretend to give; but why should we be honoured?"[49]

What begins to emerge is a cluster of veiled equivalences, with threads linking Stevenson, his creative Brownies, Edward Hyde, and the prostitute-writer within a larger web comprising middle-class ideology, commerce, and the ethics of professionalism. *Jekyll and Hyde*, I would argue, is in part a symbolic working through of these linkages. We recall for instance that bourgeois commerce is implicitly associated with whoring in Stevenson's description of the "thriving" commercial street which Jekyll's house backs on to, its "florid charms," "freshly painted shutters," and "well polished brasses" giving luster to goods displayed "in coquetry; so that the shop fronts stood along that thoroughfare with an air of invitation" (30). The doctor's house fronts on to "a square of ancient, handsome houses, now for the most part decayed from their high estate" and given over to vaguely disreputable trades, "shady lawyers, and the agents of obscure enterprises": the once-fine homes are "let in flats and chambers to all sorts and conditions of men" (40). Readers who hear in this last passage a covert reference to Besant's popular 1882 novel, *All Sorts and Conditions of Men*, might speculate that Stevenson is indirectly including professional authorship among the shady and obscure trades of modern life. Even without the specific connection to Besant, we note that Jekyll's house is surrounded front and back by the trappings of bourgeois life, a life described in terms of the seedy, the disreputable, the garish, the decayed. Such linkages – commerce and prostitution, prostitution and authorship, authorship and professionalism, professionalism and bourgeois ideology, and so on – suggest that we might usefully approach *Jekyll and Hyde* as an indirect attempt by Stevenson to size up his situation as a professional writer at the close of the nineteenth century.

The novel in fact turns out to be obsessively concerned with writing of various kinds: wills, letters, chemical formulae, bank drafts, "full statements," and the like. Like "A Chapter on Dreams," *Jekyll and Hyde* worries over the question of authenticity. Just as in the essay Stevenson feared that his writing originated not in some genuine self but in a market-driven unconscious, so in the novel he continually links writing with forgery and other kinds of "inauthentic" production. Enfield first discovers Hyde's identity when he reads his name written on a cheque that Enfield "had every reason to believe...was a forgery." That in fact "the cheque was genuine" only convinces Enfield that the deception runs deeper than he had imagined (32). Hyde was known even earlier to Utterson through Jekyll's will, which the lawyer considers an affront to "the sane and customary sides of life" (35) and whose irregularities he "never approved of" (43). Even before he makes his first appearance in the present of the novel, then, Hyde is associated with writing that is at once "professional" – bank drafts and legal testaments – and yet also somehow irregular and thus troubling. In both instances, moreover, Hyde stands to benefit financially, just as in "A Chapter on Dreams" Stevenson says his own "irregular" writings proved to be the most lucrative.

Jekyll too is implicated in the production of questionable writing. Utterson, after hearing Mr. Guest's analysis of Jekyll's letters, is driven to conclude that the doctor has begun to "forge for a murderer" (55). We also recall that Jekyll's downfall results from the "impurity" of his original chemical formulae, and that it is precisely out of that impurity that Hyde originally springs (96).[50] We cannot finally separate Jekyll's writing from Hyde's, however, since a central conceit of the story is that they write identical hands. "Of my original character," the doctor notes, "one part remained to me: I could write my own hand" (93). Hyde can sign Jekyll's cheques and Jekyll can write Hyde's letters because their "characters" (in both senses of that word) are the same. Ever vigilant, F. W. H. Myers objected to this conceit, saying that it showed a "want of familiarity" on Stevenson's part "with recent psycho-physical discussions" concerning the individuality of handwriting.[51] Once again fingering a pressure point in the novel, Myers argued that no two hands could be identical, since each individual's unique and authentic character is reproduced via the characters on the page. In a parallel vein, both Rider Haggard and E. T. Cook took exception to Jekyll's will, claiming that the law would never recognize such a document because it could not be securely attributed to Jekyll himself.[52]

Jekyll and Hyde of course takes as its explicit theme the possibility that the self is not unique and inviolable. Yet Myers, Haggard, and Cook seem relatively untroubled by the novel's "revelation" that two distinct subjectivities inhabit the same "self." All three men instead attest to the anxiety that arises from the suspicion that writing itself might be entangled in this same indeterminacy. As their appeals to science and the law further suggest, vast realms of social discourse operate on the assumption that writing and selfhood are interchangeable. Yet it is precisely this faith that both "A Chapter on Dreams" and *Jekyll and Hyde* undermine. In this context it is worth noting that Stevenson himself has often been criticized for not being sufficiently "present" in his own writings. In 1927, at the nadir of Stevenson's reputation, Leonard Woolf dismissed him as having "no style of his own." His writing is "false," Woolf contended; at best he was a mimic, "a good imitator."[53] The "no style" argument is common in Stevenson criticism, and interestingly finds its complement in the equally common claim that Stevenson is merely a stylist. During his lifetime both William Archer and George Moore criticized Stevenson for being all style and no substance.[54] What links these seemingly contradictory assessments is their shared suspicion that there may be no "self" visible in Stevenson's writing, no discernible subjectivity expressed there. Rather than style being the man, it seems that in Stevenson's case style – whether his own or borrowed – replaces the man. Stevenson occasionally critiqued himself along these same lines, claiming that as a writer he was merely "a sedulous ape" who did no more than mimic the styles of the writers who came before him.[55] This self-characterization links Stevenson back to Edward Hyde, himself a "sedulous ape" who learns to his great cost how to mimic his "betters."

Given this context, we can readily agree with Ronald Thomas's claim that *Jekyll and Hyde* enacts the modernist "disappearance of the author." Thomas notes, for instance, how often in the story writing is tied to vanishing.[56] "When this shall fall into your hands," Jekyll predicts in his last letter to Utterson, "I shall have disappeared" (72). Earlier, the lawyer's apprehensions concerning Jekyll's will centered on the provision that it come into effect upon the doctor's "disappearance or unexplained absence" (35). Hastie Lanyon likewise pens his narrative (also "not to be opened until the death or disappearance of Dr. Henry Jekyll" [58]) knowing that it will not be read until after his decease. It is thus only fitting that the novel concludes by foregrounding this link between the act of writing and the death of selfhood: "as I lay down my pen," reads the book's final sentence, "I bring the life of that unhappy Henry Jekyll to an end" (97).

That last sentence points the problem with particular sharpness, since it leaves unclear to whom "I" refers. Though the document is labelled "Henry Jekyll's Full Statement of the Case," within the statement the first person shifts referents with notorious frequency. The final few paragraphs contain sentences in which "I" means Jekyll, sentences in which "I" means Hyde, and sentences in which both Jekyll and Hyde are referred to in the third person, leaving an authorial "I" unattached to any self. The oft-cited confession of ontological anxiety – "He, I say – I cannot say, I" (84) – is in one sense misleading, since the "Full Statement" says "I" all the time. We merely do not always know who "I" is. Like the conscious self posited in "A Chapter on Dreams," the "I" of the "Full Statement" holds the pen and sits at the desk yet cannot unequivocally claim to be author of the document.

This dissociation of writing from selfhood is especially conspicuous in what is after all meant to be an autobiographical narrative. When Jekyll begins his confession in properly Victorian fashion ("I was born in the year 18— to a large fortune, endowed besides with excellent parts, inclined by nature to industry," and so on [81]), we might expect him to at last write himself into the kind of coherence ostensibly promised by the autobiographical form.[57] What he finds instead is a self increasingly fragmented and estranged from "his" own writing. "Think of it – I did not even exist!" (86).

Jekyll and Hyde covertly enacts, then, a crisis in realist writing alongside its more overt thematizing of a crisis in bourgeois subjectivity. That these crises find expression in a story "about" criminal degeneracy should not surprise us, since traditional humanist notions of both realism and identity were deeply embedded in the normative categories deployed by degenerationists. *Jekyll and Hyde* self-consciously dismantles those categories, though it does not offer any to replace them, since Stevenson too felt himself estranged both from his "professional" self and from his writing. It is easy to see his subsequent flight to Samoa as a finally futile attempt to reclaim the possibility of pure Romantic expression. The irony, of course, is that exile made him more popular than ever with the middle-class reading public in Britain.

CHAPTER 3

Wilde's trials: reading erotics and the erotics of reading

POSING

The first English edition of Nordau's *Degeneration* appeared in February 1895, the same month that the Marquess of Queensberry left a calling card for Oscar Wilde with an insult scrawled on its face. Queensberry's handwriting proved difficult to decipher, but one misspelled word – "Somdomite" – was legible enough for Wilde to feel justified in bringing a suit for libel against his tormentor. The disastrous trial that ensued led directly to Wilde's arrest and subsequent conviction for "acts of gross indecency" under the 1885 Criminal Law Amendment Act, which prohibited sexual relations between men. The press coverage of the three proceedings involving Wilde was extensive and highly sensational. During these same months *Degeneration* enjoyed mostly favorable reviews in the papers, and Nordau's book was often used to gloss the dramatic events taking place at the Old Bailey. After the inconclusive close of the second trial, for instance, an editorialist in *Reynolds' Newspaper* wrote:

> It is certain that this whole case has stamped as pernicious the kind of literature with which Wilde's name is closely identified. That literature is one of the most diseased products of a diseased time. Indeed, so far as English writers are concerned, we do not know where we should find all the worst characteristics of our decadent civilization – its morbidity, its cold heartless brilliance, its insolent cynicism, its hatred of all rational restraint, its suggestiveness – more accurately mirrored than in the writings of Oscar Wilde. In his powerful book on "Degeneration," Max Nordau has dissected Wilde's absurdities with great ability.[1]

In fact Nordau has relatively little to say about Wilde in *Degeneration*. He says nothing at all about the issue presumably being debated in court, namely Wilde's sexual activities.[2] Then again, neither does the *Reynolds'* editorialist. Despite the enormous publicity surrounding the trials, press accounts never named and seldom even alluded to the specific sexual acts

Wilde was charged with.[3] Instead – and here the editorial reproduces a procedure adopted not just by the papers but by the government prosecutors – attention was directed at Wilde's writings, which were taken as indicative of his "perverse" character as well as symptomatic of a general cultural crisis. Though Wilde was eventually convicted of "indecent acts," the focus of the trials was less on what he did than on what he was. What he was, the prosecutors argued, was revealed most clearly in his writings, which in turn "accurately mirrored," as *Reynolds'* put it, "the worst characteristics of our decadent civilization."

Nordau could be used to frame journalistic accounts of the trials because he, like Wilde's assailants in court, saw criminal deviance as arising out of the complex interactions of private character and social milieu, interactions frequently mediated through literary texts. Nordau's brief discussion of Wilde in *Degeneration* is guided by three assumptions central to his book as a whole: first, that deviance is a form of character rather than a mode of behavior; second, that individual character expresses (and thus reveals) itself most coherently through the medium of literary writing; and third, that literary works exert a profound influence over the shape and "health" of a culture. The argument forms a neat circle, since the deviant cast of an individual character could then be traced to the malign influence of a decadent culture, or even of an especially mischievous book. For Nordau, Wilde is "degenerate" not because of specific acts he performs but because of what Nordau terms his "personal eccentricities" – traits of character whose signs are outlandish dress, overweening vanity, perverse taste, and a "megalomaniacal contempt for men."[4] Working backward, Nordau traces these eccentricities to somatic disorders caused by the "vertigo and whirl" of contemporary life. Working forward, he sees in Wilde's writings an expression of his deviant character and warns that their cumulative effect on the reading public can only be pernicious.

This same method of arguing was adopted by Wilde's opponents in all three court proceedings. In the initial libel suit Edward Carson defended Queensberry by attacking Wilde's character, and he attacked Wilde's character by way of the writer's aphorisms, his letters, and *The Picture of Dorian Gray*. The prosecutors in the two subsequent trials, Charles Gill and Sir Frank Lockwood, followed Carson's successful precedent. Discussion in court was seldom allowed to drift far from dangerous Oscar and his suspicious writings. Ed Cohen contends that by the time the trials closed Wilde "had become the paradigmatic example for an emerging public definition of a new 'type'" of deviant individual, the male homosexual.[5]

Unlike the sodomist in earlier legal usages, the homosexual was defined primarily by his character rather than by his practices. Carson made no attempt to prove that Wilde had engaged in homosexual activities, only that he had "posed as a sodomite." As Cohen correctly notes, Carson thus opened up "the possibility for designating Wilde as a kind of sexual actor without explicitly referring to the specificity of his sexual acts, and thereby crystallized a new constellation of sexual meanings predicated upon 'personality' and not practices."[6]

More vividly than any event of the period, Wilde's trials illuminate the complexly interwoven anxieties inhering in the social construction of deviance. Though homosexuality was but one of many spurious forms of criminal degeneracy identified by late-Victorian pathologists, by the 1890s it was frequently used to stand for the rest. (That different forms of deviance were interchangeable is indicated by the structural homology between Nordau's discussion of Wilde and Carson's. Nordau called Wilde a decadent rather than a sodomist, but his and Carson's arguments follow nearly identical paths.) If Wilde was a paradigm of the male homosexual "type," that type in turn became a paradigm of the deviant individual.

The very statute under which Wilde was prosecuted testified to homosexuality's new paradigmatic status. Section 11 of the Criminal Law Amendment Act of 1885 prohibited "any male person" from committing "in public or private...any act of indecency with another male person." In intent and effect the act marked an important departure from earlier legislation covering sexual practices. Until 1885 sexual offenders were charged with felony under a 1533 statute outlawing "the detestable and abominable vice of buggery." The 1533 act superseded earlier ecclesiastical prohibitions against sodomy as a crime against nature. Under both sacred and secular law sodomy was defined to include all sexual acts that did not have procreation as their aim. A range of *practices* was interdicted: masturbation, bestiality, birth control, anal and oral intercourse, male–male intimacies.[7] Yet while the focus was on specific sexual acts, in the long run the 1533 statute also helped to normalize a specific sexual persona, namely the married and monogamous middle-class male. By the nineteenth century arrests for sodomy had become relatively rare (the last execution occurred in 1836, and sodomy ceased to be a capital offense in 1861), which means only that sexuality was by this time being regulated more effectively in the home, the school, the pulpit, and the clinic than in the courts.

In contrast to the 1533 statute, the Labouchère amendment to the Criminal Law Amendment Act legislated against a particular type of sexual character. "Acts of indecency" were outlawed even in private, but the acts themselves were – significantly – never specified. The 1885 statute marked the entry into legal discourse of the homosexual man as a deviant "character." Whereas the sodomist was a perpetrator of illegal acts, the homosexual, as Michel Foucault notes, became

> a type of life, a life form, and a morphology, with an indiscreet anatomy and possibly a mysterious physiology. Nothing that went into his total composition was unaffected by his sexuality. It was everywhere present in him: at the root of all his actions because it was their insidious and indefinitely active principle; written immodestly on his face and body because it was a secret that always gave itself away. It was consubstantial with him, less as a habitual sin than as a singular nature.[8]

As Wilde discovered to his cost, one need not commit sodomy to be labelled a criminal. One had only to "pose" as a sodomist. ("From a label," Lord Henry Wotton points out in *Dorian Gray*, "there is no escape."[9])

At stake was the sanctity of the middle-class home. In addition to homosexuality, the Criminal Law Amendment Act also aimed at regulating female prostitution. The initial impetus for the bill was the public outcry following W. T. Stead's lurid "Maiden Tribute of Modern Babylon" exposé, which uncovered an extensive traffic in underage girls in London's East End. As this symbolic linkage of prostitution and homosexuality suggests, the 1885 act as a whole was designed to protect bourgeois domestic spaces from various forms of contamination.[10] The bill was vigorously supported by "social purity" campaigners like Josephine Butler and Catherine Booth, not because of its strictures on homosexuality but because it promised to safeguard the middle-class home against aberrant desire. During the Commons debate the Home Secretary, Sir Richard Cross, noted that "there is nothing more sacred to the English people…as the purity of their own households," a purity the bill was intended to safeguard.[11] Proponents of the bill further argued that the strength of the home was inseparable from the health of the nation and empire. Rome, it was said, died when vice invaded the family circle.[12]

During the Queensberry case, Carson continually reiterated the danger Wilde posed for home and country.[13] In order to clear his client of the libel charge, Carson had to demonstrate not only that Queensberry's accusations were true but that publishing them was in the public interest. To do the first, he had to construct a character for Wilde more convincing to the jury than Wilde's own self-portrayal. To do the second, he had to show that this character was not merely a private matter but had wider social effects. To achieve both goals, he read *The Picture of Dorian Gray*.

Indeed, the grimmest irony of the Queensberry trial was that Carson turned it into a battle of hermeneutics, and won. In court he proved to be a more persuasive (which is not to say a better or more accurate) reader of Wilde's character and writings than Wilde himself was.[14] As I argued in Chapter 1, questions of deviance in this period inevitably resolved themselves into questions of hermeneutics. Carson did not read Wilde's body to make his case, as Lombroso or Tardieu – whose taxonomies of homosexuality's physiological signs were widely known in the 1890s – might have done.[15] Instead he read Wilde's "pose." In Carson's view, Wilde's deviance revealed itself not through stigmata but rather through the disposition of his entire self. Carson continually drew attention to Wilde's physical attitude, his projection of personality by way of carriage and demeanor. Wilde posed, said Carson, but not in the sense of pretending to be what he was not. He posed in the sense of theatrically parading what he was. In court Wilde's flamboyant acts of public self-construction were continually turned into indictments against his character. When Wilde objected to Carson's frequent use of the word "pose" during the trial, the counsel sharply retorted: "It is a favourite word of your own."[16]

At the same time Carson put *Dorian Gray* at center stage, as further evidence that Wilde's pose was that of a sodomist. If Wilde wanted to make Queensberry criminally responsible for what he wrote, Carson would see to it that Wilde was put in the same position. In his opening speech Carson told the jury, "In my judgement, if the case had rested on Mr. Wilde's literature alone, Lord Queensberry would have been absolutely justified in the course he has taken."[17] In court Carson's use of *Dorian Gray* was twofold. He argued that it, like Wilde's demeanor, revealed that its author was guilty of "a certain tendency" toward homosexual behavior. He then argued that the novel constituted a public danger through its "advocacy" of the unnamed "vice imputed to Mr. Wilde."[18]

As Carson seemed to know, both these arguments depended on his being an aggressively naive reader. Against the subtleties and delicacies of the Wildean critic, Carson opposed what he called the "ordinary individual" with his "common sense" approach to interpretation. That common sense lined up so neatly with legal and medical notions of criminal degeneracy only strengthened his position. Wilde protested that he had "no knowledge of the views of ordinary individuals," but Carson made sure that in court ordinary views prevailed.[19] Carson's common reader knew that language was transparent; that a work of literature expressed the personality of its author; that fiction could be a vehicle of either good or evil depending on the nature of the influence it exercised. Wilde spent his entire career working to undermine precisely these notions, but in court his objections to such dreary (and, as it proved, dangerous) literal-mindedness were largely ineffectual. As Carson recognized and Wilde apparently did not, the law itself was deeply imbued with common sense notions of language, representation, and their joint status as "evidence." Wilde's criticisms of the "incalculably stupid" "views of Philistines" when it came to reading were repeatedly turned against him, since the court began from the assumption that those views were normative.[20] In such circumstances, Lord Henry Wotton's offhand remark, "Nowadays most people die of a sort of creeping common sense" (66), turned out to be prophetic of Wilde's own fate.[21]

AUTHENTIC INSINCERITY

From one perspective, though, Carson was an astute reader of *Dorian Gray*. The novel is about the very things – character, deviance, influence, desire – that Carson said it was, though it everywhere resists the kinds of narrow constructions he put on those terms. Wilde's genius as a writer lay in his ability to critique common sense from within, to turn its own language against it. "Our proverbs want rewriting," Sybil Vane tells her brother (94), and this is just what Wilde does. He habitually employs the most familiar words and phrases in order to make possible entirely unfamiliar ways of thinking. As Regenia Gagnier notes, Wilde's mind "was stocked with commonplaces, and these seem to have been there for the sole purpose of their subversion."[22]

Subversion from within can be the most unsettling form of critique, since it invariably involves mockery. Carson was right to find *Dorian Gray* a threatening work. In it Wilde mimics the rhetoric of the dominant classes, in the process loosening that rhetoric from its accustomed ideological moorings. Despite his reputation for paradox, Wilde always insisted that his goal was to return words to "their proper and simple meaning." His mimicry, his alogical and unsettling inversions and reversals, were meant to release language from the "distortions" of conventional usage and restore the "right signification" of words.[23] "Names are everything," Lord Henry contends as he puts forward a "plan for rechristening everything" (230–31).

Most notably, Wilde is a key figure in the overturning of humanist ideologies of identity, ideologies that were on prominent display during the trials.[24] "Deviance" itself becomes virtually unthinkable outside the context of organicist conceptions of character. Belief in a deep authentic self, one capable of coherently expressing and revealing its essential nature, underwrites both the 1885 Criminal Law Amendment Act and the specific charges brought against Wilde. Carson, like Gill and Lockwood after him, implicitly argued that in "essence" Wilde's character was deviant whether or not he committed criminal acts.

To this argument Wilde in effect replied not, what is deviance? but rather, what is a character? In *Dorian Gray*, Basil Hallward adopts what would become the court's position when he assures Dorian that "there are no such things" as "secret vices." "If a wretched man has a vice, it shows itself in the lines of his mouth, the droop of his eyelid, the moulding of his hands even" (182–83). (In court Edward Carson read this passage aloud.) Like the *Daily Chronicle* reviewer who professed to loathe Dorian for "the moral pestilence which is incarnate in him," Basil believes that character can be read off the body.[25] Yet the presumption that "sin is a thing that writes itself across a man's face" (182), while it may serve in a world of Edward Hydes (or Edward Carsons), proves inadequate to the world Basil actually inhabits. As the novel makes clear, Dorian possesses nothing like an "authentic" identity. Repeatedly, he is described in terms that emphasize his lack of interiority. Dorian enters the story as a surface, a "visible presence" (32) who exists for Basil solely as "the curves of certain lines...the loveliness and subtleties of certain colours" (33). He is not an individual but rather a form of "abstract...beauty" (34). Henry feels sure that Dorian "never thinks" (25), and to this he attributes the young man's "purity" (39). If at the moment of its completion Basil's portrait perfectly captures its sitter, that is because the portrait, like Dorian, exists entirely on the plane of the visible.

Over the course of the novel Dorian acquires not a "character" but a "personality." Wilde habitually eschews the former term, with its aura of depth and authenticity, for the latter, which by the 1880s had begun to accrue its modern connotations of insincerity, artifice, and theatricality. If, as Wilde tells us, "now and then a complex personality took the place and assumed the office of art" (83), that is in part because both personalities and works of art are created artifacts. As Rachel Bowlby aptly puts it, Dorian "is introduced to an identity of his own" through his contact with Basil's portrait and Lord Henry's dazzling word play.[26] The young man feels that his conversations with Henry have served "to reveal him to himself" (44), but Henry recognizes that "to a large extent the lad was his own creation" (83). Similarly, the portrait functions as a kind of lacanian mirror for Dorian, who gazes at his image "as if he had recognized himself for the first time" (48). That qualifying "as if" is important, since it indicates that Dorian, like the child in Lacan's mirror stage, is not recognizing but rather beginning to constitute a self by way of the "reflected" image he sees. His encounter with the portrait in turn provides a model for Dorian's later, conscious endeavors to "multiply [his] personalities" (174). He eventually comes to

> wonder at the shallow psychology of those who conceive the Ego in man as a thing simple, permanent, reliable, and of one essence. To him, man was a being with myriad lives and myriad sensations, a complex multiform creature that bore within itself strange legacies of thought and passion. (175)

Here as elsewhere Wilde rejects humanist notions of the organic and autonomous individual. Yet – and herein lies much of their ability to unsettle – these rejections are usually couched in the language of humanist individualism. Through mimicry Wilde appropriates this language for his own antihumanist ethic. "The aim of life is self-development" (41), Henry tells Dorian, but for him the fully realized individual is defined not by an authentic interiority but by a drive to become ever more inauthentic, ever more "complex" and "multiform." True individuals, Lord Henry observes, continue to accrete new personalities. "They retain their egotism, and add to it many other egos. They are forced to have more than one life. They become more highly organized, and to be highly organized is, I should fancy, the object of man's existence" (101–02). That last sentence is straight out of Herbert Spencer, in whose writings Wilde immersed himself as an Oxford undergraduate.[27] Yet Wilde has turned Spencer's evolutionist language inside out. Where Spencer saw growth in terms of the coherent and directed realization of a potential latent in (and thus essential to) the individual, Wilde views it in terms of an undirected and largely alogical process of accretion. If we are to realize "the perfection of our development," Gilbert says in "The Critic as Artist" (1891), we must learn that "the soul within us is no single spiritual entity." Paradoxically, it is "through constant change, and constant change alone" that one finds "his true identity."[28]

Wilde's model for this mode of being is the actor. Sybil Vane can be taken as the symbol of Wilde's impossible ideal, the utopia he says must orient every philosophy.[29] In Dorian's words, she is "more than an individual" because "she has personality" – not a character – and can therefore be "all the great heroines of the world in one" (80). "'When is she Sybil Vane?' 'Never'" (80). This liberating mobility of identity is inseparable from Sybil's lack of self-consciousness. We may justifiably object to the way Dorian, not to mention Wilde, patronizes Sybil for her innocence. Yet within the terms of the novel her innocence is her power. She captivates her audiences precisely through the paradox that her poses are genuine, her insincerity authentic. She continually reproduces herself as an aesthetic artifact but does so "naturally." Wilde further heightens our sense of Sybil's unself-consciousness through contrast with her mother, whose "false theatrical gestures" (88) and self-conscious "affectations" (91) he gathers under the heading not of art but of melodrama (96, 98). Wilde engages in self-parody here as well, since Mrs. Vane's preference for the shapeliness and intensity of drama over the "vulgar details" (98) of everyday life, for phrases "vividly and dramatically expressed" (99) over mundane common speech, echoes not only Lord Henry's aesthetic (128–33) but Wilde's as well. As Mrs. Vane's covert affinities with her author indicate, Wilde recognized that Sybil's authentic insincerity was an unreachable ideal. Unself-consciousness once lost cannot be regained, as Sybil herself discovers. Her accession to "true" selfhood is also a fall into inauthenticity: once awakened into what she thinks of as "reality," Sybil becomes "unreal," "artificial," "false," "commonplace," "an absolute failure" (111–12). Given a choice between the "bad art" of the genuine (112) and the theatricality of melodrama, Wilde will always choose the latter. "Being natural is simply a pose, and the most irritating pose I know" (26).

It is vital to recognize that, in thus making a virtue of insincerity, Wilde is being neither dilettantish nor inconsequential. As "The Soul of Man Under Socialism" (1891) shows most clearly, Wilde saw his redefined individualism as the necessary ground for humanity's political and spiritual emancipation. The seeming paradox of this essay – that socialism and individualism are synonymous – dissolves once we recognize that the Wildean individual is not the private and inward subject of liberal humanism. As Rodney Shewan points out, Wilde's definition of the non-humanist individual owes much to W. K. Clifford's notion of the "tribal self." After reading Clifford's "On the Scientific Basis of Morals" (1875), Wilde wrote in his commonplace book that the basis of morality lay in the self, by which he means "not the individual self but what Clifford calls the tribal self: individualism, private property, and a private conscience, as well as the nominative case of personal pronouns, do not appear until late in all civilisations: it is the tribal self which is the...canon of right and wrong."[30]

As Wilde ironically notes in "Soul of Man," humanist subjects in bourgeois society are defined not by their autonomy but precisely by their "uniformity of type and conformity to rule," their virtual indistinguishability one from another (286). Socialism and (true) individualism work to subvert the ideological structures that produce such uniformity. The radical personal freedom Wilde preaches is inseparable from his desire for a radical reorganization of society. Reform society, and "human nature" itselfs will be different. Acknowledging that his "scheme" for a socialist individualism "is quite impractical, and goes against human nature," Wilde argues:

This is why it is worth carrying out. For what is a practical scheme? *A practical scheme is either a scheme that is already in existence, or a scheme that could be carried out under existing conditions.* But it is exactly the existing conditions one objects to; and any scheme that could accept these conditions is wrong and foolish. The conditions will be done away with, and human nature will change. (284; Wilde's italics)

Because true individuals resist conformity and struggle to change "that dreadful universal thing called human nature,"[31] they find themselves classed among the criminal and the deviant. "*Most personalities have been obliged to be rebels*"; they recognize that "disobedience…is man's original virtue" (262, 258; Wilde's italics).[32]

Wilde emphasizes the connections between individualism and art, making the artist society's master criminal – and its prototypical deviant. Characteristically, he reverses the valences of these terms. It is "the public [who] are all morbid" because, unlike the artist, they are fettered by conformity. Thus, what the ordinary reader considers "unhealthy" "*is always a beautiful and healthy work of art*" (275; Wilde's italics). Later, when critics attacked *Dorian Gray* for being, as one put it, "heavy with the mephitic odours of moral and spiritual putrefaction,"[33] Wilde responded that in reality "there is a terrible moral in the novel," one the ordinary reader "will not be able to find, but which will be revealed to all whose minds are healthy."[34]

The novel's moral, says Wilde, is that "all excess, as well as all renunciation, brings its own punishment."[35] This seems to throw us back into the very categories Wilde has rejected. It invites us to turn Dorian's life into a cautionary fable on the dangers of straying from the tepid securities of the *via media*. Yet Wilde makes clear that his hero is punished not for his transgressions against bourgeois morality but because he comes to accept its standards. Dorian dies, Wilde wrote to the *Daily Chronicle*, not of his "sins" but of "an exaggerated sense of conscience" that effectively "mars all his pleasures for him."[36] Like Edward Hyde, Dorian eventually internalizes the very ethos he claims to repudiate.

Or rather, he projects that ethos on to his portrait. Thinking of the painting as his "conscience" and "a visible symbol of the degradation of sin" (125), Dorian endows it with the power symbolically to body forth his "true" self. He thus implicitly adopts the order of values wherein true selves exist and sin "writes itself across a man's face." It is no accident that the transformed image is seen only by Dorian and by Basil Hallward, the novel's principal spokesman for conventional morality. (Nor is it coincidental that Dorian's dead body will later lie just where Basil's fell.) In his own person, on the other hand, Dorian embodies the truth of Lord Henry's claim that "to live out [one's] life fully and completely" without a sense of sin would leave one unmarked and pure (41). The contrast between the lovely Dorian and the hideous portrait can be taken to stand for the difference between Henry's ethic and Basil's. As Dorian moves from one to the other, he adopts the valuation of himself as a "monstrous and loathsome thing" (135). His move is also one from Sibyllian unself-consciousness to a melodramatic self-awareness like that of Mrs. Vane, whose histrionics Dorian mimics in his final self-accusations (260–62). Fittingly, Henry tells his young friend that, in condemning himself as a sinner and determining that hereafter he is "going to be good" (257), he is "posing for a character that doesn't suit" him (252). Dorian comes, in true Christian fashion, to believe that "each sin" must bring "its sure, swift penalty along with it" (260), a self-fulfilling prophecy that issues in his unintended suicide. In the novel's fine last moment, Dorian's sins are transferred from the portrait and literally inscribed on his body, which becomes "withered, wrinkled, and loathsome" as a result (264). Ironically, these grotesque stigmata do not signify Dorian's "deviance." Rather, they symbolize his conformity to bourgeois morality. In best Foucauldian fashion, Dorian is disciplined to an ideology that teaches him to read himself as criminal.

Like Stevenson, Wilde directs our attention to the hermeneutic acts by which deviance is constructed. Unlike Stevenson, he suffered the pain of being himself the object of such critical scrutiny. If Wilde's accusers in court and in the press seemed obsessed with Dorian's depravity, that was because the fictional character was taken as his author's self-portrait. Similarly, if critics expended inordinate amounts of energy deciphering *The Picture of Dorian Gray*, that was because the book was read as Wilde's oblique confession, his apologia for a life of wickedness. In the view of Wilde's antagonists, the novel stood in the same relation to its author that the portrait stands in relation to Dorian: as the bearer of displaced stigmata. What Wilde hid in his life was on display in his art. The novel betrayed his "real" character as surely as the portrait revealed Dorian's.

No matter that Wilde warns against reading in this manner. More exuberantly and systematically than Stevenson, Wilde overturns Romanticist notions of art as self-expression. Hence his extravagant praise of the virtues of insincerity and lying ("The Decay of Lying"), his interest in masks ("The Critic as Artist"), and his spirited defenses of forgery and plagiarism ("Pen Pencil and Poison," "The Portrait of Mr. W. H."). In his paradoxical formulation, "*Art is the most intense mode of individualism that the world has ever known*" precisely because it does not express the artist's character.[37] True to his notion of individualism as the adopting of successive identities, Wilde sees "all Art being to a certain degree a mode of acting."[38] Like Sybil Vane, the artist strives for authentic insincerity. "Is insincerity such a terrible thing?" asks *Dorian Gray*'s narrator. "I think not. It is merely a method by which we can multiply our personalities" (174). In itself the artwork bears no mimetic relation to its producer, as even Basil Hallward comes to realize. "Art is always more abstract than we fancy. Form and colour tell us of form and colour – that is all" (145).

If Wilde rejected the idea that art expressed character, he also doubted its ability to influence the characters of others. Carson described *Dorian Gray* as a kind of virus whose contagion could be passed to those whose moral constitutions were less than sturdy. Behind such attacks lies the tradition of the "fatal book," a tradition Wilde himself conspicuously invokes in his lengthy descriptions of the "poisonous book" (156) Lord Henry lends to Dorian, a book modelled on Huysmans's *A Rebours*.[39] The temptation to compare the deleterious effects of Wilde's novel to those of Huysmans's was irresistible, and Carson did not resist it. Like most subsequent readers, he accepted at face value Dorian's contention that the book ultimately "harmed" and "poisoned" him (257), that his moral degradation could be traced to its malign influence. Lord Henry's response, on the other hand, has been noticed less often: "As for being poisoned by a book, there is no such thing as that. Art has no influence upon action...It is superbly sterile" (257).

In denying that art revealed its creator or influenced its audience, Wilde attacked the kinds of interpretive practices that would later be used against him. Indeed, one effect of the trials was to highlight those practices, since Wilde's exchanges with his questioners almost invariably became battles over how to read properly. Implicit in most readings (both then and now) of *Dorian Gray* is the assumption that we can name its hero's "sins." According to a strong critical consensus stretching from Wilde's moment to the present, Dorian Gray among other things engages in homosexual acts. But our certainty about this "fact" is chimerical, since the novel nowhere specifies the content of the rumors swirling about Dorian. Wilde wrote to the *Scots Observer*: "What Dorian Gray's sins are no one knows. He who finds them has brought them."[40] We might plausibly reply to this admonishment by arguing that Dorian's acts need not be named to be discernible, that clues to their nature abound for anyone willing to read between the lines. Yet to "decode" the novel in this way is to read exactly as Edward Carson read, however far our motivations and sympathies may lie from his. It is also not to read like Wilde.

AN EROTICS OF READING

Few doubted then, and fewer doubt now, that *Dorian Gray* is in some way about homoerotic love. But in what way? Wilde, it is often said, veiled his endorsement of same-sex love so that the novel's subversive message would elude the prudish and the censorious. Yet if Wilde's ultimate intent was to "code" homosexual love into his story in such a way that only the initiate would understand, he made a stunningly inept job of it. As the novel's reception history indicates, *Dorian Gray*'s readers have always viewed its secrets as open ones.[41] In court Wilde's counsel complained that "hidden meanings have been most unjustly read into the poetical and prose works of my client," but the plea fell on deaf ears.[42] Indeed, Carson stated flatly that the story "was understood by the readers thereof to describe the relations, intimacies, and passions of certain persons of sodomitical and unnatural habits, tastes, and practices," making it "an immoral and obscene work in the form of a narrative."[43] Later critics usually discard the moralistic judgment while retaining this basic understanding of the novel. At the same time, nearly all readers acknowledge that homoeroticism is something that must be read into this narrative, since Wilde nowhere explicitly identifies same-sex love as part of its content. If *Dorian Gray* depicts the love that dare not speak its name, in other words, it does so by steadfastly refusing to speak its name. Like the body of the homosexual in late-Victorian discourses of pathology, Wilde's text seems to bear on its surface the marks of an underlying nature that is at once revealed and hidden by its stigmata. The novel irresistibly invites us to engage in acts of decoding, whereby manifest content is exchanged for latent truth. Suspicious readers, we become like Gwendolen in *The Importance of Being Earnest* (1895), who tells Algernon: "Whenever people talk to me about the weather, I always feel quite certain that they mean something else. And that makes me so nervous."[44]

If the artist's job is to talk about one thing and mean another, the critic's traditional office has been to calm our nerves by reconciling the two. More clearly than most, however, Wilde recognized that such reconciliations are themselves forms of invention, that meaning does not lie inertly in a text (or a textualized body) waiting to be uncovered but is instead produced through critical intervention. For Wilde, these interventions could be creative, even capricious. He continually reminds us that art is not coded language in need of deciphering. "The critic will certainly be an interpreter," Gilbert contends in "The Critic as Artist," "but he will not treat Art as a riddling Sphinx, whose shallow secret may be guessed and revealed...He will not be an interpreter in the sense of one who simply repeats in another form a message that has been put into his lips to say" (373). A desire to tweak those seeking shallow secrets beneath inscrutable signs seems to have animated Wilde's decision to distribute green carnations to his friends on the opening night of *Lady Windermere's Fan* in 1892. When Graham Robertson asked, "What does it mean?" Wilde replied, "Nothing whatever, but that is just what nobody will guess."[45]

Similarly, "Lord Arthur Savile's Crime" (1887) satirizes this same, apparently inevitable need to find the truth of signs. Savile is told by "Mr. Septimus R. Podgers, Professional Cheiromantist," that he will murder someone. His fate is inscribed on his body: "written on his hand, in characters that he could not read himself, but that another could decipher, was some fearful secret of sin, some blood-red sign of crime."[46] Lord Arthur – moral, earnest, "essentially practical," and endowed with "excellent common sense" (33, 41) – appears to himself as anything but a murderer, yet he also believes that the signs of the body do not lie, that an individual's innate character must eventually express itself whatever efforts one may make to act otherwise. Therefore he tries, with comic ineptness, to live in accordance with the "true" identity that has been revealed to him. After two unsuccessful attempts at murder, he at last fulfills his biological destiny by killing Mr. Podgers, the professional reader.

Like *Dorian Gray*, "Lord Arthur Savile's Crime" effectively critiques the kinds of reading strategies by which criminal deviance was constructed, the same strategies that would later contribute to Wilde's own downfall. Extracting sodomy from a pose, Carson practiced a form of cheiromancy akin to Septimus Podgers's. Likewise, in approaching the text of *Dorian Gray* as evidence of a hidden truth, Carson treated the novel in precisely the way that Gerald Murchison treats Lady Alroy in "The Sphinx without a Secret" (1887). Murchison is obsessed with discovering what his veiled lover is hiding but, as the story's title suggests, her secret is that she does not have one. Like Wilde's green carnation, Lady Alroy's air of mystery means nothing at all, though this is just what Murchison does not guess.

Given that Wilde's works are for the most part notoriously evasive on the issue of homoeroticism, we may suspect that they too are secretless sphinxes. Yet to say that desire is absent from the content of a work is not to deny that the work itself generates a potent erotic charge. Instead, it is to relocate the source of that charge. As Wilde knew, the act of reading is itself erotic, especially when reading takes the form of critical apprehension – with apprehension being understood in all three of its senses at once: anxiety, perception, seizure. Deciphering brings its own libidinal pleasures. In "The Sphinx without a Secret," Murchison's arousal is due not to Lady Alroy herself but to "the indefinable atmosphere of mystery that surrounded her," a mystery which, he acknowledges, "excited my most ardent curiosity."[47] Indeed, this ardor survives even the revelation that Lady Alroy's veil veils nothing. As Murchison's last words – "I wonder" – nicely suggest, the ultimate source of his passion lies in a kind of epistemophilia: an unassuageable urge to know.

The entanglement of passions sexual and hermeneutic is at the heart of a story Wilde completed just prior to *Dorian Gray*. Like the novel, "The Portrait of Mr. W. H." (1889) centers on the beguiling painting of an attractive adolescent. Unlike the novel, it takes homoerotic love as its overt subject. The plot involves a quest, undertaken by three men at different moments, to discover the identity of the young man of Shakespeare's sonnets. The problem is a venerable, not to say a hoary, one in literary scholarship. So is Wilde's proposal of a boy actor named Willie Hughes as the poet's beloved, the "Mr. W. H." whom the sonnets' dedication calls their "onlie begetter." Wilde revivifies this familiar subject by making the story not just about Shakespeare's sexual desire for Willie Hughes but also about the hermeneutic frenzy that grips the three men as they pursue Mr. W. H. across the sonnets until, as Wilde's unnamed narrator says, "I...saw his face in every line" (168).

In the context of the tale, this interpretive quest is inextricable from the homoerotic bonds linking the story's three men, as each character's pursuit of W. H. is motivated by a desire to "capture" another by persuading him of the truth of the theory. The two forms of passion substitute for each other throughout the narrative. The name "Willie Hughes" comes to stand for the hidden object of readerly desire, the elusive truth that incites the hermeneutic endeavor. At the same time, the men's passion for the textual Willie mimics Shakespeare's passion for the supposedly real young man, which in turn provides a model for the erotically charged relationships among the story's three men.

"The Portrait of Mr. W. H." dramatizes the workings of two kinds of interpretive acts that would later be practiced by Wilde's accusers at the Old Bailey: reading a character out of a text, and reading desire into it. In the story Willie Hughes is taken to be "hidden" within the sonnets, just as the portrait of W. H. is supposedly discovered secreted inside a wooden chest (163–64). Graham, Erskine, and the narrator approach the poems as encoded messages – "secret things," Erskine calls them (160) – which deciphered will produce a lovely young man "as real...as Shakespeare" (162). Yet within the terms of the story Willie Hughes exists only as the residue of interpretation. As all three men admit, no external evidence corroborates their theory. Cyril Graham "discovers" the identity of the poet's lover "working purely by internal evidence" (157). His theory "evolved...purely from the Sonnets themselves" and thus depended "for its acceptance not so much on demonstrable proof of formal evidence as on a kind of spiritual and artistic sense, by which alone he claimed could the true meaning of the poems be discerned" (160–61). Later the narrator relies on the same kind of thorough close reading – "week after week, I pored over these poems" (212) – to establish W. H.'s identity, a procedure that necessarily leaves him "always on the brink of absolute verification" without ever attaining it (188–89). Yet, as the story makes clear, the "truth" of the interpretation out of which Mr. W. H. arises is finally irrelevant, except in the sense that the desire to possess truth drives the interpretive enterprise.

Indeed, in Wilde's view this is the scandal as well as the joy of reading: that it is not a science but an erotics. Critical understanding derives less from the workings of reason than from the libidinal investments that all reading demands. In "The Portrait of Mr. W. H." Wilde foregrounds this eroticism as he marks the cycles of critical tumescence and detumescence undergone by each reader in the story.[48] The processes of interpretation, figured as the gradual unveiling of Willie Hughes, are presented in sexual terms, culminating in a critical conviction that is also a form of arousal. When Graham first becomes convinced of Willie Hughes's existence, Erskine says: "I arrived to find him in a state of great excitement" (157). When Erskine in turn is at last persuaded, the narrator says: "I had never seen him so excited" (217). The narrator himself, "counting each pulse and throb of passion" (168) in the sonnets, slowly becomes enamored of the young man his readings create for him. His ardor for the boy actor's "golden hair...delicate mobile limbs, and...white lily hands" (177) finds release in a "passionate reiteration of the arguments and proofs that my study had suggested to me" (212). When the narrator concludes, "I had gone through every phase of this great romance" (213), the context leaves it unclear whether he is referring to the poet's affair with Mr. W. H. or his own with the sonnets.

As each of the three men in turn grasps the hermeneutic truth named

Willie Hughes, he must convince another whose ardor has waned. This is the other half of the critical enterprise: not only to take possession of the truth oneself, but to persuade others to do so. As William Cohen notes, Wilde figures belief in the Willie Hughes theory as something that passes between men.[49] Again, these passings-on are presented in sexual terms. In his last, "passionate" attempt to persuade Erskine, for instance, the narrator writes a long letter. "I put into the letter all my enthusiasm. I put into the letter all my faith." Yet

> no sooner...had I sent it off than a curious reaction came over me. It seemed to me that I had given away my capacity for belief...that something had gone out of me, as it were, and that I was perfectly indifferent to the whole subject. What was it that had happened? It is difficult to say. Perhaps by finding perfect expression for a passion, I had exhausted the passion itself. (212)

That last sentence, with its play on the word "expression," nicely captures the way criticism for Wilde is both verbal and physical, at once an affair of language and of the body. His passion spent, the narrator discovers that the sonnets now "revealed to me nothing of what I had found hidden in their lines" (214). This notion of criticism as dissemination leads to some characteristically salacious punning by Wilde.[50] Given the amount of time devoted in the story to explicating Elizabethan word play, for example, it is difficult not to hear a double entendre in the narrator's first response to Erskine's suicide: "To die for a literary theory! It seemed impossible" (217). Erskine blames his death on the narrator for, in effect, refusing to believe that his theory is indeed to die for. Likewise, if to persuade is to find "that something had gone out of" you and passed into another, to fail to persuade is to be reduced to a kind of critical onanism. "By the time you read this," Erskine writes in his suicide note, "I shall have died by my own hand" (217). Earlier, we recall, Cyril Graham also dies by his own hand after failing to convince Erskine. As he dies, a spurt of blood from his wound falls on the portrait of W. H., covering the name written there. "Master Will Hews" is thus once more hidden from view, prompting a new round of critical attempts to unveil him.[51]

The acute discomfort Wilde caused among many late-Victorian readers, Jonathan Dollimore suggests, was due in part to the "perceived connection between his aesthetic transgression and his sexual transgression."[52] "The Portrait of Mr. W. H." dramatizes how these two forms of transgression impinge on one another. Wilde endorses "deviant" love at the same time that he celebrates a readerly jouissance that is itself at odds with the paradigms of responsible reading adumbrated in, say,

Matthew Arnold's "The Function of Criticism at the Present Time" (1864). Moreover, as we have seen, in Wilde's tale each of these pleasures mirrors the other. Like Plato's *Symposium*, which Wilde's narrator pores over in admiration, "The Portrait of Mr. W. H." is notable for "the curious analogies it draws between intellectual enthusiasm and the physical passion of love" (184). The scandal of the story does not lie in the revelation of Shakespeare's love for a young man – by 1889 this could be considered old news – but in the notion that the critical act of compelling the sonnets to confess their sexual secrets could be itself an erotic experience. Desire, Wilde suggests, "deviant" or otherwise, may ultimately be traced not to the content of a text but to the dynamics of interaction between text and reader.

In working to expose the "secrets" of Wilde's works, late-Victorian reviewers often revealed an uneasy if indistinct awareness of their complicity in this dynamic. Hence the frequent recourse to the language of contagion in reviews of *Dorian Gray*. "Perversity" seemed to hang heavy in the air *between* text and reader. The *Daily Chronicle* called *Dorian Gray* "unclean" and "leprous"; Wilde's words exuded a "moral pestilence" capable of "defiling" those whom they touched. The *Scots Observer* claimed that the novel would "taint every young mind that comes in contact with it." *Punch*, calling the novel a "leprous distillment," advised readers to "take it in homeopathic doses."[53]

Yet the danger seemed to lie more in the quality of Wilde's writing than in its content. Contagion was carried along the very rhythms of his prose. Wilde's flamboyant rejection of the plain style was taken by contemporaries as the linguistic equivalent of his sexual transgressions. What Gagnier calls his "style of jeweled seduction" enticed and alarmed in equal measure. What Wilde said often seemed to matter much less than the way he said it. If, as he claimed, "Truth is entirely and absolutely a matter of style," then to seek the truth of Wilde's writings would mean being enthralled by his language.[54] That language glittered, beguiled, tempted. In *Lady Windermere's Fan* Wilde coyly claimed that "to be intelligible is to be found out."[55] To be indirect, on the other hand, is to be sought out. It is to encourage a kind of aggressive overreading that seeks to unravel paradoxes and unmask secrets. Yet precisely in yielding to the seduction of words one risked being contaminated by them. As Joseph Bristow suggests in an analogous context, Dorian Gray himself "is surely seduced by aphorisms."[56]

As reviewers of Nordau knew, "deviant" literature seduces and infects in just this manner. Significantly, Nordau's discussion of what he calls "sexual psychopathies" in modern literature stresses the *reader's* role in the movement of perverse desire from printed page to human organism. According to him, only those who are unnaturally attuned to a text's perverse emanations are endangered by them:

> All persons of unbalanced minds – the neurasthenic, the hysteric, the degenerate, the insane – have the keenest scent for perversion of a sexual kind, and perceive them under all disguises. As a rule, indeed, they are ignorant of what it is in certain works and artists which pleases them, but investigation always reveals in the object of their predilection a veiled manifestation of *Psychopathia sexualis*...Works of a sexually psychopathic nature excite in abnormal subjects the corresponding perversion (til then slumbering and unconscious, perhaps also undeveloped, although present in the germ), and give them lively feelings of pleasure, which they, usually in good faith, regard as purely aesthetic or intellectual, whereas they are actually sexual. (*Degeneration*, 452–53)

Nordau throws the burden of guilt squarely on to those with "too keen a scent for" what is "disguised" or "veiled" in a book. In his formulation, perverse desire remains latent in both text and reader until their interaction makes it manifest. Like Lord Arthur Savile, readers may be entirely unaware of what lies "slumbering and unconscious" within them; like the men in "The Portrait of Mr. W. H.," they do not distinguish between aesthetic and sexual pleasure. One's critical response to a literary work becomes a litmus test of moral health, since only those with a "predilection" toward perversion are infected by the "corresponding perversion" in the text.

In Nordau's view, reading can be a dangerous enterprise. He thought it so for precisely the reason that Wilde found it liberating: because it is apt to result in "lively feelings of pleasure." For Nordau, the willingness to indulge such pleasures is a clear sign of pathology, an indication of moral weakness and possibly of physical debility. He opens up the possibility that reading itself can, under certain conditions, be practiced in a "degenerate" manner. Here as elsewhere, he contrasts the pathological reader with the healthy and dispassionate critic – dispassionate because healthy – whose reason and objectivity render him immune to textual seduction. Yet the possibility always remains that a reader has discovered "perversion" in a text for the wrong reason: not because one engages in scientific inquiry but because one shares the perversion. This takes-one-to-know-one specter hovered over Wilde's court proceedings. The prosecutors argued that Wilde's works would especially endanger youths with a "tendency" toward homosexuality, a tendency that might under "normal" conditions remain unrealized. Yet because perversion was hidden in Wilde's texts, because it had to be teased out from the folds of his jewelled and elusive style, the prosecutors laid themselves open to the charge that they too had betrayed perverse tendencies.

In no respect is Wilde less of his age than in his notion of reading as erotic play. Yet it is also the case that he simply develops "tendencies" that were latent in Victorian criticism. Nordau, for instance, banishes the cathected body from proper acts of reading, only to allow it to return in a more palatable guise. The key word here is "sympathy," which, he argues, governs all healthy reader–text interactions. Not coincidentally, Nordau uses Wilde as his occasion for elaborating on the importance of sympathy. His argument rests on three interlocked claims: that art's purpose is not simply to be beautiful (a position he attributes, reductively, to Wilde) but to be socially useful; that its utility consists in binding men together "in emotional communion" with one another, a communion that is the "organic basis of the social edifice" (325); and that the artist achieves this effect by inducing audiences to enter into a bond of sympathy with the work of art. The artist wishes "to impart his own emotions" to others through the medium of art while the audience is motivated by a desire to "participate in the emotions" thus imparted (325). Nordau then gathers all these emotional interchanges, aesthetic and social alike, under the general heading of sympathy.

Stripped of their vituperative tone, Nordau's arguments concerning the dynamics of reader–text interaction and the social utility of art are staples of Victorian literary theory. As George Mosse has noted, Nordau stands firmly in "the mainstream of European middle-class thought of the late nineteenth century."[57] Few terms are as deeply enwoven in the critical history of fiction as "sympathy," and Nordau's use of it is solidly traditional. Here is George Eliot: "The greatest benefit we owe to the artist is the extension of our sympathies.... [A] picture of human life such as a great artist can give, surprises even the trivial and the selfish into that attention to what is apart from themselves, which may be called the raw material of moral sentiment."[58] As her last clause indicates, Eliot views the novel as playing a vital role in the moral education of a community. Though sympathy begins as an aesthetic issue, a matter, as Eliot says, of "direct observation" and "concrete presentation" leading to accurate depiction, it opens up to become a political maxim: without insight into "what is apart" from ourselves, no viable society is possible. Thirty years after Eliot, here is Walter Besant in "The Art of Fiction": "The especial quality" of the novel is that "it not only requires of its followers, but creates in readers, that sentiment which is destined to be a most mighty engine in deepening and widening the civilization of the world. We call it Sympathy....Surely it is a wonderful Art which endows the people...with this power of vision and feeling."[59] In their separate replies, Henry James and Robert Louis Stevenson dissented from nearly everything their colleague said concerning the art of fiction, but both acknowledged the importance of sympathy to the life of the novel.

I cite Eliot and Besant to underline how securely Nordau fits with the main tradition of Victorian criticism, as well as to suggest in what ways Wilde's criticism deviates from that tradition. If Nordau appealed to a wide range of fin-de-siècle readers, that was in part because he seemed to ground traditional aesthetics in modern biological paradigms, thus giving to the critic a new status as a kind of scientist. Yet he scientized bourgeois aesthetics without altering them in any significant way.

In *Degeneration* Wilde is condemned for privileging pleasure over utility, the body over rationality, yet we are more likely to be struck with how his radical aesthetic develops possibilities already present in Nordau's more traditional formulations. Wilde's joyous erotics of reading find their muted counterpart in the more decorous notion of readerly sympathy, just as the homoerotic bonds celebrated in "The Portrait of Mr. W. H." modulate into the kinds of homosocial ties that, as Eve Sedgwick has shown, are integral to the functioning of modern patriarchal societies. For Eliot, Besant, and Nordau no less than for Wilde, such affective bonds govern not only interactions of readers and texts but also social interactions "between men." Nordau criticizes Wilde for "laboriously seeking the opposite pole to sound common-sense" (320), yet he seems aware that the real problem is not that Wilde has discarded common sense views of art and society, rather that he has "perverted" them to new ends.

On the one hand, Wilde makes visible the ideological underpinnings of the critical doctrine of sympathy. This critique is explicit in "The Soul of Man Under Socialism," which argues that sympathy, instead of relieving suffering, at best deflects attention from and at worst contributes to the real, material causes of suffering. "Sympathy with pain does not really diminish the amount of pain. It may make man better able to endure evil, but the evil remains" (286). In as far as writers – artists and critics alike – strive to do no more than induce readerly sympathy, they simply help institutionalize the suffering they wish to alleviate. Humanism, Wilde argues, serves not Truth but specific, historically contingent truths, regardless of whether one's humanism is compassionate and intelligent like Eliot's or James's, complacent like Besant's, or intolerant like Nordau's.

On the other hand, Wilde appropriates "sympathy" to the service of his own antihumanist aesthetic. The term recurs throughout his great essays of 1889–91, where it denotes a kind of criticism that is at once playful, adversarial, creative, and erotically charged: a criticism of art and life that, rejecting objectivity and truth as goals, becomes "large, healthy, and spontaneous."[60] The spontaneity and play he advocates are not forms of hedonistic indulgence, just as Wildean individualism is not selfishness. Instead they are ways to aestheticize ourselves and our worlds, to make, as Wilde famously put it, life imitate art. In his essays and in *Dorian Gray* Wilde contends that in a well-ordered world art would not exist, since we would ourselves be forms of art. Art, in other words, is for Wilde the sign of our fallen condition, and in a fallen world those who strive to aestheticize themselves will always be outcast. At the same time aesthetic experience is our only solace and refuge in a suffering world. "Must we go, then, to Art for everything?" asks Ernest in "The Critic as Artist," to which Gilbert replies, in words that no one at Wilde's trials seemed capable of hearing: "For everything. Because Art does not hurt us" (380).

PART TWO

Between the body and history

CHAPTER 4

Men at work: from heroic friendship to male romance

"But suppose, Harry, I became haggard?"

The Picture of Dorian Gray[1]

From Oscar Wilde to Rider Haggard is a long journey, but worth making. In this chapter I want to delineate some of the continuities between the homoeroticism celebrated by Wilde and the kinds of conservative homosocial ties found in the works of late-Victorian "male romancers," specifically those of Haggard. Between Wilde and Haggard I situate John Addington Symonds, who combined the former's sexual preferences with the latter's ideological leanings. In Symonds's writings the erotic bonding of man to man is figured as heroic and conservative rather than, as in Wilde's work, subversive. From Symonds's position it is but a short step to the fantasies of male adventure, at once homosocial and homophobic, characteristic of the late-Victorian romance genre.

As Eve Sedgwick has argued, the continuum linking the homoerotic and the homosocial is central to modern Western cultures, yet it is also invariably occluded.[2] Making the links visible can help us better to see, among other things, the specific historical circumstances to which the differing forms of male bonding respond. The same issues involving identity, the body, sexuality, and writing that occupy Wilde occupy Haggard too; they provide the key coordinates for Symonds as well. All three men locate value within a structure of male relationships, though the values espoused could hardly be less alike. That each of these men would repudiate his connections with the other two does not alter the structural similarities among their positions.

At the same time, the journey from Wilde to Haggard moves us outward, from the domestic to the imperial arena. The most visible feature of the late-Victorian male romance is its engagement with issues of empire. Yet that turn outward to the frontiers is itself entangled with anxieties about domestic decay. The romance genre, like late-Victorian imperialist ideology generally, is centrally concerned with the possibility of renewal. As David Trotter points out, the typical romance tale takes "exhausted, purposeless men...whom we expect to degenerate or wither away, and transposes them to a new territory, the frontier, where a more vigorous identity can be created."[3] The same promise of national and personal regeneration was at the heart of most populist defenses of imperialism as well.[4] It was precisely in order to avoid what Lord Curzon called "the corroding ease and the morbid excitements" of a degenerate contemporary world that one embraced the empire and what it ostensibly represented.[5]

Yet while the empire in the works of male romancers provides a stage on which fantasies of a revitalized masculinity are played out, it also generates problems of its own: problems having to do with racial integrity, national decline, and the collapse of the great tradition of English letters. From Haggard I will be turning in succeeding chapters to works by Stoker, Wells, Doyle, and Kipling, all of whom situate questions of "degeneration" – personal, cultural, aesthetic – within the context of fin-de-siècle imperial politics.

"WE CANNOT BE GREEK NOW"

Like Wilde, John Addington Symonds tied art firmly to eros, though he was often troubled by the connection. At seventeen Symonds read the *Phaedrus* and the *Symposium* for the first time, and "it was just as though my own soul spoke to me through Plato."[6] He felt that his true identity as a homosexual man had been revealed to him. Reading Plato, Symonds recalled, was "the revelation I had been waiting for." Inchoate desires coalesced, and the "discords of [his] instincts" resolved into "a practical harmony." A lifelong "enthusiasm for male beauty" was given the dignity of a name. "I had touched solid ground," he wrote in his posthumously published *Memoirs*. "I had obtained the sanction of the love which had been ruling me since childhood" (*M* 99).

Reading Plato transformed Symonds, yet it was an experience he thought others were best spared. Writing to Benjamin Jowett in 1889, Symonds contends that "the study of Plato is injurious to a certain number of predisposed young men" because it leads to a destructive self-knowledge. While the passions of "inverted" young men are as natural as those born with "ordinary sexual appetites," Symonds argues, they are so "wholly out of accord with the world" that it is best to suppress them.[7] Victoria's Britain, unlike Plato's Greece, did not provide the social conditions under which a healthy homoeroticism could flourish. "What is left for us modern men?" Symonds asks in his memoir. "We cannot be Greek now" (*M* 69). In the contemporary world nature and culture clash, at least for those whose natures incline them to love other men. This was a formula for tragedy, Symonds wrote to Jowett, one he himself had lived. Better not to read Plato, then: without "the allurements of inspired art" one's "inborn natural passion" might never know itself, might therefore be spared "a struggle which thwarts and embitters."[8]

As this suggests, Symonds was no rebel. Like Wilde he helped give self-consciousness to modern homosexuality, but where Wilde strove to undermine traditional ideological structures with his anti-humanist "critiques from within," Symonds pursued more modest goals. Conservative by temperament, he sought to reconcile same-sex desire with conventional notions of identity and masculinity. Where Wilde rejected the terms under which deviance was constructed, Symonds accepted them in the belief that they could be made to serve more humane ends.

Thus, Symonds's defenses of homoerotic love often resemble the arguments of fin-de-siècle homophobes. Though he writes that homosexual men "are neither physically, intellectually, or psychically inferior to normally constituted individuals," he also depicts same-sex desire as a regrettable "perversion of appetite," a fall away from the "normally constituted." The homosexual man is "born with his sexual instincts improperly correlated to his sexual organs."[9] In contending that "sexual inversion" is an inborn condition, a matter of embryology not ethics, Symonds rejects Lombroso's and Krafft-Ebing's moralistic attacks on homosexuality as either a form of criminal atavism or else an acquired pathology (*ME* 15–53). Yet he also frequently slips into the language of his oppressors. The *Memoirs* are full of tortured self-accusations concerning what Symonds at one point calls "the congenital disease of my moral nature" (*M* 239), at another "an incurable malady" (*M* 281). This same tension pervades the life histories that Symonds collected for Havelock Ellis's *Sexual Inversion* (1897). Despite the laudable intentions of both men, *Sexual Inversion* effectively pathologizes its subjects, in part by turning them into "case studies." Symonds himself is Case XVII.

Moreover, by arguing that homosexuality is inborn, Symonds committed himself to the essentialism that Wilde rejected. As I noted in Chapter 3, such essentialist arguments effectively redefined homosexuality in terms of character rather than behavior. Symonds believed that no aspect of his life was uncolored by his sexual identity, an identity he might repress or ignore but which he could not alter. Though at times he defiantly embraces this identity, Symonds habitually represents his "condition" as abnormal and himself as an object of interest primarily to "the ethical psychologist and the student of mental pathology" (*M* 182).

Like many such students, Symonds posits an intimate connection between sexual identity and the written word. Like Nordau and Lombroso, he argues that certain kinds of writing could bring one's inborn "disposition" to homosexuality into active self-consciousness. Symonds's reservations concerning Plato, for instance, anticipate Nordau's warnings about the way "deviant" literature awakens in certain readers the "slumbering and unconscious germ" of perversity. Symonds laments where Nordau deplores, but they share the belief that an immutable identity lies beneath the accidents of circumstance and behavior. Like Nordau too, Symonds invests writing with the power to lead one to self-knowledge by giving coherence and direction to otherwise inchoate desires. The *Memoirs* recount numerous occasions on which the writing of others suddenly makes Symonds "known" to himself.[10] The most striking involves an obscene graffito which he encounters shortly after being solicited by a young soldier. Though "strongly attracted by his physical magnetism," Symonds had rejected the man's advances and run away (186). Confused and troubled by an "undefined craving coloured with a vague but poignant hankering" (187), he happens upon the graffito. The undefined now becomes definite, the vague is given a sharp clarity. The writing

> was of so concentrated, so stimulative, so penetrative a character...that it pierced the very marrow of my soul...My malaise of the moment was converted into a clairvoyant and tyrannical appetite for the thing which I had rejected. The vague and morbid craving of the previous years defined itself as a precise hunger after sensual pleasure, whereof I had not dreamed before. (*M* 187–88)

What is important here is not that Symonds has been aroused by an obscenity, but that he represents this moment as one of profound self-illumination. He has been revealed to himself, and this awareness in turn leads directly to his decision to begin actively seeking the "audacious comradeship" (*M* 188) offered by other men.

This essentialism is also linked to a belief in the expressive nature of art. Symonds accepts the view that the work of art reveals, more or less directly, the character of the artist.[11] In one respect he anticipates Freud by suggesting that art is sublimated libido, sexual energy that has been deflected from its original goal. *A Problem in Greek Ethics* (1883) is devoted in part to proving that poetry and paederastia are differing manifestations of the same underlying impulse.[12] "Expression" is vital according to Symonds, who consciously sought to relieve sexual tension by way of writing. Barred from openly practicing the audacious comradeship he valued, Symonds continually finds himself possessed by what he refers to as the *cacoethes scribendi*: "the frenzied itch to write" (*M* 156). Throughout his life he produced, as a "palliative treatment" (*M* 188), long poem cycles in praise of homoeroticism; poetry became "the vehicle and safety valve for my tormenting preoccupations" (*M* 189). So closely entwined are artistic and sexual expression that, as he puts it, "the writing of these poems was a kind of mental masturbation" (*M* 189). On occasion he allowed bowdlerized verse to appear in print. Sending the manuscript poems of *New and Old* (1880) to Graham Dakyns, Symonds asked his friend to go through them and "cut off the offending members." He told Dakyns that he would then alert his publisher "of the imminent coming of poems...sans testicular appurtenances."[13]

As Wayne Koestenbaum notes, Symonds "was the first writer in British history who felt that his sexual preference was central to his literary career."[14] Yet it is also the case that Symonds saw that career – which included not only the influential, seven-volume *Renaissance in Italy* (1875–86) but also dozens of works of literary criticism, biography, history, translation, and travel – as one long public disavowal of his "true nature." Shadowing the published oeuvre is an abundant mass of private writing which Symonds produced for himself or for distribution among his friends. (The outstanding example is the *Memoirs*, unpublished until 1984.[15]) Because these private writings were "expressive" in a way that his public works could not be, Symonds felt that they were essential to his health. When the ten copies of *A Problem in Modern Ethics* were published in 1890 Symonds told Dakyns that they would "go to slumber in a box of precious writings, my best work, my least presentable, until its day of doom."[16] Symonds referred to this receptacle as "the desolation box." Twenty years earlier he had briefly buried it as a prelude to composing *The Renaissance in Italy*, hoping, as he wrote to Henry Sidgwick, that by "trundl[ing] away [his] stumbling blocks" he could transform himself into a respected "historian of Italian literature."[17]

Symonds found this public/private split nearly intolerable. After reading *Jekyll and Hyde* in 1886, he confided to Stevenson that the experience had "left such a deeply painful impression on my heart that I do not know how I am ever to turn to it again." The story, he confessed, "touched one too closely."[18] The influence of Stevenson's tale can be felt in the searing final paragraph of Symonds's *Memoirs*, which recalls Henry Jekyll's "Full Statement" in its description of the conflict between instinct and moral precept. Like Jekyll, Symonds closes his autobiographical narrative in the third person. He fears, again like the doctor, that he must end by becoming a "self-destroyer."

When instinct prevails over reason, when the broadway of sensual indulgence invites his footing, the man plucks primroses of frank untutored inclination... But, when he comes to frigid reason's self again, when he tallies last night's deeds with today's knowledge of fact and moral ordinance, he awakes to the reality of a perpetual discord between spontaneous appetite and acquired respect for social law. By the light of his clear brain he condemns the natural action of his appetite; and what in moments of self-abandonment to impulse appeared a beauteous angel, stands revealed before him as a devil abhorred by the society he clings to... When he obeys the flesh, he is conscious of no wrong-doing. When he awakes from the hypnotism of the flesh, he sees his own misdoing not in the glass of truth to his nature, but in the mirror of convention... The quarrel drives him into blowing his brains out, or into idiocy. (*M* 283)

I quote at length because this passage so clearly delineates the terms of Symonds's dilemma. In doing so it also marks his distance from Stevenson and Wilde, who invoke "the mirror of convention" primarily in order to shatter it. By contrast, Symonds's loyalties are conspicuously divided: "spontaneous appetite" and "social law" equally claim his allegiance. Precisely because Symonds can neither "condemn the natural action of his appetite" nor revoke his "acquired respect" for social convention, he contemplates suicide. If his embrace of an outlawed love is fervent and sincere, so too is his commitment to the proprieties.

Indeed, much of Symonds's interest for us lies in his attempts to reconcile his conception of homoerotic passion with traditional middle-class notions of love and masculinity. His advocacy of same-sex love, in other words, is never meant to be transgressive. Unlike Wilde's, Symonds's critique of bourgeois ideology is not utopian: it does not seek to overthrow existing structures but to rehabilitate them. Where Wilde worked on behalf of a future imagined as discontinuous with the present, Symonds – and in this respect he moves in the mainstream of Victorian social thought – tried to heal a perceived rupture between the present and an ideal past. Such a healing, he believed, would lead to a reintegration of homoerotic desire into everyday culture.

This is the explicit message of Symonds's two privately printed treatises on homosexuality, *A Problem in Greek Ethics* (1883) and *A Problem in Modern Ethics* (1890). Both works argue for the centrality in Western history of what Symonds calls the paederastic passion. This passion, far from being deviant, is in fact enwoven in the fabric of the normal.

We find it present everywhere and in all periods of history. We cannot take up the religion books, the legal codes, the annals, the description of the manners of any nation, whether large or small, powerful or feeble, civilized or savage, without finding it in one form or another...Endowed with inextinguishable life, in spite of all that has been done to suppress it, this passion survives at large and penetrates society, makes itself felt in every quarter of the globe. (*ME* 3–4)

The importance of this argument rests in its three interlocked claims: that homosexuality is neither deviant nor pathological nor a symptom of modern life. Where late-Victorian pathologists traced the etiology of homoerotic desire to the disjunctures of a decadent modernity, Symonds argues that decadence originates in the suppression of such desire. In *A Problem in Greek Ethics*, having attributed the vitality of Hellenic society to its cultivation of the "paederastic institution," Symonds then maps out the "descent" of homoerotic desire through history (*GE* 27). The same libidinal energy that animates Hellas reappears in various guises – as "the joy of medieval amorists," as Dantesque divine love, and finally as Renaissance humanism (*GE* 74).

This is perhaps Symonds's finest legacy: his contribution to the struggle to give homosexuality a history. (In a similar manner, *Sexual Inversion* tried to give individuals the chance to reclaim their specific life stories.) Wilde's debt to Symonds is often overlooked: his impassioned defense on the witness stand of "the love that dare not speak its name" is in effect an oral redaction of the arguments in *A Problem in Greek Ethics*.[19] According to both Wilde and Symonds, the history of homosexuality is not an "alternate" history. It is simply History, coterminous with the story of Western culture. Indeed, for the late-Victorian public the scandal of Wilde's speech lay precisely in its impertinent co-opting of a familiar heroic narrative. As Ed Cohen notes, Wilde appealed to "the same cultural genealogy used by his contemporaries to assert the 'greatness' of Victorian Britain's imperial tradition."[20]

Symonds makes this same connection, but for unWildean reasons. Himself resolutely middle class in outlook and taste, Symonds endeavors to make same-sex desire palatable to middle-class sensibilities. He therefore represents the "healthy" homosexual man as the very embodiment of an ideal masculinity seen in bourgeois terms. Linda Dowling has shown how Symonds's conception of male love was decisively formed in the 1860s by his experiences at Oxford, where, thanks largely to the efforts of Benjamin Jowett, Greek studies in general and Plato in particular were moved to the heart of the *Literae humaniores* curriculum. In Jowett's hands, Hellenism was transformed into a discourse of civic virtue and moral regeneration, a ground of transcendent value which could supplement an increasingly beleaguered Christianity. Jowett stressed the Platonic ideal of "spiritual procreancy," the intellectual and spiritual communion of mentor and pupil from which flows art, culture, law – civilization itself. Jowett's own charisma as a tutor made such an ideal seem realizable. But he neither forsaw nor could forstall the appropriation of Hellenism in the name of a newly self-conscious homosexuality. For followers like Symonds, the notion of spiritual procreancy was inseparable from an idealized male love. Jowett was also instrumental in bringing Germanic historiography into the Oxford curriculum. The importance for Symonds of a work like Karl Muller's *Dorians* (1824) lay in its revelation that Greek paederastia was martial in origin. The ideal of male love Symonds imbibed at Oxford was thus neither decadent nor effeminate. Rather it was assertive, productive, "manly," and culturally indispensable. As Dowling notes, for men like Pater and Symonds "the language of male love could be triumphantly proclaimed the very fountain of civic health."[21]

This context helps account for Symonds's sharp distinctions between "vulgar" and "heroic" forms of homoerotic love. The former, which he associates with public school buggery and male prostitution, is labelled decadent, corrupt, unmanly: a wallowing in physicality marked by "effeminacies, brutalities, and gross sensualities" (*GE* 16, 33). Heroic love, by contrast, originates in a kind of chaste hypermasculinity. It is not sensual but spiritual, not effeminate but virile, "tolerating no sort of softness" (*GE* 33). In his autobiography Symonds insists that he is no "vulgar and depraved sensualist" (*M* 183) but one who is by nature robust and manly. He rejected "the belief that all subjects of inverted instinct...are pale, languid, scented, effeminate, painted, timid" (*GE* 33). In like manner, his defense of Greek homoeroticism rests on the assertion that it realized an "ideal of passion purged from sensuality" (*GE* 74). It is easy enough to see that Symonds's portrayal of Hellenic Greece is a displaced and idealized vision of nineteenth-century Britain. Indeed, in *Greek Ethics* heroic love is linked to a long catalog of Victorian virtues and practices: "manly sports, severe studies, enthusiasm, self-sacrifice, self-control, and deeds of daring" (*GE* 64). In *Studies in the Greek Poets* (1875) Symonds offers a portrait of the perfect Hellenic youth, who combines physical beauty with moral purity: such "a man in perfect health of mind and body, enjoying the balance of mental, moral, and physical qualities which health implies, carried within himself the norm and measure of propriety."[22] A more succinct exegesis of the Victorian ideal of *mens sana in corpore sano* is difficult to imagine.[23] Lest we miss the class-bias of this vision of heroic homoeroticism, Symonds links it to "gentlemanliness," that supremely middle-class construct. Paederastia in Hellas, Symonds writes, formed part of "the code of honour among gentlemen" (*GE* 33). In other words, where the effete Wildean dandy mockingly parodies the gentlemanly code, Symonds's noble youth becomes its very paragon.

A Problem in Modern Ethics continues Symonds's exploration of the difference between heroic and vulgar love, but in a new vocabulary. By the late 1880s Symonds had systematically studied the "professional" literature on homosexuality: the works of Tarnowsky, Moreau, Lombroso, Krafft-Ebing, and, most notably, Karl Heinrich Ulrichs. In *Modern Ethics* Symonds adapts Ulrichs's taxonomy of inversion in order to argue for the existence of a "non-deviant" form of homosexuality. Distinguishing first between acquired and congenital inversion, Symonds subdivides men in the latter category into hermaphrodites, androgynes, and "Urnings." This last group, Ulrichs's "middle sex," comprises men whose instincts are not "in harmony" with their sexual organs. Symonds numbers himself among the Urnings, then goes on to emphasize Ulrichs's further distinction between Urnings who are "Weiblinge" (effete) and Urnings who, like Symonds, are "Mannlinge" (virile). Having thus located himself "scientifically," Symonds is more than willing to consign all other forms of homoerotic desire to perdition. While *A Problem in Modern Ethics* is a careful critique of professional discourses on homosexuality, it also effectively reproduces the distinctions Symonds ostensibly seeks to break down. Here as elsewhere, his disgust at "sick" forms of homosexual behavior is palpable. In contrast, the heroic friendship of manly Urnings is in Symonds's view the most noble love imaginable. Such a love does not overturn conventional notions of masculinity but instead represents their ideal fulfillment.

In addition, the existence of such bonds between men provides for the transmission of culture by means of that "spiritual procreancy" that Jowett preached. In *Greek Ethics* Symonds stresses "the importance of the paiderastic institution" in ensuring that fundamental values are passed on from one generation to the next. In Hellenic Greece the love between an older and a younger man "became a potent instrument of education…The lover taught, the hearer learned; and so from man to man was handed down the tradition of heroism, the peculiar tone and temper of the state" (*GE* 27, 26). As such passages indicate, Symonds's vision could hardly be more patriarchal or more invested in the notion of culture as a male inheritance. In his autobiography Symonds repeatedly attempts to segregate the two halves of his genetic inheritance. From his mother came his illnesses: noting that her family "was tainted with...extreme nervous excitability, eccentricity, even madness" (*M* 64), Symonds concludes that "there is every reason to suppose that...she transmitted a neurotic temperament to certain of her children" (*M* 38). His father (also named John Addington, as was his father before him, a fact Symonds highlights to indicate the continuity of his heritage) by contrast comes to stand for an enriching cultural legacy, one that the son strives to be worthy of inheriting. "Open at all pores to culture, to art, to archeology, to science, to literature," the elder man "yielded his spirit up to beauty and imbibed the well-spring of modern philosophy" (*M* 52). Symonds attributes his own scholarly and artistic achievements to the influence exerted by his father, "the author of [his] being and the moulder of [his] character" (*M* 53).

At the same time, Symonds contends that his own generation marks a distinct decline from that of its fathers. He feels this most strongly in his own case – "How immeasurably superior my father was to me, as a man, as a character, as a social being, as a mind, I feel, but I cannot express" (*M* 56) – but he also suggests that his case is, in this one respect at least, representative. Like many of his contemporaries, Symonds felt that he was living in a diminished age, one that had mishandled its cultural legacy. In particular, he is harshly critical of the age for making impossible certain heroic forms of male expression and action. To him, modern British society had become alarmingly sensual, morbid, weak, effeminate. (That he recognized these tendencies in himself only alarmed him the more.[24]) Symonds saw in Wilde the epitome of an age in which the ideals of heroic friendship had been degraded into a luxurious hedonism. He dismissed *Dorian Gray* as "unwholesome in tone" and warned of the dangers of its "unhealthy, scented, mystic, congested touch."[25] Symonds's celebrations of the "manliness" of Homeric poetry were in part attempts to counteract modern unwholesomeness, to inculcate the virtues associated with heroic masculinity into an effeminized and decadent world.

At such moments – and they permeate his critical writings – Symonds situates himself ideologically alongside late-Victorian male romancers like Haggard, Conan Doyle, and Kipling. For him, the key structural distinction is finally not between hetero- and homosexuality but between masculinity and femininity. What Sedgwick calls his "aggressive lack of interest" in women and women's issues was an inevitable result of his privileging of heroic virility.[26] For Symonds "sickness" and "effeminacy" are always synonyms. He thus worked to repress the "feminine" aspects of his own psyche, just as he urged his compatriots to begin purging the culture of *its* feminine weaknesses. Symonds's interest in classical Greece is finally not that of Arnold or Pater, who saw in Hellenism a potentially softening influence on the harsh puritanism of Victorian England. Instead, Symonds's position is more akin to that of someone like Andrew Lang, who tirelessly proselytized for the tonic, invigorating effects of immersing oneself in Hellenic culture. Though Lang would have denied the connection, he shared Symonds's intense interest in promoting the benefits – cultural, political, psychological – of a revitalized masculinity. He did this in part by disseminating popularized versions of Greek epic and myth, in part by promoting the benefits of a new fictional genre, the male romance.

SMALL THINGS, SMALL PEOPLE

To its many devotees, the late-Victorian romance was of value precisely through its interest in maleness. Among the vocal supporters of the form were Andrew Lang, Rider Haggard, Hall Caine, Arthur Conan Doyle, and George Saintsbury, all of whom championed the romance as an antidote to an effeminate modernity. Given such self-definition, we should not be surprised to find that the genre is rich in expressions of male bourgeois vitriol and angst. Though it has often been read by later critics as unambiguously celebratory of late-Victorian masculinist ideals, the male romance is in fact deeply imbued with a sense of loss. Through this genre male middle-class writers responded, not always coherently, to their sense of disenfranchisement in the world. That this disenfranchisement was more perceived than real is indisputable. Yet the theory and practice of the male romance reveals an array of anxieties at once personal, "racial," political, and aesthetic: anxieties concerning the dissolution of masculine identity, the degeneration of the British "race," the moral collapse of imperial ideology, and the decline of the great tradition of English letters.

Consider a brief exchange between Lang and William Watson. In late 1888 Watson, writing in *The Fortnightly Review*, lamented what he called "the fall of fiction" in contemporary Britain. Fiction had lapsed into a sad decline, he wrote, largely because the national character as a whole had done the same. Novels had lost the "old merits of fulness and 'body'," themselves the products of "robust minds." Such virtues had been "hereditary" in a "lineage...which can be traced backward without a break from George Eliot to Fielding." Now, however, they are "growing rarer and rarer." In one kind of modern novel, fulness and body give way to introspection and an increasingly rarefied sensibility. Instead of Fielding, there is Henry James; instead of Scott, Ouida. Such fictions are "miracles of inexhaustible nothingness," exuding little but "languor and *ennui* and enervation." This literary lassitude, Watson contends, had inevitably produced "a frantic rebound" to its equally dismal opposite, namely to the violent adventure novels of Rider Haggard. "From elegant listlessness fiction has suddenly leapt into paroxysmal life. From coma it has passed into convulsions."[27] Each of these extremes represents, in Watson's view, a decisive break in the "hereditary" line of British novels. Watson associates that line with the great tradition of English realism, which in turn he implicitly links to Britain's world ascendancy in the eighteenth and nineteenth centuries. The era of literary realism thus coincides with an extended moment of high national prestige. Both, Watson suggests, have declined precipitously during the present generation.[28]

"The Fall of Fiction" provoked a quick response from Lang, who ambivalently defended his contemporaries against Watson's attack. Modern writers possess the same qualities we admire in their predecessors, Lang contends, only in reduced form. "We have not a Thackeray, we have not a Dickens. But have we not…the small change, la monnaie, of those authors?" If we look at Besant, for instance, do we not see a little Dickens? Is Stevenson not a smaller Scott? Does Norris not qualify as "the Thackeray of a later age?" In short, is not fiction in the 1880s simply Victorian fiction writ small? While denying that there has been a "break" in English fiction's hereditary line, Lang nonetheless admits the validity of Watson's main charge: that the British novel is in a diminished state. Its best energy, Lang says, has been "spent," an image that neatly connects his "small change" metaphor to the notion of a declining genealogical line. Ever sanguine, Lang holds out hope that the novel will eventually reinvigorate itself, that the diminished sons of Victorian giants will themselves give way to grandsons of renewed stature.[29]

Lang disagreed with Watson's assessment of Haggard, but in one respect the critics are in perfect accord, since both consider "overrefinement" the primary danger confronting modern culture. Together the two men rehearse widespread late-Victorian concerns about the decline of the novel, and they do so in an utterly familiar vocabulary of heredity, evolution, and descent. For both critics this vocabulary permits easy transitions between discussions of national character on the one hand and literary merit on the other. In a similar vein, George Saintsbury argues in "The Present State of the English Novel" (1888) that fiction had been "'bred in and in' until the inevitable result of feebleness of strain had been reached." This literary enfeeblement, he continues, finds its inevitable counterpart within the current "habits and public opinion of the nation."[30] The year before his exchange with Watson, Lang had wondered in print what the "Man of the Future" would read, given the current drift of human evolution. Predictably, this Eloi-like reader – "bald, toothless, [and] highly 'cultured'" – turns out to be "addicted to tales of introspective analysis."

> I don't envy him when he has got rid of that relic of the ape, his hair; those relics of the age of combat, his teeth and nails; that survival of barbarism, his delight in the last battles of Odysseus, Laertes' son. I don't envy him the novels he will admire, nor the pap on which he will feed.[31]

Lang imagines decay not as the reversal of progress but as its culmination. His Man of the Future is the victim of a "degeneration" resulting not from Lombrosan reversion to savagery but instead from an unhealthy excess of civilized refinement. As I noted in Chapter 1, it was generally agreed that degeneration was an affliction peculiar to modernity. Maudsley and Lankester had each argued that degeneration was simply another word for evolution under civilized conditions. Advanced culture breeds degenerates, Maudsley wrote, who cannot be considered "savages with the simple mental qualities of children" but who are instead "repulsive characters...of the worst kind, because bred of the best organic developments."[32] As Sander Gilman and J. E. Chamberlin have noted, degeneration was "the dark side of progress" in nineteenth-century thought precisely because the two terms so easily became entangled.[33]

The ever-energetic Lang attempted to combat the creeping enervation of modern life by vigorously promoting "primitive" forms of literature, among them what Saintsbury had dubbed the "pure romance of adventure." Lang had long been persuaded by the anthropologist E. B. Tylor's argument that the poetic impulse was a "savage survival" from humanity's ancient past. In *Primitive Culture* (1871), Tylor had claimed that the "mental condition of the lower races is the key to poetry, nor is it a small portion of the poetic realm" in contemporary life which could be explained by the notion of savage survivals.[34] Lang, taking Tylor's argument as evidence of the innate doubleness of the modern psyche, argues that this split expresses itself as a contradiction in aesthetic taste. While the "civilized" self finds pleasure in modern tales of introspective analysis, "the natural man within" us still responds viscerally to certain "primitive" forms of art – ballads, folk stories, fairy tales, sagas. In the march of progress those forms have been largely superseded, replaced by genres that more accurately mirror the sophistications of modern life. In Lang's schematic evolutionism, just as civilization "has turned customs into codes...myth into science...magic mummery into gorgeous ritual" so too has it transformed "nursery tales into romance" and "ballad into epic."[35] Yet because of what Lang calls "our mixed condition, civilized at top with the old barbarian under our clothes," we still hunger for the older literary forms. The "survival of some blue-painted Briton or of some gipsy" in the contemporary reader ensures that "primitive" art retains its power.[36]

Hence the importance, in Lang's view, of the new barbarians of the literary world, the romancers. His defenses of Haggard (and later of Kipling) are grounded in the belief that the novel of adventure possessed therapeutic value. It could help reverse the effects of an enervated and overly self-conscious modernity by returning literature to its "authentic" roots in song and saga. Immersion in vigorous primitive narratives could itself invigorate, could stir healthy energies long muffled by culture. Saintsbury concurred: with realism "gone hopelessly sterile," a "return to the earliest form of writing, to the pure romance of adventure" was the only hope for salvation.[37] Himself a resolute guardian of high culture, Saintsbury nevertheless allows that culture may become too rarefied for its own continuance, and thus in need of revivifying by lower forms of art. In this spirit Lang, an accomplished popularizer, worked to revive interest in "fundamental" forms of art. Through surveys like *Custom and Myth* (1885) and *Myth, Ritual, and Religion* (1889) plus numerous anthologies of ballads, fairy tales, and sagas, Lang attempted to counteract modern ennui. His translations of the Icelandic sagas are explicitly motivated by a desire to reawaken what he calls that strong "Norse blood" now lying "dormant" within the British race.[38] Lang's public defenses of Haggard's fictions (about which he expressed reservations in private) were similarly motivated.

In its self-representations, then, the romance was a conscious response to late-Victorian realism and the "evolutionary" conditions that produced it. Contemporary realist fiction spoke only to the "emasculated specimens of an overwrought age," Haggard wrote, "with culture on their lips, and emptiness in their hearts."[39] As this formulation suggests, romancers straightforwardly figure the decline of modern culture as a fall into the feminine. More generally, Sandra Siegel has shown how the equation of "decadent" and "feminine" permeated thought across a wide range of late-Victorian intellectual disciplines.[40] By contrast, the maleness of the romance is its self-proclaimed defining feature. As Elaine Showalter points out, the celebration of King Romance (the designation is Lang's) in the 1880s formed part of "a men's literary revolution" against the novel of (feminine) domestic realism.[41] The genre's pointed misogyny and aggressive anti-intellectualism – Haggard often boasted of what he liked to call his dullness – help to distance the genre from an established literary form and a specific ideology, both represented as feminine. Within what Haggard termed the "safe and secret place" of the romance, male authors worked to articulate masculinity's often dubious virtues against an effeminized modern world.[42]

In this context we can also note how the accelerating push to professionalize the author's trade was used in some quarters as a means to marginalize women writers and "women's" writing. The Society of Authors refused initially to admit women as members, for instance, despite the fact that women formed the majority of writers and readers of fiction. "It is a lady-like age," sneered Frederic Harrison in 1894, "and so it is the age of ladies' novels... Let us accept what the dregs of the nineteenth-century can give us."[43] Significant changes in methods of publication and distribution in the 1880s and 90s served to curtail the publication of three-decker novels, a format that had come to be associated almost exclusively with women.[44] Haggard explicitly makes this connection when he claims that the heroes of modern fiction do little more than "dangle round the heroines till their three-volume fate is accomplished."[45] By contrast, male romances were almost invariably published in inexpensive one-volume editions.

Showalter quite reasonably therefore sees male romances as acts of aggression. Yet the form's virulence only partially masks the fears it was meant to assuage. It offered itself as a refuge for a class still very much in power but feeling itself besieged from many sides. Even in the eyes of its theoreticians, the romance was a debased form, one that, no less than the "novel of introspection," marked a falling away from the tradition embodied in Fielding, Scott, Dickens, Thackeray, and Eliot. Contrary to Showalter's claim that the form constitutes a simple repudiation of Victorian realism, romance writers continually announce their inferiority to their predecessors. This is the best our shrunken age can produce, they say. In a "day of small things, and small people," Lang counsels, let us embrace the vicarious and compensatory pleasures offered by the adventure story without pretending it forms "the highest class of fiction."[46] "Small is the word," Stevenson agrees. "It is a small age, and I am of it."[47] Speaking at a Royal Literary Fund dinner in 1893, Arthur Balfour lamented that

> the great names which rendered illustrious the early years of the great Victorian epoch are, one by one, dropping away...I do not know that any of us can see around us the men springing up who are to occupy the thrones left

vacant...[W]e do not see a rising generation of men of letters likely to rival those of old times...It is a most interesting situation, because I am prepared to admit that we live in an age which bears upon it the marks of decadence.[48]

In considering the kinds of cultural work the romance performs in this period, then, we must recognize in its aggressive optimism a desire to compensate for perceived losses: for the decline of English letters, for the degeneration through overrefinement of bourgeois society, for the "emasculation" of the middle-class male, and so on. It is in this context that we should understand the genre's deep ideological investment in the empire as a place of renewal.[49] Transformed into a fantasy space "elsewhere," the empire is imagined by romancers as a realm free from the various debilities of modernity. To be sure, a certain logic inheres in romance's embrace of empire, since the rhetoric of late-Victorian imperialism was itself organized in terms of loss and compensation. Bernard Porter notes that "'Imperialism,' as the word is generally understood, was for Britain...a symptom and an effect of her decline...and not of strength."[50] As early as 1902, J. A. Hobson described imperialist fervor as a displaced response to economic and social troubles at home.[51] Hobson also recognized that the emergence of imperialism as a conscious ideology was inseparable from anxiety over the decline of the British race figured in masculinist terms.[52]

Thus, what Joseph Bristow calls "reading for the empire" was at the heart of middle-class efforts to revitalize the nation. By the turn of the century, "imperialism took on all the attributes of moral and educational improvement" that had, for an earlier generation, been associated with the term "culture."[53] Young men were encouraged to embrace the imperial ideal not simply for the sake of the empire itself, but also because it helped inculcate those sturdy virtues – austerity, self-control, determination, practicality, and so on – which were thought to be ebbing from the world. Baden-Powell's Boys Scouts (an organization he originally thought to name the Young Knights of the Empire) are only one example of the way that imperial ideology could be put in the service of character-building.[54] Bristow notes how the tenets of imperialism began to shape school curricula at all levels, and also how neatly the new curricula dovetailed with the lessons offered by adventure fiction and the male romance.[55] Like Arnoldian culture, imperialism was said to dissolve differences of class and gender and to transcend the vicissitudes of time. To internalize the imperialist ethos was thus to find oneself in solidarity with right-thinking, right-feeling individuals of all epochs and places. In like manner, the appeal of the male romance was said to be universal. This is what Lang is getting at when he writes that the romance appeals to the "natural man within" us; what Haggard means when he claims that "the love of romance" is "an innate quality of mankind" and is thus "probably coeval with the existence of humanity."[56]

"To celebrate adventure was to celebrate empire," Martin Green reminds us, to which we can add that to celebrate adventure and empire was also to universalize a conception of the world that was in reality class- and gender-specific.[57] Yet that is finally only half the story. The celebrations of empire found in the male romance are edgy, defensive. The very need to celebrate seems to arise from a mood of incipient despair. This is assuredly the case with the preeminent example of the genre, Rider Haggard's *She* (1887). If, as many recent critics have argued, this novel is central to an understanding of the Victorian fin de siècle, that is because Haggard managed to channel so many of the period's anxieties through the figure of Ayesha.

HOC FECIT

Sigmund Freud for one found Ayesha suggestive. The heroine of *She* makes a brief but highly charged appearance in another paradigmatic fin de siècle text, *The Interpretation of Dreams* (1899). Late in that book Freud recounts a dream in which he watches himself dissect his own pelvis. He plausibly reads the operation as an expression of fears of self-exposure, brought on by the difficult decision to publish his own dreams in the *Interpretation.* This reluctance "to give away so much of my own private character" in print is translated into "the task which was imposed on me...of carrying out a dissection of my own body."[58] In Freud's reading, in other words, this is in part a dream about interpreting dreams. It is also one of many moments when the act of writing his book explicitly becomes a topic within that book.

If the self-dissection dream points to fears of public exposure, however, Freud's telling of it points to fears of public neglect and professional failure. In the dream Freud is assisted by Louise N., a friend whom he later identifies as "the occasion of the dream." Visiting on the previous day, Louise had requested something to read.

> I offered her Rider Haggard's *She.* "A *strange* book, but full of hidden meaning," I began to explain to her; "the eternal feminine, the immortality of the emotions ..." Here she interrupted me: "I know it already. Have you nothing of your own?" – "No, my own immortal works have not yet been written." – "Well, when are we to expect these so-called ultimate explanations of yours...?" she

asked, with a touch of sarcasm. At that point I saw that someone else was admonishing me through her mouth and I was silent. (490)

Freud goes on to equate Leo Vincey's and Horace Holly's quest in *She* with his own ambitions for psychoanalysis. Both involve "perilous journeys" over "an adventurous road that had scarcely ever been trodden before, leading into an undiscovered region" (491). Like Haggard's heroes, Freud is in search of "hidden meaning" and "ultimate explanations," and like them he expects to be rewarded for his toils with a glimpse of "the eternal feminine, the immortality of the emotions."

Yet in recounting the "occasion of the dream" – his conversation with Louise N. – Freud situates these matters within a significantly different context, one in which the real issue is not "ultimate explanations" but Freud's continuing failure to produce the "immortal works" in which those explanations will appear. The impetus for the dream likewise has less to do with Freud's interest in the eternal feminine than with his muted irritation at a particular woman, who chides him for his ambitions and for his desire to compel the eternal feminine to yield its secrets. Having so far failed in his tasks, Freud is humbled into silence by the sarcasm of one who "already knows" what the analyst is struggling to discover. As he often acknowledges within *The Interpretation of Dreams*, Freud saw that book as, in part, a vehicle for satisfying his desire for professional success. He may therefore have taken special pleasure in the anecdote of Louise N.'s skepticism, since the very fact of our reading it proves that she was wrong to doubt, wrong to be sarcastic. Freud gets the last word: the threats to his professional competence posed by Louise N.'s dismissive "admonishments" are finally contained within, and defused by, the would-be "immortal work" itself, Freud's dream-book.

She does double duty in this episode. Within the dream Haggard's story becomes an allegory for the psychoanalytic quest. In the dream frame, on the other hand, *She* operates as a symbol of Freud's anxieties as a writer. The novel itself comes to stand for his own as yet unwritten works. The account of his exchange with Louise N. focusses attention not so much on the "truths" of psychoanalysis as on the relation between those truths and the discourse that Freud was at that moment working to articulate.

The whole episode thus turns on an occluded struggle between "eternal" femininity on the one hand and male writing on the other. That Freud uses *She* to express such a struggle suggests that he "unconsciously" recognized that Haggard's novel is structured in precisely these terms. A generation later a teenaged Elizabeth Bowen, upon first reading *She*, likewise responded to the agonistic conflict between Ayesha's magic femininity and what Bowen calls "the power of the pen...the inventive pen" associated with Horace Holly. Bowen consciously chose the pen, and with it a power traditionally associated with men.[59] So too Henry Miller, who in his notorious essay on *She* wrote that Ayesha stood for the "endless immolation" of man, which could be warded off only through "the magic of words."[60]

Certainly, Ayesha's sororial ties to other nineteenth-century fatal women – Lamia, Carmilla, Faustine, Lilith, Salome – are highly visible. Like them, she is presented as a figure of enormous power, possessed of a beauty at once enslaving and destructive. Closely associated with chthonian Nature as well as with the supernatural, she is depicted as the source and the negation of life. She is the veiled woman, that ubiquitous nineteenth-century figure of male desire and anxiety, whose body is Truth but a Truth that blasts.

Against the threat Ayesha poses, Haggard offers us the all-male professional world of the university where Holly and Vincey reside. Having agreed to take on Vincey as his ward, Holly determines that he "would have no woman lord it over [him] about the child, and steal his affections."[61] He is more than willing, however, to share his symbolic paternity with his professional colleagues. Vincey quickly establishes himself as the "favorite of the whole College," pampered and petted by every don. "The offerings made at his shrine were simply without number" (20). Just as Vincey becomes in effect the child of the patriarchy, Cambridge itself is transformed into an extended domestic sphere, one reimagined in exclusively male terms. As the site of scholarship and practical knowledge (Holly is a mathematician, traditionally figured as the most masculine of disciplines), moreover, the university is implicitly offered as a bulwark against Ayesha's magic femininity.

Yet, as Freud's example suggests, structuring the situation in these terms can be deceptive. Invoking the "eternal feminine" can be a way of deflecting attention away from other, more historically specific sources of anxiety. Similarly, to read Ayesha simply as the embodiment of a transhistorical femaleness is to miss distinctive features of this novel. Haggard employs a figure who is "outside" time, but he does so in order to articulate timely concerns. Once in Africa, Holly and Vincey traverse a heavily symbolic landscape that appears to move them backward in and finally out of history as they travel forward in space, yet at journey's end they find a being who is at once archaic and very up to date. Waiting for Ayesha to make her first appearance, Holly wonders whether he will encounter "some naked savage queen, a languishing Oriental beauty, or a nineteenth-century young lady" (141). The answer of course is: all three. Haggard's portrayal of Ayesha draws on European legends of African tribes ruled by despotic white women, while also invoking familiar stereotypes of "Oriental" decadence and sensuality. Yet in tracing Haggard's sources we must also look closer to home, at that "nineteenth-century young lady" mentioned by Holly.

More specifically, Haggard's novel needs to be situated in the context of late-Victorian gender politics.[62] As Sandra M. Gilbert and Susan Gubar point out, Haggard took care to set the action of *She* in 1881, the year Cambridge first allowed women to sit for the same Previous and Tripos examinations as men.[63] The presence and pressure of the New Woman makes itself felt in Ayesha's confident forays into intellectual disciplines usually barred to women: theology (192–93), philology (146), political science (255–56), biology (154), and chemistry (194, 240) to name but a few. Outstripping Francis Galton and Karl Pearson, she has even mastered eugenics, that cutting-edge of late-Victorian science (154). Holly may be quick to place her power under the rubric of feminine magic, but Ayesha insists in best empiricist fashion that "there is no such thing as magic, though there is such a thing as knowledge of the secrets of Nature" (151–52). Her impertinent incursions into the realms of male scholarship are particularly galling to Holly, the unregenerate misogynist. The two men may flee the university's breached bastion, yet it is only to discover the very image of the New Woman enthroned in the heart of Africa. By the time Holly's servant Job suggests "that that there She is the old gentleman himself" (245), we may suspect that Haggard is thinking not of the devil but of the various secular patriarchs She threatens symbolically to displace.

A more effective talisman against Ayesha's power than the university turns out to be the Sherd of Amenartas. Indeed, since the single and unchanging message written all over the Sherd is, Take Revenge on Her, we can see this artifact as representing a male force opposed to Ayesha's magic femininity. Where Ayesha is aligned with pure speech and the body,[64] the Sherd is associated with writing, culture, learning, genealogy, history – with patriarchy in its broadest self-delineation. Symbolically, the Sherd of Amenartas performs the same function for the Vinceys that the Pillar of Life performs for Ayesha: it staves off death. The unbroken male line given on the Sherd – father to son through twenty-two generations – is equivalent to Ayesha's perpetual and celibate self-regeneration. (It also has clear affinities to the paederastic model of cultural transmission that John Addington Symonds idealized.) Within *She*, the potent fantasy of an uninterrupted male genealogy accords the Vinceys the same immortal status that Ayesha enjoys.

The importance Haggard attached to this talisman can hardly be overestimated. Following *She*'s magazine serialization, Haggard extensively revised the text for book publication. Many of the revisions occur in Chapter 3, where Holly and Vincey first examine the contents of the chest bequeathed by Leo's father. Haggard's descriptions of the Sherd of Amenartas, already lengthy in the serial version, were lengthened some more for the first edition, with Haggard meticulously correcting mistakes in his "scholarship."[65] Generally disdainful of learning, he took unusual care to ensure the accuracy of the Greek and Latin passages on the artifact, going so far as to enlist the aid of a classicist, Hubert Holden, and an archeologist, John Raven, in their composition. In the novel these passages together with their English counterparts run on for many more pages than can easily be justified. In one sense they are entirely superfluous, since they merely repeat in different languages and scripts the same story, which is the story of Amenartas's oath of revenge and its aftermath.

Haggard's obsession extended further. As he began to revise *She*, he asked his friend Agnes Barber to construct an "authentic" Sherd of Amenartas for him, complete with markings, scratches, chips as well as inscriptions in uncial and cursive Greek, classical and medieval Latin, and Middle English. A color facsimile of her handiwork formed the frontispiece to the first English edition of the novel. Barber had been involved in a similar project the year before, when at Haggard's request she drew up Jose da Silvestra's treasure map exactly as described in *King Solomon's Mines*: on a scrap of white linen, in blood. In both cases Haggard self-consciously drew attention to the "authenticity" of the artifacts. He displayed them in the midst of his collection of Egyptian antiquities, and he liked to tell of having taken the Sherd to Sir John Evans, the noted antiquary, who was dubious about its origins but admitted he could say no more than that "it might *possibly* have been forged."[66]

In the context of a novel as relentlessly concerned with permanence and change as *She* is, Haggard's overdetermined desire to give the Sherd a durable "body" takes on added significance. The Sherd testifies to the persistence of the Vincey line, a line that apparently requires no women for its continuance. On the Sherd men beget men, whereas Ayesha begets only herself. Within the novel male generativity is figured in terms of the passing on of written language, specifically of the family name, that most patriarchal of inheritances. "Through this link of pen and paper," the elder Vincey writes to his son, "I stretch out my hand to you" in order to "hand on these the results of my labour" (27, 29). (We note the pun on "labour" here.[67]) On the Sherd itself writing and male genealogy are made synonymous. The history of Leo's family, "one of the most ancient families in the world" (10), is also the history of the written languages (Egyptian, Greek, Latin, English) that tell of his family. The family name itself reveals this same progression of scripts, with the Egyptian cartouche translated into the Greek Tisisthenes or "Avenger," which in turn becomes the Latin Vindex, the Norman de Vincey, and finally the "plain modern Vincey" of English (37). As Holly notes, the Vinceys are defined by their name, which has etymologically "embalmed" within it "the idea of revenge" that continues to motivate them (37).

The Sherd also situates the Vinceys within a specific historical trajectory, one from which Ayesha is barred. As Laura Chrisman argues, the origin of the Vincey line – the marriage of an Egyptian princess and a Greek priest – makes the family "a sign for the inauguration of Western civilization itself, achieved at the expense of Ayesha who herself desires to be the mate of the Greek."[68] The Vinceys' subsequent migrations, from Asia Minor to Italy to Norman France to England, likewise follow the historical progression of Western culture as Haggard and his contemporaries conceived it. The Sherd offers an heroic narrative of civilization, one which aligns Leo's family with political imperium (Nectanebes, Charlemagne, William the Conqueror, Elizabeth), learning (Herodotus, Erasmus, William Grocyn), art (Shakespeare), and religion (Isis, the Crusades). The Vinceys become in effect a synecdoche for Western civilization.

Given this context, it makes perfect sense that the family in modern times has been most notable for maintaining "a dead level of respectability" (11). The Vincey narrative culminates in the petty bourgeoisie – the merchants, soldiers, brewers, and tradesmen who comprise the family tree from the late seventeenth century forward (11–12). At the terminus and apex of Western history stands the Victorian middle class. Leo himself is a veritable catalog of middle-class virtues. He is loyal, sturdy, commonsensical, extroverted, addicted to sporting, suspicious of learning, and proud to be intellectually undistinguished. As the unnamed editor of Holly's manuscript admits, "he is not…particularly interesting" (6). Yet that very dullness, what Leo's father calls the invincible Vincey "mediocrity" (11), is finally figured as the source of his strength. As an antidote to "the very excess and splendour" (6) of Ayesha's nature, in other words, Haggard offers the moderation and common sense of the Vinceys' bourgeois respectability. Leo's "spark of greatness" derives from these same class-bound virtues, the unnamed editor concludes, and they are finally what move Ayesha to "worship" at his "shrine" (6).

For Haggard, then, the Sherd of Amenartas represents a stay against the ravages of time.[69] It is also a hinge that connects concerns over the decay of individual bodies with the decline of nations. The sadness of passing time is one of Haggard's most persistent themes, and it is nowhere more evident than in *She*.[70] The banality of his laments – "The arising sun; the setting sun!" (57) – does not detract from their sincerity, nor does it obscure Haggard's insistent equating of biological and imperial decay. The novel encourages us to see Great Britain's fate presaged in the history of Kor, the once great, now annihilated race whose ruins house the savage Amahagger. The cry that Holly finds so moving, "Kor is fallen!...Kor is fallen!" (179), becomes a proleptic lament for Britain itself.[71] Throughout his narrative Holly misses no chance to indulge in the lachrymose pleasures of *ubi sunt*. "Time after time have nations...been and passed away and been forgotten, so that no memory of them remains" (180). These apostrophes to the world's many "long dead and forgotten civilisations" (62) in turn find their counterparts in Haggard's frequent lamentations over the corruption and death of the individual body.

Ayesha's physical perfection of course serves as a continual reminder of "man's" mortal lot. Yet it is finally through this contrast that Haggard "manages" Ayesha. If virtual immortality and perfection make Ayesha immensely attractive, they are also presented as the ultimate signs of her monstrosity. The combination of immortality and perfection is one Ayesha shares with the novel's most uncanny figures, the embalmed corpses of Kor. Having, like her, escaped "the crumbling hand of Decay" (111), the corpses provoke wonder and horror in equal measure. With appalled fascination Haggard repeatedly directs our attention to these "perfect" figures. "Nearly all the bodies...were as perfect as on the day of death" (184). "The whole mountain is full of dead, and nearly all of them are perfect" (170).

Like Ayesha, the corpses give rise to perverse desire in the living, as Billali's necrophilic yearning for the embalmed "body of a fair woman" (110) preserved in one of the caves attests. Ayesha herself worships the "white and perfectly preserved" body of the dead Kallikrates (238). With physical perfection thus yoked to death and to unnatural desire, it is no accident that, though Ayesha at first reminds Holly of "a corpse in its grave-clothes," he nevertheless finds this vision "instinct with beauty" (142). (Later Job "ejaculates" when Ayesha appears: "Here's a corpse a-coming!" [195].) The mixture of uncanniness, desire, death, perfection, and immortality is neatly captured in the "Wedded in Death" tableau that Holly finds so strangely attractive: "a young man and a blooming girl...clasped heart to heart," their youth and love "preserved" along with their embalmed bodies (185).

By making perfection the sign of perversity, Haggard "recuperates" decay and death, investing them with an ethical significance they do not usually possess. As the novel progresses, his laments over devouring time begin to sound more like celebrations of nature's moral and beneficent order. Nations fall, empires crumble, races decline, men die – and this is all to the good. By the time Holly tells Ayesha, "I will live my day and grow old with my generation, and die my appointed death" (252), he seems not to be bowing to necessity but staking out the ethical high ground. Significantly, Holly's, and later Leo's, refusal of immortality repeats the refusal of the wise philosopher Noot, who teaches Ayesha about the Pillar of Life but "for his conscience' sake would have none of it" himself (281).

Haggard thus attempts to lend moral grandeur to what would otherwise be simply a distressing fact, namely that human beings and their institutions do not last forever. Given this context, Holly unsurprisingly presents Ayesha's death as fitting punishment for transgressions against the order of things. She "opposed herself against the eternal Law," he writes, and pays for her hubris by being "swept back to nothingness...with shame and hideous mockery" (295). Yet as Holly's words also suggest, it is not enough for Ayesha simply to fall. She must also be humiliated. Her death-agonies, presented at length and in excruciating detail (Haggard was proud of this scene and has often been praised for it), transform her from an object of awe and dread to one of contempt or, at best, pity. Forced to live evolution backward, she endures the rapid deterioration of her body from "the most splendid...the world has ever seen" to one "too hideous for words" (294). Holly may see "the finger of Providence in the matter" (295), but we are more likely to be aware of the "hideous mockery" involved in his prolonged descriptions of her painful descent from goddess to "baboon...of unutterable age" (294).

This physical devolution is accompanied by Ayesha's intellectual and moral abasement at the feet of Leo Vincey. Shortly before entering the fire Ayesha willingly prostrates herself "in token of submission" to her beloved, thus achieving what she calls the "first most holy hour of completed Womanhood" (284). Having sworn to "abandon Evil...eschew Ambition...[and] be ever guided by thy voice in the straightest path of Duty" (284), Ayesha pledges fealty to the domestic ideology she earlier scorned. The fatal woman is to become an angel in the house. This unlikely transformation validates an earlier observation of Holly's: "I saw that after all she was only a woman, although she might be a very old one" (157). Even more than the spectacle of her devolution, Ayesha's abasement into "completed Womanhood" marks her submission to patriarchy's "eternal law."

It is also symbolically a submission to the power of male writing. As Ayesha's body first begins to deteriorate, Holly notes that her skin loses "the perfect whiteness of its lustre" and turns "dirty brown and yellow, like an old piece of withered parchment" (293). He later repeats the metaphor: the "hideous little… frame" of the corpse, he writes, looks as if it were "covered with crinkled yellow parchment" (295). In effect, Ayesha is at last fit to be inscribed upon with the "inventive pen" of the male writer, to be brought into the realm of writing in the form of Holly's narrative. This same uncanny conjunction of masculine art and the degraded female body had been made earlier in the book. In a bizarre and apparently irrelevant footnote, the unnamed editor of Holly's manuscript interrupts the action to note the various practical uses to which embalmed corpses can be put. "Mummy, that is pounded ancient Egyptian," he says, is among other things "a pigment much used by artists, especially those of them who direct their talents to the reproductions of the works of the old masters" (262). Ground-up mummy is literally the stuff of which great art, the art of the "old masters" and their imitators, is made. This highly overdetermined image of the female body transfigured – or, more accurately, disfigured – into art is then indirectly invoked at the moment of Ayesha's death.

In this context it is difficult not to recall Haggard's own mother, Ella Haggard, if only because Rider was obsessed with her influence over him and his writing. If the image of "pounded mummy" brutally subordinates female to male, it also situates the female in a position prior, and indispensable, to the male act of creation. We know from Haggard's autobiography that he considered Ella, herself a writer, the source of his artistic talent and yet also a suffocating influence from which he needed to break free.[72] (Hence, perhaps, the double insistence in *She* that Leo is an exact replica of his mother and that he killed her.) Haggard's conflicted response to Ella – whose name, as Koestenbaum notes, is Spanish for "She" – repeats on a personal level the widespread anxiety among fin-de-siècle male writers over the "priority" of feminine creativity, an anxiety the male romance form implicitly attempts to allay.[73]

In the end, Haggard's novel acknowledges this priority in the very act of repressing it. If the Sherd of Amenartas stands for a male self-generative power opposed and finally superior to Ayesha's magic creativity, it nonetheless acknowledges the female as origin and begetter. The first writing on the Sherd is that of Amenartas herself, who inaugurates the line that eventually produces Leo.[74] One other woman's name appears, momentarily interrupting the two-thousand-year sequence of fathers and sons. "Dorothea Vincey," reads Holly, who immediately feels "perfectly bewildered" (35). The name prompts us to recall the two heroines of *Middlemarch* as well as their creator, a woman (Mary Ann Evans) who wrote "beneath" a man (George Eliot). As Showalter reminds us, in the 1880s Eliot's work stood for the kind of domestic realist High Victorian fiction that male romancers loudly disparaged and secretly despaired of measuring up to.[75]

Unlike the other writing on the Sherd, Dorothea Vincey's contribution does not refer to the family curse or quest. She instead offers a doggerel couplet – "In earth and skie and sea/Strange thynges ther be" – to which she appends a telling tag. "Hoc fecit": in effect, "She made this." While "this" presumably refers to the lines of verse, it can easily be extended to encompass more symbolic referents. In Haggard's novel female "making" is shown to precede and thus take precedence over its belated male counterpart. To find further evidence of such precedence we need look no further than the epigraph to *She* itself, which turns out to be – no surprise – Dorothea's couplet. That couplet inaugurates Holly's story. His "inventive pen" merely elaborates and rewrites what she has already written: "strange things there be." In a like manner, through Dorothea Vincey's epigraph George Eliot can be said to put her ghostly signature on Rider Haggard's novel. Hoc fecit: She made this.

PART THREE

The sins of empire

CHAPTER 5

The Occidental tourist: Stoker and reverse colonization

THE MISERABLE SKEDADDLE

Roughly speaking and with notable exceptions, High Victorian fictions banish problems by throwing them outward, toward the colonies. In this way they rid themselves of figures who disrupt or trouble the domestic order, or who simply find no suitable place within established hierarchies: Jem Wilson in *Mary Barton*, Alton Locke and John Crossthwaite in *Alton Locke*, St. John Rivers in *Jane Eyre*, Lady Collins in *Orley Farm*, the Micawbers and Peggottys in *David Copperfield*, Pip in *Great Expectations*, to name only a few. This evacuation often serves of course to highlight domestic ills. Emigration, enforced or voluntary, is represented as the only option for the casualties – political, social, economic – of Victorian England. Yet the movement outward can also indicate a certain confidence. "Problem" characters like the Micawbers, once relocated, often lose their problematic status. Misfits at home, they succeed famously abroad. Having failed to find a place in Great Britain, they are nevertheless integrated into what Charles Dilke in a famous coinage called Greater Britain: the world brought safely (and profitably) under English cultural hegemony.[1] Exile serves a double function in such novels. Providing fantasy solutions to the problems besetting mid-century Britain, it also leads to the pleasures attendant on narrative closure.

By the end of the century, however, the thrust is more often inward. Problematic or disruptive figures come from the periphery of the empire to threaten a troubled metropole. Midway through *She*, for instance, Ayesha reveals that she is considering traveling to Britain in order to overthrow her sovereign counterpart, Victoria. The proposal brings a joint "exclamation of dismay" from Holly and Vincey, who "absolutely shudder to think what would be the result of her arrival" in England. "In the end," Holly speculates, "she would...assume absolute rule over the British dominions, and probably over the whole earth" (255–56).

Moments like this recur with remarkable frequency in late-Victorian popular fiction, embedded in what can be called narratives of reverse colonization. In such narratives what has been represented as the "civilized" world is on the point of being overrun by "primitive" forces. These forces can originate outside the civilized world (as in *She*) or they can inhere in the civilized itself (as in Kurtz's emblematic heart of darkness). In each case a fearful reversal occurs: the colonizer finds himself in the position of the colonized, the exploiter is exploited, the victimizer victimized. The reversals are in turn linked to perceived problems – racial, moral, spiritual – within Great Britain itself. Having recovered from his initial shock, Holly allows himself to wonder whether Ayesha's arrival in England might not have its benefits.

> After much thinking I could only conclude that this wonderful creature...was now about to be used by Providence as a means to change the order of the world, and possibly, by the building up of a power that could no more be rebelled against or questioned than the decrees of Fate, to change it materially for the better. (256)

He adds: "I was sure that she would speedily make ours the most glorious and prosperous empire that the world has ever seen" (256). Despite his disclaimers, in other words, Holly admits that Britain sorely needs someone like Ayesha. Replacing an aged queen with an ageless one, the nation itself might resist the ravages of time. Holly's fantasy of an empire as immortal and implacable as fate would have had special resonance in the aftermath of not only the Home Rule conflict but also the 1884 Berlin Conference and the debacle at Khartoum, events which underscored the increasing fragility of British imperial dominion.

Yet if fantasies of reverse colonization are products of the geopolitical fears of a troubled imperial society, they are also responses to cultural guilt. In the marauding, invasive Other, British culture sees its own imperial practices mirrored back in monstrous forms. Stoker's Count Dracula and Haggard's Ayesha frighten not least because their characteristic actions – appropriation and exploitation – uncannily reproduce those of the colonizing Englishman.[2]

Reverse colonization narratives thus contain the potential for powerful critiques of imperial ideology. H. G. Wells, for instance, located the "point of departure" for *The War of the Worlds* (1898) in a discussion with his brother concerning the eradication of indigenous Tasmanians by Western colonists. Speculating on this "very frightful disaster," Frank Wells imagined the positions reversed. "Suppose some beings from another planet were to drop out of the sky suddenly...and begin laying about them here!"[3] In the novel Wells's narrator never tires of equating Britain's fate with that of colonized peoples: we are to the pitiless and exploitative Martians, he says, as "the poor brutes we dominate" once were to us. "I was no longer a master," he laments.[4]

The fear aroused by the spectacle of England laid waste by alien invasion is coupled with, and oddly augmented by, a strong suspicion that the devastation may, after all, be deserved, that it may be a form of punishment for the nation's destructive imperial practices. "What sins have we done?" asks the anguished curate in the midst of the carnage (216). Such sins, Wells suggests, are not far to seek. Chief among them is the "ruthless and utter destruction" of the world's "inferior races" (155). Wells's narrator asks whether, given Britain's own "war[s] of extermination," one can "complain if the Martians warred in the same spirit?" (155). Suffering the invasion becomes a form of atonement.[5] Significantly, one of the first buildings destroyed by the aliens is the Oriental College (187, 196), that symbol of Western appropriations of the East.

In Wells's invader, the late-Victorian reader could discover, distorted but recognizable, both his own face and that of the colonized Other.[6] They were equally disturbing. On the one hand, the Martians' straightforwardly imperial motives parody those of the colonizing Englishman. Their journey earthward, Wells ironically suggests, is a "missionary enterprise" (153). An implicit parallel is drawn between British expansion in the tropics and the Martians' urge to "carry warfare sunward" (155) from their cold planet.

Superimposed on this self-portrait, however, is another image. In addition to themselves, Wells's readers would also have recognized in the Martians a nightmarish vision of the colonized Other, come to overthrow their oppressors and begin "the rout of civilisation" (252). A thinly concealed racialism underlies both the depiction of the Martians and the British response to them. Wells's brushstrokes are broad, but the stereotypical features of the "primitive savage" are carefully delineated nonetheless. The aliens are dark, oily, unclean, inarticulate, sexually perverse, and cannibalistic: "unspeakably nasty," as the narrator insists. "What ugly *brutes*!" (170; emphasis in original).

In Wells's fantasy, the colonized Other thus returns both to haunt the culture for its sins and to threaten its destruction as a form of retribution. In addition, the British seem to invite their subjugation through the weakness of their national character, a weakness Wells figures in racial terms. If the British are "no longer masters," Wells's narrator implies, it is largely because they have lost their collective will. The principal spokesman for this position within the novel is the artilleryman on Putney Hill, who rails against his countrymen's enervation and welcomes the cleansing offered by the Martians.[7] The Utopia he envisions to replace the current "miserable skedaddle" (304) is a genetic engineer's fantasy of a race of "able-bodied, clean-minded" men and women, their stock untainted by the blood of the "useless and cumbersome and mischievous" (305–06). As Wells's own lifelong attraction to Carlylean heroes and Nietzschean samurai indicates, he likewise yearned for the kind of forcible "renewal" of the national character ostensibly offered, for instance, by the eugenicist movement.[8] While the artilleryman is eventually discredited (he turns out to be a drunkard and a loafer), his position is not. Indeed, his very weakness proves his point. He himself is evidence of the truth of his accusations.[9]

In its concern for the nation's vulnerability, *The War of the Worlds* springs from the same font of cultural anxiety that produced the innumerable "invasion scare" and "dynamite" novels of the period. After the stir caused by *The Battle of Dorking* (1871), Sir George Chesney's cautionary tale of a successful German attack on England, the invasion scare novel became a staple of British fiction.[10] These tales played on late-Victorian fears of national decline, urban degeneration, and the threat to English racial "purity" posed by increased immigration. As Daniel Pick has shown, such stories frequently raised the specter of a Channel Tunnel (often proposed after 1880 but never begun) which, in linking England to the Continent, would lay open the nation to all sorts of cultural, sexual, and racial impurities.[11] Rivalling the invasion scare novel in popularity were the dynamite novels of the 1880s and 90s, tales that drew on fears of anarchist and nihilist groups in fin-de-siècle London. Henry James in *The Princess Casamassima* (1886) and Joseph Conrad in *The Secret Agent* (1907) provide largely ironic high culture reworkings of this tradition.[12]

There are distinctions between these subgenres and reverse colonization narratives, however. Invasion scare novels focus on the threat posed to Britain by other industrial nations. As Clarke shows, changes in international power relationships are mirrored in these stories, as different foreign powers were in turn perceived as the most likely invader of England's shores. Dynamite novels originated partly in the Victorian fascination with the "criminal element," especially as it was thought to exist among the growing urban underclass. These stories articulate a middle-class fear both of foreign revolutionaries (like the mysterious Hoffendahl of James's novel) and of an industrial underclass that was itself becoming increasingly politicized.

By contrast, reverse colonization narratives are obsessed with the spectacle of the primitive and the atavistic. The "savagery" of Haggard's Amahagger or Wells's Morlocks both repels and captivates; their proximity to elemental instincts and energies, energies seen as dissipated by modern life, makes them dangerous but also deeply attractive. Patrick Brantlinger has linked this interest in the primitive to the late-Victorian fascination with the occult and the paranormal, and by extension to the Gothic. The primitive and the occultist alike operated beyond or beneath the rational mind, tapping into unconscious resources as well as into deep-rooted anxieties and fears. Brantlinger identifies a body of fiction he terms "imperial Gothic" in which the conjunction of imperialist ideology, primitivism, and occultism produces narratives that are at once self-divided and deeply "symptomatic of the anxieties that attended the climax of the British empire." The "atavistic descents into the primitive" characteristic of imperial Gothic "seem often to be allegories of the larger regressive movement of civilization" and of the ease with which it could be overcome by the forces of barbarism.[13] Another way to put this is to say that in this period political and cultural concerns about the decline of empire often become gothicized. Which brings us to *Dracula.*

HISTORY AND THE GOTHIC

Dracula (1897) participates in that modernizing of Gothic which occurs at the close of the nineteenth century. Like *Jekyll and Hyde* and *The Picture of Dorian Gray*, Stoker's novel achieves its effects by bringing the terror of the Gothic home. Whereas earlier Gothic novelists had often displaced their stories in time or locale, these later writers root their action firmly in the modern world. Yet critics have until recently ignored the historical contexts in which these works were written and originally read. The divorce of Gothic from "history" can be traced as far back as Walter Scott's famous distinction between the two in his introduction to *Waverley* (1814). We do better, however, to approach this genre by way of David Punter's sensible claim that the Gothic contains "a very intense, if displaced, engagement with political and social problems."[14] The neglect of history in Gothic studies has in part resulted from the various psychoanalytic approaches taken by most critics of the genre. While such approaches have greatly enriched our understanding of *Dracula*, and while nothing in psychoanalytic theory precludes an historicist reading of literary texts, that theory has in practice been used almost exclusively to demonstrate, as a recent critic puts it, that *Dracula* is a "representation of fears that are more universal than a specific focus on the Victorian background would allow."[15] Yet the novel's very attachment to the "Victorian background" – what *The Spectator* in 1897 called its "up-to-dateness" – is a primary source of Stoker's continuing power.[16]

Dracula's up-to-dateness is nowhere more evident than in its articulation of anxieties generated by the prospect of imperial and racial decline.[17] Several critics have noted the political overtones of Count Dracula's excursion to Britain. Carol Senf suggests that Dracula manifests "the threat of the primitive trying to colonize the civilized world," while Burton Hatlen argues that the Count "represents a dark, primitive strata of civilization" come to disrupt further an already beleaguered Victorian culture. Judith Wilt emphasizes the connection between Dracula's "awful visitations" and the "willful penetration" of Transylvania by the emissaries of Western imperial might.[18] These accounts quite rightly stress the archaic forces unleashed by the Count, forces that threaten to overturn the progressive, scientific world of contemporary Britain. More can be said, however, both about the nature of the highly overdetermined threat posed by Count Dracula and about the relation of that threat to the problems of late-Victorian imperial culture.

Largely overlooked in most readings of *Dracula* is the fact that the novel participates in more than one genre. Stoker maps his story not simply onto the Gothic but also onto a second, equally popular late-Victorian form, the travel narrative. Like fin-de-siècle Gothic, the travel narrative clearly displays aspects of imperial ideology. Like Gothic, too, the travel narrative concerns itself with boundaries – both with maintaining and with transgressing them. The blurring of psychic and sexual boundaries that occurs in Gothic is certainly evident in *Dracula* (and is one reason the novel is so accessible to psychoanalytic interpretation), but for Stoker the collapse of boundaries resonates culturally and politically as well. The Count's transgressions and aggressions are placed in the context, provided by innumerable travel narratives, of late-Victorian forays into the "East." For Stoker, the Gothic and the travel narrative problematize, separately and together, the very boundaries on which British imperial hegemony depended: between civilized and primitive, colonizer and colonized, victimizer (either imperialist or vampire) and victim. By problematizing those boundaries, Stoker probes the heart of the culture's sense of itself, its ways of defining and distinguishing itself from other peoples, other cultures, in its hour of perceived decline.

FOLLOWING THE WAKE OF EMPIRE

In many respects, *Dracula* represents a break from the Gothic tradition of vampires. It is easy, for instance, to forget that the inevitable association of vampires with Transylvania begins with, rather than predates, Stoker's novel. The site of Castle Dracula was in fact not determined until well after Stoker had begun to write. In his working notes for the novel, Stoker signalled his debt to his countryman Le Fanu's *Carmilla* (1872) by locating the castle in "Styria," the scene of the earlier novella.[19] In rewriting *Dracula*'s opening chapters, however, Stoker moved his Gothic story to a place that, for readers in 1897, resonated in ways Styria did not. Transylvania was known primarily as part of the vexed "Eastern Question" that so obsessed British foreign policy in the 1880s and 90s. The region was first and foremost the site, not of superstition and Gothic romance, but of political turbulence and racial strife. Victorian readers knew the Carpathian Mountains region largely for its endemic cultural upheaval and its fostering of a dizzying succession of empires. By moving Castle Dracula there, Stoker gives distinctly political overtones to his Gothic narrative. In Stoker's version of the myth, vampires are intimately linked to military conquest and to the rise and fall of empires. According to Van Helsing, the vampire is the unavoidable consequence of any invasion: "He have follow the wake of the berserker Icelander, the devil-begotten Hun, the Slav, the Saxon, the Magyar."[20]

Given this link between empire and the undead, nowhere else in the Europe of 1897 could provide a more fertile vampiric breeding ground than the Count's homeland. The Western accounts of the region that Stoker consulted invariably stress the ceaseless clash of antagonistic cultures in the Carpathians.[21] The cycle of empire – rise, decay, collapse, displacement – was there displayed in a particularly compressed and vivid manner. "Greeks, Romans, Huns, Avars, Magyars, Turks, Slavs, French and Germans, all have come and seen and gone, seeking conquest one over the other," opens one late-century account.[22] The Count himself confirms that his homeland has been the scene of perpetual invasion: "there is hardly a foot of soil in all this region that has not been enriched by the blood of men, patriots or invaders," he tells Harker (33). His subsequent question is thus largely rhetorical: "Is it a wonder that we were a conquering race?" (41).

The "race" in which Dracula claims membership is left ambiguous here. He refers at once to his Szekely warrior past and to his vampiric present. The ambiguity underscores the impossibility of untangling the two aspects of Dracula's essential nature, since his vampirism is interwoven with his status as conqueror and invader. Here Stoker departs significantly from his literary predecessors. Unlike Polidori and Le Fanu, for instance, who depict their vampires as wan and enervated, Stoker makes Dracula vigorous and energetic. Polidori's Count Ruthven and Le Fanu's Carmilla represent the aristocrat as decadent aesthete; their vampirism is an extension of the traditional aristocratic vices of sensualism and conspicuous consumption.

Dracula by contrast represents the nobleman as warrior. Stoker's Count belongs in the tradition of aristocratic rakes like Richardson's Lovelace, who in turn have their roots in the medieval lord with his demands for the *droit de seigneur*. Indeed, *Dracula* can be read as a bourgeois fantasy of aristocratic power and privilege. Like the hereditary nobleman, Dracula derives his power from land (he must stay in contact with his native soil to survive), wealth (which he literally digs out of the land on the night of Harker's arrival in Transylvania), family (his name is transmitted through generations without the line being interrupted), and of course blood, which in turn is connected with the other three: when Harker cuts Dracula with his knife, for instance, the Count "bleeds" a "stream of gold" coins (364). For a middle-class Victorian audience, the vision of aristocratic power embodied by the vampire could be deeply attractive, especially given the ineffectuality of the novel's only English aristocrat, Lord Godalming.

Dracula's activities after death thus simply carry on his former activities in life. In both cases the Count successfully engages in forms of conquest and domination. *Racial* conquest and domination, we should immediately add. In *Dracula* Stoker draws on the common perception of Eastern Europe as a place of endemic racial strife. For Stoker, the vampire "race" is simply the most virulent of the numerous warrior races – Berserker, Hun, Turk, Saxon, Slovak, Magyar, Szekely – inhabiting the area. Nineteenth-century accounts of the Carpathians repeatedly stress its polyracial character. The standard Victorian work on the region, Charles Boner's *Transylvania* (1865), begins by marveling at this spectacle of variety:

> The diversity of character which the various physiognomies present that meet you at every step, also tell of the many nations which are here brought together... The slim, lithe Hungarian... the more oriental Wallachian, with softer, sensuous air, – in her style of dress and even in her carriage unlike a dweller in the West; a Moldavian princess wrapped in a Turkish shawl... And now a Serb marches proudly past, his countenance calm as a Turk's; or a Constantinople merchant sweeps along in his loose robes and snowy turban. There are, too,

Greeks, Dalmatians, and Croats, all different in feature: there is no end to the variety.[23]

Transylvania is what Dracula calls the "whirlpool of European races" (41), but within that whirlpool racial interaction usually involved conflict, not accommodation. Racial violence could in fact reach appalling proportions, as in the wholesale massacres, widely reported by the British press, of Armenians by Turks in 1894 and 1896, the years in which *Dracula* was being written. For Western writers and readers, these characteristics – racial heterogeneity combined with racial intolerance considered barbaric in its intensity – defined the area east and south of the Danube, with the Carpathians at the imaginative center of the turmoil.

By situating Dracula in the Carpathians, and by continually blurring the lines between the Count's vampiric and warrior activities, Stoker forges seemingly natural links among three of his principal concerns: racial strife, the collapse of empire, and vampirism. It is important too to note the sequence of events. As Van Helsing says, vampires follow "in [the] wake of" imperial decay (286). Vampires are generated by racial enervation and the decline of empire, not vice versa. They are produced, in other words, by the very conditions many perceived as characterizing late-Victorian Britain.

Stoker in this way transforms the materials of the vampire myth, making them bear the weight of the culture's fears over its declining status. The appearance of vampires becomes the sign of profound trouble. With vampirism marking the intersection of racial strife, political upheaval, and the fall of empire, Dracula's move to London indicates that Great Britain, rather than the Carpathians, is now the scene of struggle. The Count has penetrated to the heart of modern Europe's largest empire, and his very presence seems to presage its doom. "This was the being I was helping to transfer to London," Harker writes in anguish, "where, perhaps for centuries to come, he might, amongst its teeming millions, satiate his lust for blood, and create a new and ever widening circle of semi-demons to batten on the helpless" (67).

The late-Victorian nightmare of reverse colonization is expressed succinctly here. Harker envisions semi-demons spreading through the realm, colonizing bodies and land indiscriminately. The Count's "lust for blood" points in both directions: to the vampire's need for its special food, and also to the warrior's desire for conquest. The Count endangers Britain's integrity as a nation at the same time that he imperils the personal integrity of individual citizens. Harker's lament highlights this double thrust –

political and biological – of Dracula's invasion, while at the same time conflating the two into a single threat. Dracula's twin status as vampire and Szekely warrior suggests that for Stoker the Count's aggressions against the body are also aggressions against the body politic.

Indeed, the Count can threaten the integrity of the nation precisely because of the nature of his threat to personal integrity. His attacks involve more than an assault on the isolated self, the subversion and loss of one's individual identity. Again unlike Polidori's Count Ruthven or Le Fanu's Carmilla or Thomas Prest's Sir Francis Varney, Dracula imperils not simply his victims' personal identities, but also their cultural, political, and racial selves. In *Dracula* vampirism designates a kind of colonization of the body. Horror arises not because Dracula destroys bodies, but because he appropriates and transforms them. Having yielded to his assault, one literally "goes native" by becoming a vampire oneself. As John Allen Stevenson argues, if "blood" is a sign of racial identity, then Dracula effectively deracinates his victims.[24] In turn, they receive a new racial identity, one that marks them as literally "Other." Miscegenation leads not to the mixing of races but to the biological and political annihilation of the weaker race by the stronger.

Through the vampire myth, Stoker gothicizes the political threats to Britain caused by the enervation of the Anglo-Saxon "race." These threats also operate independently of the Count's vampirism, however, for the vampire was not considered alone in its ability to deracinate. Stoker learned from Emily Gerard that the Roumanians were themselves notable for the way they could "dissolve" the identities of those they came in contact with:

> The Hungarian woman who weds a Roumanian husband will necessarily adopt the dress and manners of his people, and her children will be as good Roumanians as though they had no drop of Magyar blood in their veins; while the Magyar who takes a Roumanian girl for his wife will not only fail to convert her to his ideas, but himself, subdued by her influence, will imperceptibly begin to lose his nationality. This is a fact well known and much lamented by the Hungarians themselves, who live in anticipated apprehension of seeing their people ultimately dissolving into Roumanians.[25]

Gerard's account of the "imperceptible" but inevitable loss of identity – national, cultural, racial – sounds remarkably like the transformations that Lucy and Mina suffer under Dracula's "influence." In life Dracula was a Roumanian (Gerard designates the Szekelys as a branch of the Roumanian race); his ability to deracinate could thus derive as easily from his Roumanian as from his vampiric nature.

The "anticipated apprehension" of deracination – of seeing Britons "ultimately dissolving into Roumanians" or vampires or savages – is at the heart of the reverse colonization narrative. For both Gerard and Stoker, the Roumanians' dominance can be traced to a kind of racial puissance that overwhelms its weaker victims. Given, too, widespread British fears over the degeneration of their "stock," especially in the cities, Dracula's threat would inevitably have been perceived in racial terms. The vampire is the disseminator of "bad" blood.[26] The racial context also helps account for what critics routinely note about Dracula: that he is by his very nature vigorous, masterful, energetic, robust. Such attributes are conspicuously absent among the novel's British characters, particularly the men. All the novel's vampires are distinguished by their robust health and their equally robust fertility. The vampire serves, then, to highlight the alarming decline among the British, since the undead are, paradoxically, healthier and more fertile than the living. Perversely, a vampiric attack can serve to invigorate its victim. "The adventure of the night does not seem to have harmed her," Mina notes after Lucy's first encounter with Dracula. "On the contrary, it has benefited her, for she looks better this morning than she has done in weeks" (115). Indeed, after his attack, Lucy's body initially appears stronger, her eyes brighter, her cheeks rosier. The corresponding enervation that marks the British men is most clearly visible in Harker (he is "pale," "weak-looking," "exhausted," "nervous," "a wreck"), but it can be seen in the other male British characters as well. Harker and Dracula in fact switch places during the novel. Harker becomes tired and white-haired as the action proceeds, while Dracula, whose white hair grows progressively darker, becomes more vigorous.

The vampire's vigor is in turn connected with its virility, its ability to produce literally endless numbers of offspring. Van Helsing's concern that the earth in Dracula's boxes be "sterilized" (347, 355) underlines the link between the Count's threat and his fecundity. In marked contrast, the non-vampires in the novel seem unable to reproduce themselves. Fathers in particular are in short supply: most are either dead (Mr. Westenra, Mr. Harker, Mr. Murray, Mr. Canon), dying (Mr. Hawkins, Lord Godalming, Mr. Swales), or missing (Mr. Seward, Mr. Morris), while the younger men, being unmarried, cannot father legitimately. Even Harker, the novel's only married man, is prohibited from touching Mina after she has been made "unclean." In *Dracula*'s lexicon, uncleanliness is closely related to fertility, but it is the wrong kind of fertility. Mina, the men fear, is perfectly capable of producing "offspring," but not with Jonathan. The prohibition regarding Mina is linked to the fear of vampiric fecundity, a fecundity that threatens to overwhelm the far less prolific British men. Thus, as many critics have pointed out, the arrival of little Quincey Harker at the story's close signals the final triumph over Dracula, since the Harkers' ability to secure an heir – an heir whose racial credentials seem impeccable – is the surest indication that the vampire's threat has been mastered. Even this triumph is precarious, however. Harker proudly notes that his son is named after each of the men in the novel, making them all figurative fathers (449), yet Quincey's multiple parentage only underscores the original problem. How secure is any racial line when five fathers are needed to produce one son?

Such racial anxieties are clearest in the case of Lucy Westenra. If Dracula's kiss serves to deracinate Lucy, and by doing so to unleash what the male characters consider her incipiently monstrous sexual appetite, then the only way to counter this process is to "re-racinate" her by reinfusing her with the "proper" blood. But Stoker is careful to establish a strict hierarchy among the potential donors. The men give blood in this order: Holmwood, Seward, Van Helsing, Morris. Arthur Holmwood is first choice ostensibly because he is engaged to Lucy, but also because his blood is, in Van Helsing's words, "more good than" Seward's (149). As the only English aristocrat in the novel, Holmwood possesses a "blood so pure" (149) that it can restore Lucy's compromised racial identity. Dr. Seward, whose blood though bourgeois is English nonetheless, comes next in line, followed by the two foreigners, Van Helsing and Morris. (We note that Van Helsing's old, Teutonic blood is still preferred over Morris's young, American blood, for reasons I will take up in a moment.) Even foreign blood is better than lower-class blood, however. After Lucy suffers what proves to be the fatal attack by Dracula, Van Helsing, looking for blood donors, rejects the four apparently healthy female servants as unsafe: "I fear to trust those women" (180).

More precisely, Van Helsing's distrust of "those women" marks a point of intersection between his usually covert class prejudices and his often overt misogyny.[27] That Dracula propagates his race solely through the bodies of women suggests an affinity, perhaps even an identity, between vampiric sexuality and female sexuality. Both are represented as primitive and voracious, and both threaten patriarchal hegemony. In the novel's (and Victorian Britain's) sexual economy, female sexuality has only one legitimate function, propagation within marriage. Once separated from that function, as Lucy's desire is, female sexuality becomes monstrous. The violence of Lucy's demise is grisly enough, but we should not miss the fact that her subjection and Mina's final fate parallel one another. They differ in degree, not kind. By the novel's close, Mina's sexual energy has been harnessed for purely domestic use. In the end, women serve identical purposes for both Dracula and the Western characters. If in this novel blood stands for race, then women quite literally become the vehicles of racial propagation. The struggle between the two camps is thus on one level a struggle over access to women's bodies, and Dracula's biological colonization of women becomes a horrific parody of the sanctioned exploitation practiced by the Western male characters.

By considering the parallel fates of Lucy and Mina, moreover, we can see how the fear and guilt characteristic of reverse colonization narratives begin to overlap. The fear generated by the Count's colonization of his victims' bodies – a colonization rightly designated monstrous – modulates into guilt that his practices simply repeat those of the "good" characters. Dracula's appropriation of female bodies does not distinguish him from his Western antagonists as much as at first appears. Instead of being uncannily Other, the vampire is here revealed as disquietingly familiar. And since the colonizations of bodies and territory are closely linked, the same blurring of distinctions occurs when we consider more closely the nature of the Count's invasion of Britain. Just as Dracula's vampirism mirrors the domestic practices of Victorian patriarchs, so his invasion of London in order to "batten on the helpless" natives there mirrors British imperial activities abroad.

As a transplanted Irishman, one whose national allegiances were conspicuously split, Stoker may have been particularly sensitive to the issues raised by British imperial conquest and domination. Britain's subjugation of Ireland was marked by a brutality often exceeding what occurred in the colonies, while the stereotype of the "primitive...dirty, vengeful, and violent" Irishman was in most respects identical to that of the most despised "savage."[28] The ill will characterizing Anglo-Irish relations in the late-nineteenth century, exacerbated by the rise of Fenianism and the debate over Home Rule, far surpassed the tensions that arose as a result of British rule elsewhere. For Stoker's audience, Dracula's invasion of Britain would conceivably have aroused seldom dormant fears of an Irish uprising.

The paucity of autobiographical materials makes it difficult to determine the extent, if any, to which Stoker consciously felt himself in solidarity with his Irish brethren. On the one hand, his few published essays, particularly one advocating censorship, reveal a deeply conservative outlook in which "duty to the [British] state" outweighs all other considerations, even those of a dubious freedom or self-determination.[29]

On the other hand, through Stoker's very adherence to what he calls "forms of restraint" runs a deeply anarchic streak. The attraction of forbidden, disruptive action is evident enough in *Dracula* as well as in Stoker's other fictions; the same tension between restraint and rebellion may have characterized his relation to the ruling state. It probably also characterized his professional life. Certainly his status as glorified manservant to the autocratic Henry Irving almost uncannily reenacted, on the personal level, the larger cultural pattern of English domination and Irish subservience. Stoker's lifelong passion for Irving had its dark underside: the rumors, persistent in Stoker's lifetime, that Count Dracula was modeled on Irving suggests the deep ambivalence with which the transplanted Irishman regarded his professional benefactor. Like Quincey Morris, Stoker seems finally to stand in alliance with his English companions without ever being entirely of their camp.

Dracula suggests two equations in relation to English–Irish politics: not just, Dracula is to England as Ireland is to England, but, Dracula is to England as England is to Ireland. In Count Dracula, Victorian readers could recognize their culture's imperial ideology mirrored back as a kind of monstrosity. Dracula's journey from Transylvania to England could be read as a reversal of Britain's imperial exploitations of "weaker" races, including the Irish. This mirroring extends not just to the imperial practices themselves, but to their epistemological underpinnings. Before Dracula successfully invades the spaces of his victims' bodies or land, he first invades the spaces of their knowledge.

The Count operates in several distinct registers in the novel. He is both the warrior nobleman, whose prowess dwarfs that of the novel's bourgeois Englishmen, and the primitive savage, whose bestiality, fecundity, and vigor alternately repel and attract. But he is also what we might call an incipient "Occidentalist" scholar. Dracula's physical mastery of his British victims begins with an intellectual appropriation of their culture, which allows him to delve the workings of the "native mind." As Harker discovers, the Count's expertise in "English life and customs and manners" (30) provides the groundwork for his exploitative invasion of Britain. In Dracula the British characters see their own ideology reflected back as a form of bad faith, since the Count's Occidentalism mimics and reverses the more familiar Orientalism underwriting Western imperial practices.

OCCIDENTALISM

To understand fully how the Count's Occidentalism functions, however, we must relate it to the second literary genre visible in *Dracula*, the travel narrative. Jonathan Harker's initial journey to Castle Dracula constitutes a travel narrative in miniature, with the opening entries in his journal reproducing the conventions of this popular genre. Critics have occasionally noted the travel motifs in *Dracula*, but have not pursued the implications of Stoker's mixing of genres. To be sure, Gothic has always contained a strong travel component. The restless roaming found in many Gothic fictions – Victor Frankenstein's pursuit of his monster, Caleb Williams's distracted flight, Melmoth's wanderings, Mr. Hyde's perambulations of London – suggests that an affinity between the two genres has always existed. Stoker's use of travel conventions is new, however. Earlier Gothic writers are interested primarily in the psychological dimensions of travel; the landscape traversed by the Gothic protagonist is largely symbolic.[30] Stoker on the other hand is chiefly interested in the ideological dimensions of travel.

Early in his stay at Castle Dracula, Harker to his great surprise finds his host stretched upon the library sofa reading, "of all things in the world," an English Bradshaw's Guide (34). We probably share Harker's puzzlement at the Count's choice of reading material, though like Harker we are apt to forget this brief interlude amid ensuing horrors. But why is Dracula interested in English train schedules?

The Count's absorption in Bradshaw's in fact echoes Harker's own obsessive interest in trains. (Later we discover that Mina, attempting to secure Harker's affections, has herself become a "train fiend," memorizing whole sections of Bradshaw's for his convenience.) Harker's journal opens with the terse note: "should have arrived at 6.46, but train was an hour late" (9). The next morning, more delays give him further cause to grumble: "It seems to me that the further East you go the more unpunctual are the trains. What ought they to be in China?" (10–11).

An obsession with trains – or, as in Harker's case, an obsession with trains running on time – characterizes Victorian narratives of travel in Eastern Europe. Even Emily Gerard, whose enthusiasm for all things Transylvanian seldom flagged, had little patience with its trains. "The railway communications were very badly managed," she writes of one journey, "so that it was only on the evening of the second day (fully forty-eight hours) that we arrived at Klausenberg...It would hardly have taken longer to go from Lemberg to London."[31] Harker immediately invokes a second convention of the travel genre when, having crossed the Danube at Budapest, he invests the river with symbolic significance. "The impression I had was that we were leaving the West and entering the East; the most Western of splendid bridges over the Danube...took us among the traditions of Turkish rule" (9). In crossing the Danube, Harker maintains, he leaves "Europe" behind, geographically and imaginatively, and approaches the first outpost of the "Orient."[32]

Harker's first two acts – noting that his train is late, and then traversing a boundary he considers symbolic – function as a kind of shorthand, alerting readers that Harker's journal is to be set against the background of late-Victorian travel narratives. Once the travel genre is established, there is an inevitability about Harker's subsequent gestures. Not only does he continue to gripe about the trains, he also searches for quaint hotels (12), samples the native cuisine (10), ogles the indigenous folk (11), marvels at the breathtaking scenery (11), wonders at local customs (15), and, interspersed throughout, provides pertinent facts about the region's geography, history, and population. Harker's first three journal entries (Chapter 1 of the novel) are so thoroughly conventional as to parody the travel genre. Such conventions constitute what Wolfgang Iser calls the "repertoire of the familiar" that readers can be expected to bring to texts.[33] If Harker is an adept imitator of travel narratives, that is in part because he has been such an assiduous reader of them. Like Stoker himself, Harker "had visited the British Museum and made search among the books and maps in the library regarding Transylvania" in order to gain "some foreknowledge of the country" (9).

This foreknowledge – the textual knowledge gathered before the fact, the same knowledge that any casual reader of contemporary travel narratives would also possess – structures Harker's subsequent experiences. In assuming the role of the Victorian traveler in the East, Harker also assumes the perspective that allows him to "make sense" of his experiences there. The contrast between British punctuality and Transylvanian tardiness stands, in Harker's view, as a concrete instance of more fundamental and wide-ranging oppositions: between Western progress and Eastern stasis, between Western science and Eastern superstition, between Western reason and Eastern emotion, between Western civilization and Eastern barbarism. The "backwardness" of the Carpathian races displayed itself most surely in what one traveler called their inability to "[settle] themselves down to the inexorable limits of timetables."[34] As Harker moves further east toward Castle Dracula, he leaves even the railroads behind and is forced to travel by stagecoach. Simultaneously, he leaves Western rationality behind: "I read that every known superstition in the world is gathered into the horseshoe of the Carpathians" (10).

Harker may marvel and wonder at this strange world he has entered, but he does not expect to be disconcerted. He trades extensively on his "foreknowledge," which allows him to retain a comfortable distance from the scene. He views it simply as a diverting spectacle, imagining the "barbarian" Slovaks he sees by the roadside as "an Oriental band of brigands" performing "on the stage" (11). At first, Harker's descent into the dark heart of the Carpathians serves only to titillate, not to unsettle. Throughout his journey, he is able to reduce everything he encounters to an example of the picturesque or the poetic.

Until he reaches Castle Dracula, that is. There, everything is disrupted. Stoker abruptly undermines the conventions of the travel narrative, just as Dracula undermines all the stable oppositions structuring Harker's – and his readers' – foreknowledge. For the fact is, by Harker's own criteria, Dracula is the most "Western" character in the novel. No one is more rational, more intelligent, more organized, or even more punctual than the Count. No one plans more carefully or researches more thoroughly. No one is more learned within his own spheres of expertise or more receptive to new knowledge. A reading that emphasizes only the archaic, anarchic, primitive forces embodied by Dracula misses half the point. When Harker arrives at the end of his journey East, he finds, not some epitome of irrationality, but a most accomplished Occidentalist. If Harker has been diligently combing the library stacks, so too has the Count. Harker writes: "In the library I found, to my great delight, a vast number of English books, whole shelves full of them, and bound volumes of magazines and newspapers...The books were of the most varied kind – history, geography, politics, political economy, botany, geology, law – all relating to England and English life and customs and manners" (30). Displaying an epistemophilia to rival Harker's own, Dracula says: "'These friends' – and he laid his hand on some of the books – 'have been good friends to me, and for some years past, ever since I had the idea of going to London, have given me many, many hours of pleasure. Through them I have come to know your great England'" (31).

The novel thus sets up an equivalence between Harker and Dracula: one can be seen as an Orientalist traveling East, the other – unsettling thought for Stoker's Victorian readers – as an Occidentalist traveling West. Dracula's absorption in Bradshaw's timetables echoes Harker's fetish for punctual trains, just as the Count's posture – reclining comfortably on a sofa – recalls the attitude of the casual Western reader absorbed in a late-Victorian account of the exotic.

But of course Dracula's preoccupation with English culture is not motivated by a disinterested desire for knowledge, but represents instead the essence of bad faith, since it promotes and masks the Count's sinister plan to invade Britain and subdue her people. By insisting on the connections between Dracula's growing knowledge and his power to exploit, Stoker also forces us to acknowledge how Western imperial practices are implicated in certain forms of knowledge. Stoker continually draws our attention to the affinities between Harker and Dracula, as in the oft-cited scene where Harker looks for Dracula's reflection in the mirror and sees only himself (37). The text's insistence that these characters are capable of substituting for one another becomes most pressing when Dracula twice dons Harker's clothes to leave the Castle (59, 64). Since on both occasions the Count's mission is to plunder the town, we are encouraged to see a correspondence between the vampire's actions and those of the traveling Westerner. The equivalence between these two sets of actions is underlined by the reaction of the townspeople, who have no trouble believing that it really is Harker, the visiting Englishman, who is stealing their goods, their money, their children. The peasant mother's anguished cry – "Monster, give me my child!" (60) – is directed at him, not Dracula.

The shock of recognition that overtakes Harker, and presumably the Victorian reader, when he sees Dracula comfortably decked out in contemporary garb is, however, only part of the terror of this scene. The truly disturbing notion is not that Dracula impersonates Harker, but that he does it so well. Here indeed is the nub: Dracula can "pass." To impersonate an Englishman, and do it convincingly, is the goal of Dracula's painstaking research into "English life and customs and manners," a goal the Count himself freely, if rather disingenuously, acknowledges. When Harker compliments him on his command of English, Dracula demurs:

"Well I know that, did I move and speak in your London, none there are who would not know me for a stranger. That is not enough for me. Here I am noble…I am master…[In London] I am content if I am like the rest, so that no man stops if he sees me, or pause in his speaking if he hear my words, to say 'Ha, ha! a stranger!' I have been so long master that I would be master still – or at least that none other should be master of me." (31)

To understand fully how disquieting Dracula's talents are, we have only to remember that in Victorian texts non-Western "natives" are seldom – I am tempted to say never, since I have not come up with another example – permitted to pass successfully. Dracula is different, however. A large part of the terror he inspires originates in his ability to stroll, unrecognized and unhindered, through the streets of London. As he tells Harker, his status as "master" resides in this ability. So long as no one recognizes him as a "stranger," he is able to work his will unhampered. Stoker's text never explicitly acknowledges the continuity between Dracula's actions and British imperial practices, but it continually forces us to see the first as a terrifying parody of the second. In the Gothic mirror that Stoker holds up to late-Victorian culture, that culture, like Harker peering into the glass at Castle Dracula, cannot see, but is nevertheless intensely aware of, its monstrous double peering over its shoulder.

Dracula not only mimics the practices of British imperialists, he rapidly becomes superior to his teachers. The racial threat embodied by the Count is thus intensified. Not only is he more vigorous, more fecund, more "primitive" than his Western antagonists, he is also becoming more "advanced." As Van Helsing notes, Dracula's swift development will soon make him invincible:

> "In some faculties of mind he has been, and is, only a child; but he is growing, and some things that were childish at the first are now of man's stature...That big child-brain of his is working. Well for us, it is, as yet, a child-brain; for had he dared, at the first, to attempt certain things he would long ago have been beyond our power." (360)

Van Helsing's metaphor of the child growing into manhood is a familiar and homely way to explain Dracula's progress, but the image deflects attention from the notion of racial development that is the real source of the vampire's threat. Since Dracula's growth is not bound by a single lifetime, but instead covers potentially limitless generations, the proper analogy for his development is not that of an individual but of a race. A passage from Emily Gerard is relevant here, since Stoker seems to have had it in mind when he made his vampire a Roumanian. In discussing the various races in Transylvania, Gerard singles out the Roumanians as representing what she calls "manhood in the future tense":

> It is scarcely hazardous to prophesy that this people have a great future before them, and that a day will come when, other nations having degenerated and spent their strength, these descendants of the ancient Romans, rising phoenix-like from their ashes, will step forward with a whole fund of latent power and virgin material, to rule as masters where formerly they have crouched as slaves.[35]

Gerard's prophecy sounds much like Van Helsing's metaphor for Dracula's development. What Gerard again allows us to see is that the anxieties engendered by Count Dracula do not derive wholly from his vampirism. He is dangerous as the representative or embodiment of a race which, all evidence suggested, was poised to "step forward" and become "masters" of those who had already "spent their strength." Even Dracula's destruction (which, if he stands in for an entire race, becomes a fantasized genocide) cannot entirely erase the moral endorsed by the rest of the story: that strong races inevitably weaken and fall, and are in turn displaced by stronger races. The novel provides an extraordinarily long list of once-proud peoples, now vanquished or vanished – not just the Huns, Berserkers, Magyars, and others who have passed through Carpathian history, but the Romans who gave their name, and perhaps their blood, to the modern Roumanians, as well as the Danes and Vikings who, Mina tells us, once occupied Whitby (80–81).

BLOTTED TRACES

Dracula, then, is what Ann Williams aptly calls a "public nightmare."[36] It articulates, in distorted but vivid fashion, some of the culture's more harrowing anxieties. Yet one can argue that it is precisely the business of Gothic fiction to articulate anxieties as a prelude to mastering them. Indeed, most readers agree that Stoker's novel displays what Christopher Craft calls the "triple rhythm" of the Gothic. It "first invites or admits a monster, then entertains or is entertained by monstrosity for some extended duration, until in its closing pages it expels or repudiates the monster and all the disruption that he/she/it brings."[37] There is also wide agreement that this mastering of the threats posed by the Count is closely tied to Stoker's narrative procedures. David Seed notes the abrupt diminishment in stature suffered by Dracula over the final third of the novel, arguing that this "progressive scaling down" of the monster is tied to the increasing power felt by the Western characters as they knit together their disparate documents into a coherent narrative. "As the gaps between individual accounts close, so Dracula becomes better known, better defined, and therefore the easier to resist."[38] Much energy is expended in order to produce what Seward calls a "whole connected narrative" (269) out of the mass of diaries, journals, letters, memoranda, telegrams, and cylinders at their disposal. From this jumble is distilled a text that unites isolated experiences into a communal story and also makes sense of that story in relation to Dracula. No longer passive victims of Dracula's aggression, the Western characters in turn become the aggressors. The last third of the novel, as Franco Moretti notes, is in effect narrated collectively. Though the tale continues to be told through the diaries of different figures, their telltale idiosyncrasies have been erased. The characters (more accurately, the male characters) all come to speak with the same voice.[39] The power of narrative to order and manage reality, and thereby to produce "truth," is thus strikingly foregrounded in *Dracula*.

Yet Stoker also embeds within his tale a telling critique of the procedures by which the narrative as a whole is constructed. "He has evidently some deep problem on his mind," Dr. Seward writes of the "lunatic" Renfield, "for he keeps a little notebook in which he is always jotting down something" (88). In a novel where *everyone* is always jotting down something, Renfield's notebook takes on added significance. We quickly discover that the form of Renfield's jottings mocks the very criteria used by the other characters to produce their master narrative. Confiscating the notebook, Seward cannot help but admire the orderliness of Renfield's accounts, just as he cannot help but sympathize with the way Renfield conducts the experiments those accounts record. "How well the man reasoned," Seward marvels (90). What he does not mention is that Renfield's "cumulative" method (90) of notekeeping blatantly parodies the accumulating of diaries, journals, and letters that Mina supervises, a process Seward later refers to as a "knitting together" of "evidence" (269). Renfield's neat columns carefully tabulated find their counterpart in the skillfully arranged, properly sequenced documents that make up the text of *Dracula* itself. Seward in fact underlines the continuity between the lunatic's jottings and the writings of the remaining characters when he compares Renfield's notebook to his own newly begun journal (90).

In mimicking the novel's narrative strategies, Renfield also calls attention to the distortions they produce. As Seward notes, Renfield's reasoning makes sense, but only "within [its] own scope," which is that of a "lunatic" (90). His columns of figures, added up, do not in fact add up. In other words, they give Renfield merely the answer he wants them to. In the same way, the accumulation of documents produces a coherent, intelligible narrative, one that allows for the mastering of Dracula's threat, but it does so only by covering over troubling gaps, silences, inconsistencies. The novel's unsigned prefatory note makes this same point obliquely by first claiming that all the available "papers have been placed in sequence" yet then admitting that "all needless matters have been eliminated" from the printed text precisely so that the story "may stand forth as simple fact" (8). There unquestionably are gaps in the text, some more intriguing than others: surely Jonathan's account of his escape to Sister Agatha's hospital, or Mina's of the Count's night visit, do not seem "needless."[40] Dracula himself, we learn from Harker's opening diary entries, is a copious writer, though we are permitted to read only one of his compositions – the short note welcoming his guest to the Carpathians (12).

Each of these silences is telling, and complicates the novel's status as "simple fact." Through Renfield, Stoker reflects self-consciously on his own narrative project, in the process forcing us to attend to what has been occluded or repressed in the story. This self-reflexivity finally troubles the solace that might otherwise be derived from the novel's concluding sections. Indeed, *Dracula* ends divided against itself: while it works, as Craft and Seed suggest, to master the monstrosity embodied by the Count, that mastery is never entirely achieved. The novel in fact ends twice. The narrative proper closes with a fantasy of revitalized English supremacy. But this temporary satisfaction is immediately disrupted by Harker's "Note," which constitutes *Dracula*'s second ending.

Dracula at last succumbs, appropriately enough, to the weapons of empire. Harker's "great Kukri knife," symbol of British imperial power in India, and Morris's bowie knife, symbol of American westward expansion, simultaneously subdue the vampire (447). The triumph extends even further for the British, since the Count is not the book's only fatality. The American Quincey Morris dies too. His demise is not simply gratuitous, for the American represents, however obliquely, a second threat to British power hidden behind Dracula's more overt antagonism.[41] A shadowy figure throughout, Morris is linked with vampires and racial Others from his first appearance. When he courts Lucy, Morris reminds her of Othello. Aroused and frightened by his words, she compares herself to "poor Desdemona when she had such a dangerous stream poured in her ear, even by a black man" (74). Morris's dangerous hunting expeditions are a modern equivalent to the Count's warrior exploits, while Lucy's fascination with his stories of adventure repeats Harker's initial response to Dracula's tales. Later, it is left to Morris to pronounce the word "vampire" for the first time in the novel, when he compares Lucy's condition to that of a mare on the Pampas "after one of those big bats that they call vampires had got at her in the night" (183). Morris's familiarity with vampirism apparently exceeds even Van Helsing's, since he correctly diagnoses the etiology of Lucy's symptoms the first moment he sees her.[42]

There are even hints that the American is at times leagued with Dracula against the others. Morris leaves, without explanation, the crucial meeting in which Van Helsing first names the Count as their enemy; a moment later he fires his pistol into the room where they are seated (288–89). He quickly explains that he was shooting at a "big bat" sitting on the windowsill, but this brief and easily missed tableau – Morris standing outside the window in the place vacated by Dracula, looking in on the assembled Westerners who have narrowly escaped his violence – suggests strongly that Stoker wants us to consider the American and the Roumanian together.[43]

Morris thus leads a double life in *Dracula*. He stands with his allies in Anglo-Saxon brotherhood, but he also, as representative of an America about to emerge as the world's foremost imperial power, threatens British superiority as surely as Dracula does. "If America can go on breeding men like that," Seward remarks, "she will be a power in the world indeed" (209).[44] If *Dracula* is about how vigorous races inevitably displace decaying races, then the real danger to Britain in 1897 comes not from the moribund Austro-Hungarian or Ottoman empires, but from the rising American empire. Without at all dismissing the powerful anxiety that the Count produces, we can say that Stoker's attention to Dracula screens his anxiety at the threat represented by Morris and America. Stoker insistently directs our gaze East, all the while looking back over his shoulder. It is appropriate, then, that Morris's death, not Dracula's, closes the story proper; appropriate, too, that the confrontation between England and America is displaced to the Balkans, traditionally the arena where Western powers conducted their struggles with one another indirectly, or by proxy.

England's triumph is immediately troubled and qualified, however, by Harker's appended "Note," written seven years later. In announcing the birth of his son Quincey, Harker unwittingly calls attention to the fact that the positions of vampire and victim have been reversed. Now it is the Count whose blood is appropriated and transformed to nourish a faltering race. As Mark Hennelly has noticed, in Quincey Harker flows the blood not only of Jonathan and Mina, but of Dracula as well.[45] Little Quincey, who is not conceived until after Mina drinks the Count's blood, is, moreover, born on the anniversary of Dracula's and Morris's demise. Through Roumania, the English race invigorates itself by incorporating those racial qualities needed to reverse its own decline. American energy is appropriated as well, since, as Jonathan tells us, Quincey Morris has also contributed to his namesake's racial makeup: "His mother holds, I know, the secret belief that some of our brave friend's spirit has passed into" their son (449). The "little band of men" can thus rest assured that the threats to English power have been neutralized on both fronts, East and West, through the appropriation of Dracula's blood and Morris's spirit.

The remainder of Harker's "Note" is taken up with two related projects: his account of a return visit to Transylvania, and an apology for the "inauthenticity" of the documents comprising the novel. These two projects point back, in different ways, to the two genres – travel and Gothic –

in which *Dracula* participates. Harker first relates that he has recently revisited the Carpathians:

> In the summer of this year we made a journey to Transylvania, and went over the old ground which was, and is, to us so full of vivid and terrible memories. It was almost impossible to believe that the things we had seen with our own eyes and heard with our own ears were living truths. Every trace of all that had been was blotted out. The castle stood as before, reared high above a waste of desolation. (449)

In his working notes, Stoker titled this section of his novel "A Tourist's Tale."[46] Indeed, the text seems to have come full circle and returned securely to its starting point. The conventions of the travel genre are once more invoked. Harker's return to Transylvania ostensibly reenacts the trip that opened the novel; or rather, it attempts to reinstate the conditions and attitudes which preceded and in a sense enabled that trip. By returning simply as a tourist (this time he has not even the excuse of business to take him there), Harker implicitly asserts that nothing has intervened to make the tourist outlook problematic. The disruption caused by Dracula is entirely erased; the story ends where it began.

But Harker's words are strikingly tentative. In their general movement, his first two sentences assert that things have indeed returned to "normal." The old ground was once full of vivid and terrible memories; we once believed (but do no longer) that what we experienced constituted a living truth. Yet each sentence is significantly qualified, and qualified in such a way as to reverse its effects. The ground not only was, but still is, full of terrible memories; the living truths are not impossible to believe, but almost impossible, which means that belief in them is, at bottom, almost inevitable. The overall effect of the sentences is to exacerbate the anxieties they are presumably intended to assuage. The unalloyed confidence and security of the novel's opening pages cannot be recaptured. Any return to the beginning is barred.

The linchpin of the passage is Harker's overdetermined assertion, "Every trace of all that had been was blotted out." On the manifest level, Harker means simply that all evidence of the Count's horrific presence is gone from the land. His next comment contradicts this claim, however, since "the castle stood as before." We might see this "blotting out," then, in psychological terms, as a repression of the insights, the "living truths," revealed by the narrative as a whole. Alternately (or simply in addition), what has been "blotted out" is precisely that vision of Transylvania – landscape, people, culture – which Harker, as a traveling Westerner secure in his "foreknowledge" of the region, "saw" on his initial visit. The ideological foundations of that vision having been disturbed, Harker can no longer perceive the land or its people in the same way. Significantly, he now sees nothing at all, only "a waste of desolation." The wasteland is the result not of Dracula's activities – if that were the case, Harker would have noted such a wasteland on his earlier, not his later, visit – but of the desolation that has occurred to Harker's and the Victorian reader's accustomed modes of perception.

Finally, though, both these kinds of erasures, psychological and epistemological, lead to a different kind of obliteration. The "blotting out" of "traces" points to the cancellation of writing, to Harker's (though not necessarily Stoker's) attempt to disavow the Gothic narrative preceding the "Note." When he returns from Transylvania, Harker retrieves the mass of papers comprising the narrative – diaries, journals, letters, memoranda, and so on – which have remained buried and unread in a safe. "We were struck by the fact," he writes in an oft-cited disclaimer, "that, in all the mass of material of which the record is composed, there is hardly one authentic document!"

Such disclaimers are often found in Gothic fictions. Harker's "Note" invokes the narrative framing devices that are one of Gothic's distinctive features. But Harker uses this device to *repudiate* parts of his narrative, whereas in Gothic the function of the frame is precisely to *establish* the narrative's authenticity. Indeed, this is the function of the unsigned note that opens *Dracula*: to overcome readerly skepticism "so that a history almost at variance with the possibilities of latter-day belief may stand forth as simple fact" (8). For Harker, however, the inauthenticity of the documents (what would make for authenticity is unclear) casts further doubt on the veracity of portions of the narrative. "We could hardly expect anyone, even did we wish to, to accept these [documentsl as proofs of so wild a story" (449). Not only does Harker not expect us to believe the collected accounts, he does not even "wish [us] to."

At the same time that he tries to recapture the comforting tourist outlook, Harker also tries to erase the Gothic parts of his story, to blot out all their traces. The two gestures are complementary. In effect, Harker asserts the story's "truth" up until the moment he enters Castle Dracula, the moment, in other words, when his travel narrative, disrupted by the Count's Occidentalism, becomes a Gothic narrative. The trouble, in Harker's view, starts there. Once the dichotomies on which Harker's (and imperial Britain's) tourist perspective rest are exploded, anything is possible. The "Note" tries to recontain the anxieties generated by that moment of rupture by invalidating what follows, by calling into question its authenticity as narrative. The "realism" of the travel narrative gives way to the fantasy constructions of the Gothic, which can be dismissed – as Harker urges us to do – as untrue. "We want no proofs; we ask none to believe us," Van Helsing says in the novel's final moments, and his words sound remarkably like a plea.

As the examples of Haggard, Wells, and Stoker indicate, the problems of empire are continually yet covertly "worried at" across a wide range of late-Victorian popular fictions directed at male readers. None of the genres considered thus far – adventure, science fiction, Gothic – has any inevitable connection to imperial issues. Indeed, if imperial problems are seldom allowed to surface *as* problems in these works, that is in part because they tend to be subsumed by the kinds of issues appropriate to their specific generic forms. One attraction of formulaic genres is that they effectively manage unruly anxieties by rearticulating them within the conventions of the genre, thereby draining or at least redirecting much of their troubling energy.

Such rearticulations are most discernible in the detective story, which for the past century has been recognized as the formulaic genre *par excellence.* More insistently than any other genre, the detective story manages ideological or social questions by turning them into formal questions. If (to echo Edmund Wilson's famous complaint) we do not care who killed Roger Ackroyd, that is because Agatha Christie encourages us to attend closely instead to her dexterity in manipulating the conventions of the genre. In the next chapter I turn to the most famous late-Victorian detective fictions, those of Arthur Conan Doyle. In considering Doyle's Sherlock Holmes tales, we should not be surprised to find this same "binding" of social problems to formal problems, nor to discover that the problems thus bound have to do with empire and the body.

CHAPTER 6

Strange events and extraordinary combinations: Sherlock Holmes and the pathology of everyday life

Arthur Conan Doyle was happy to number himself among Lang's "new barbarians." He always professed to prefer those of his works that fit within the romance tradition: historical novels like *The White Company* (1893), *Micah Clarke* (1893), and *Sir Nigel* (1906) and exotic adventure tales like *The Lost World* (1912) and *The Poison Belt* (1913). To later readers, the Sherlock Holmes tales are at once more familiar and less likely to read in terms of male romance conventions. Yet those stories display many of the same anxieties that we have been examining, anxieties concerning the erotics of interpretation, the pathologized body, and the decline of empire. If we tend not to approach the Holmes canon in this way, that is in part because the detective genre actively discourages certain forms of attention. As Fredric Jameson points out, the classic detective story is usually said to be "about" nothing beyond the logic of detection. The genre represents itself as a "form without ideological content," concerned only with ahistorical questions of epistemology and rationality.[1] This is certainly Holmes's view of detection, and he has been singularly successful in dictating the terms within which his cases have been understood.

As a way to begin opening up the Holmes tales to other kinds of understanding, I want to set *The Sign of Four* (1890) against one of its unacknowledged (by Doyle, at any rate) sources, Wilkie Collins's *The Moonstone* (1868). The surface similarities between the two works make a comparison especially useful. Doyle's debt to his predecessor is on one level clear enough. Holmes's creator owes much to Collins's influential elaborations of detective paradigms. In *The Sign of Four* that debt extends in other directions as well. The two novels address many of the same issues, both domestic and imperial. And, since Doyle shamelessly lifted the main features of Collins's story, the two works also share a plot. In each book an unscrupulous imperial soldier steals an Indian treasure and returns with it to England, setting off a series of events that result in mystery, crime, and domestic unrest. Both novels establish lines of connection between imperial politics and troubles at home. After protracted dalliances with exoticism and decadence, each finally celebrates the power of reason and science to master the world.

Yet their similarities serve ultimately to underscore the important differences between these novels. If they take up like problems, they treat them in unlike ways. A comparison will allow us to see how literary representations of the empire shift during this relatively brief period and to tie that shift not only to changes in public perceptions of imperialism, masculinity, and pathology but also to changes in the cultural uses of detective fiction. Genres never exist in pure states. While both *The Moonstone* and *The Sign of Four* rely heavily on the paradigms of detective fiction, those paradigms are themselves inflected by other novelistic traditions. In many respects Collins's book moves squarely within the mainstream of Victorian domestic realism, while Doyle's operates within the purlieu of the male romance. Recognizing their respective generic affiliations can help us account for the differing emphases the two novels put on the same basic material. To state that difference schematically at the outset: Collins uses an imperial indiscretion to tell a tale of domestic turmoil, while Doyle uses an instance of domestic mystery to tell a tale of imperial crime.

THE SECRET THEATER OF HOME

The Moonstone calls our attention to two dates, 1799 and 1848. For Collins's Victorian readers the first marked a moment of imperial high adventure, the capture of Seringapatam by British troops during the Fourth Anglo-Mysore War, an event commemorated in the novel's prologue. The British victory under Wellesley effectively consolidated English rule in the Indian subcontinent, in the process dispelling any lingering illusions that the East India Company, now under government control, was simply a commercial operation.[2] Wellesley's actions as Governor-General were controversial in 1799, but they were much less so in 1868, when Collins's novel began its serial run. Imperial policy had shifted dramatically in the aftermath of the 1857 Indian uprising, an occurrence, historians unanimously agree, whose long-term effects on public opinion in Britain are difficult to overestimate. As news of the mutiny reached England, Charles Dickens declared that, were he Commander in Chief in India ("and I wish I were," he wrote), he would "do [his] utmost to exterminate the Race upon whom the stain of the late cruelties rested...and raze it off the face of the earth."[3] From a post-1857 perspective, the storming of Seringapatam was easily transformed into an uncomplicated story of British valor and Indian treachery.

Indeed, John Clark Marshman's 1869 *History of India* sets up a stark contrast between Wellesley's integrity and the incompetence and decadence of Tipu, the Sultan of Mysore. At the moment of battle Tipu "discarded the advice of his most experienced officers, and surrounded himself with boys and parasites, who flattered him." The English General Sir David Baird by contrast "ascended the parapet...and exhibited his noble military figure to the view of both forces, and then...desired his men 'to follow him, and show themselves worthy of the name of British soldiers.'"[4]

Given this atmosphere, Collins's brief account of the battle is remarkably cynical. Narrated by one of Baird's officers, the prologue focusses not on the soldiers' valor but on their plundering of the town and its palace. "The camp-followers committed deplorable excesses; and, worse still, the soldiers found their way, by an unguarded door, into the treasury of the Palace, and loaded themselves with gold and jewels...There was riot and confusion enough."[5] The officer partially excuses such behavior by saying that the men "disgraced themselves good-humouredly" (36), but disgrace themselves they do. At the climax of the prologue is John Herncastle's theft of the moonstone and his murder of three Hindu officers. His actions are denounced by the narrator, but they represent just one (albeit extreme) instance of a widespread looting and pillaging. Collins moreover reverses the typical roles of Briton and Indian found in works like Marshman's. While Herncastle, his "fiery temper...exasperated to a kind of frenzy," loses all self-possession and begins to act "like a madman" (36, 37), his victims are accorded some nobility of purpose in their hopeless defense of the jewel. Even Tipu acquires a modicum of pathos as his dead body is discovered "under a heap of the slain" (36).

These and similar details have led some readers to suggest that one of Collins's purposes in *The Moonstone* was to pierce the hypocrisy of imperial fervor by exposing the criminality of British actions in India.[6] Certainly, Collins's few direct responses to the 1857 Mutiny lack the paranoia and vengefulness that consumed Dickens.[7] Moreover, *The Moonstone* portrays the brahmins' quest to recover their diamond in a charitable light. Though Collins frequently resorts to stereotype in his depictions, he emphasizes the brahmins' resourcefulness and intelligence, as well as their courage in sacrificing caste to redeem the moonstone. Indeed, they exhibit the traditional Victorian virtues of faith, steadfastness, and a tireless devotion to the work ethic.[8] We can also point to Ezra Jennings, "born, and partly brought up, in one of our colonies," whose blood contained "the mixture of some foreign race" (420). Persecuted and outcast in English society, Jennings proves to be the novel's most sympathetic figure. He is also of course instrumental in solving the mystery of the diamond's disappearance. In all, then, Collins offers about as unjingoistic a picture of British colonial practices and racial attitudes as can well be expected in a High Victorian novel.

Yet it would be misleading to call this novel a *critique* of imperialism. I do not deny that the information provided by *The Moonstone* can be used as part of such a task; it can. But the novel itself does not organize or present that information in such a way as to constitute a critique, even a masked one. Though the narrative is framed fore and aft by episodes in India, they only tangentially inform our understanding of the novel's main action. As many readers have noted, once the diamond is stolen from Rachel Verinder, India and the brahmins cease to matter much to the story. "They [the Indians] have no more to do with the actual loss of the jewel than you have," Cuff tells Betteredge (189), an assessment no one disputes. And so the brahmins disappear from view. Reminded later of their continued existence at Frizinghall, Betteredge turns to the reader to exclaim: "The Indians had gone clean out of my head (as they have, no doubt, gone clean out of yours)" (175).

Replacing them in our heads is the "family scandal" (181, 205, 218) threatening the Verinder household. Throughout the novel the moonstone operates as a symbol not of Britain's imperial transgressions but of Rachel's compromised virtue. The sexual allegory is transparent enough: a rifled cabinet, a lost jewel, a stained nightgown, a locked box buried in the ooze of the Shivering Sand.[9] Cuff does not hesitate to identify the events surrounding the moonstone's disappearance as constituting a "family secret" that must be kept "within the family circle" (209). "I shouldn't be surprised," the detective announces, "if a scandal was to burst up in the house to-night" (171). Though Cuff eventually misnames the thief, he correctly identifies sexual impropriety as forming the basis of the mystery. Indeed, within *The Moonstone*'s economy, the true culprit is unregulated desire. Rachel's undisguised passion for Franklin Blake (and vice versa), Rosanna Spearman's impossible love for the same gentleman, and Godfrey Ablewhite's criminal promiscuity provide the plot's motivating energies. Only when such desire is punished (Rosanna and Godfrey die) or properly channeled (Rachel and Franklin marry) can the family and the social order be made safe once more.

One can argue, as Ronald Thomas does in a subtle reading, that Collins raises the issue of imperial guilt only to repress it, deflecting attention away from the colonies and onto domestic matters. "The crime of the novel is displaced...from the original scene of imperial conquest and murder upon the body of a promiscuous womanizer. This mystery, which begins as a violent military invasion, gradually degenerates into nothing more than the unmasking of a spurned lover and an incorrigible chaser after women."[10] Yet the novel does not in fact degenerate into a tale of domestic misconduct; it is one from the start. We are explicitly asked to understand Herncastle's actions in India in the context of a family quarrel. The document which narrates these events, produced by Herncastle's cousin, is "Extracted from a Family Paper" (33). Addressed "to my relatives in England," it tells of a "private difference" (33) that ended in a permanent falling out between the cousins. Though the quarrel takes place during "a great public event," the narrator is more concerned to supply details "for the information of my family only" (33, 37). When the scene shifts to England, then, we are already more than prepared for Franklin Blake to tell us that the novel's events comprise a "strange family story" (39).

At no point does Collins portray Herncastle's actions as "effects" of Britain's imperial presence in India.[11] He is not, in other words, a synecdoche for his country. Instead, the novel takes pains to explain the theft solely in terms of Herncastle's personal failings. He is simply a bad man, "one of the greatest blackguards that ever lived" (63). His actions originate in a character evil by nature, "one that closed the doors of all his family against him" (63). (In this respect he differs significantly from Doyle's villain, Jonathan Small, whose failings are in part blamed on an unjust society.) Herncastle steals the moonstone out of avarice, keeps it out of pride, and wills it to Rachel out of malice. In the context of the novel he is guilty of enormous sins, but no crimes. Having shown himself unworthy to be a member of a "civilized" society, he is punished by being ostracized by his community. Herncastle's conduct, says Betteredge, has "outlawed him, as you may say, among his own people" (64).

Herncastle thus directs us to the novel's most pressing concerns, which turn out to be those of the High Realist novel. Collins is less interested in the politics of empire than in negotiating the conflicting demands of individual desire and communal norms. Indeed, as the trappings of the mystery begin to peel away, we discover beneath it a familiar courtship plot. Like Elizabeth Bennett and her many successors, Rachel Verinder finds herself subjected to various kinds of gratuitous pain, chastisement, and suspicion until she learns to distinguish bad suitors (Wickham/Ablewhite) from good (Darcy/Blake).[12] In like manner, as the trappings of exoticism and imperial intrigue fall aside, we find that *The Moonstone*'s most trenchant criticism is directed at injustices involving class rather than race. The bulk of the novel is set in 1848, that year of revolution across Europe, and the anxiety of class strife is never far off. Rosanna Spearman is arguably Collins's most tragic figure; her thwarted desire for Franklin Blake – her forced exile, in other words, from the novel's courtship plot – and her suicide constitute a damning indictment of contemporary mores. When Betteredge "out of pure pity for the girl" laments that Rosanna "had been mad enough to set her heart" on Blake, Cuff sharply retorts: "Hadn't you better say she's mad enough to be an ugly girl and only a servant?" (151). The larger political issues raised by her situation are underlined by Limpin' Lucy when she tries to deliver Rosanna's letter to Blake. "Where's this gentleman that I mustn't speak of, except with respect?...The day is not far off when the poor will rise against the rich. I pray Heaven they may begin with *him*" (227).

The Moonstone stands firmly within the English tradition of domestic realism, a tradition whose primary cultural work, as Nancy Armstrong has demonstrated, has always centered on the creation of gendered and class-determined domestic subjects.[13] Indeed, Collins is at times criticized by historians of detective fiction for "succumbing" to the conventions of the domestic novel and thus perverting an otherwise excellent mystery. Yet as D. A. Miller points out, if *The Moonstone* does not adhere to the detective formula, that is simply because Collins does not wish it to. Though it "invokes the norms of detective fiction," this novel quickly "moves from a story of police action to a story of human relationships in less 'specialized' contexts. The move seems a shift in genre as well: from the detective novel to what can only be called the Novel *tout court*."[14] Though one may dissent from Miller's reading of *The Moonstone*'s disciplinary functions, he is surely correct to say that Collins's work moves within the mainstream of Victorian realism. Begun just after the passing of the second Reform Bill (1867), this is a novel whose attention first and last is directed inward. Its concerns are domestic: both in the sense that it works to forge a secure and stable family unit, and in the sense that the true horizon of its vision coincides with the nation's borders. Its anxieties are domestic, too, consisting primarily of panic at the idea of excessive (usually feminine) desire and fascinated horror at the prospect of class conflict. The empire plays only a peripheral part in all this, since the novel's emotional cathexes are all elsewhere.

In fact, one can argue that the empire *must* be peripheral to all this. Martin Green has noted how, from the eighteenth century forward, the novel of domestic realism has been "employed to carry...key values of the ruling mercantile class," values which existed in usually unacknowledged tension with "the crudest expansive thrusts of the modern system – including imperialism and adventure." If a prejudice against the adventure story was coterminous with the rise of the novel in Britain, and if the domestic novel of courtship "preempted the prestige of literary seriousness" in England, this was largely because the militarist-aristocratic values implicit in the adventure genre could not be assimilated into bourgeois ideology.[15] The empire may have depended on the John Herncastles of the world for its efficient running, but such men could not be admitted into most Victorian novels except under the sign of moral disgrace.

Late-Victorian romancers, in rejecting the "effeminacy" of modern bourgeois life, tried to rehabilitate such figures and make them heroic once more. The hyper-masculinist, ultra-jingoist heroes of G. A. Henty's novels, for example, are direct descendants of Herncastle, but with the moral valences reversed. Yet in so far as romance writers were themselves products of the middle class, their championing of imperialist ideologies leaves gaps through which critique may enter. Doyle's early Sherlock Holmes stories reveal this tension clearly. These tales introduce figures from the colonies – beginning with Dr. Watson himself – with surprising frequency, but in such a manner as to make the empire a problem in a way it is not for Collins. Publicly the most vocal of imperialists – Jon Thompson justly calls him "one of the great Victorian apologists of empire" – Doyle in his fiction cannot prevent even his staunchest defenses from being hounded by doubt.[16] Where John Herncastle's actions betray only his own moral turpitude, Jonathan Small's serve inadvertently to illuminate the criminality of empire itself. At the same time, taken as a group the Holmes stories of the late 1880s and early '90s constitute an extended if usually clandestine indictment of the domestic ideology purveyed by Victorian realism. Here again a productive ambivalence can be felt. Though Doyle explicitly portrays the detective as the great guardian of bourgeois practices and beliefs, the stories themselves are more likely to show their bankruptcy. It is precisely such ambivalence that marks the male romance as a genre.

THE CESSPOOL OF EMPIRE

The Holmes canon begins under the shadow of empire. As all readers recall, the first tale, *A Study in Scarlet* (1887), opens with Watson's description of his experiences as an army surgeon in Afghanistan. They have not been good ones. Though colonial service "brought honours and promotion to many," to Watson it offered "nothing but misfortune and disaster."[17]

Wounded in battle, struck by enteric fever, "worn with pain," "weak and emaciated," his "health irretrievably ruined" (*SS* 9, 10), the good doctor lasts but a short while in the colonies before being sent home.

Yet Watson's ravaged body is only part of his problem. He has also been psychically maimed by his experience, and in this he is not alone. Once discharged, the ex-serviceman "naturally gravitated to London, that great cesspool into which all the loungers and idlers of the Empire are irresistibly drained. There I stayed for some time...leading a comfortless, meaningless existence, and spending such money as I had, considerably more freely than I ought" (*SS* 10). Drifting, unemployed, improvident, feckless – this is not the Watson we remember. More troubling still is Doyle's suggestion that Watson's experience has become typical. He is but one of many "loungers and idlers" who straggle back from the colonies to disappear into London's cesspool. The class is portrayed as incipiently criminal. Watson himself, it can be argued, is saved from a fatal dissolution only by being brought under the watchful eye of the metropolis's great detective.

What we can call the "maimed colonial" is in fact a recurring figure in the Holmes stories.[18] Returned from the outposts of empire, these men become the locus of crime and corruption. Unlike John Herncastle, wicked by nature, Doyle's colonials have been corrupted by their experiences. Moreover, the crimes they commit – and here Jonathan Small's theft of the Agra treasure in *The Sign of Four* provides the best example – constitute implicit indictments of imperial practices. "We only ask you to do that which your countrymen come to this land for," Abdullah Khan urges Small. "We ask you to be rich."[19]

In private life Doyle passionately defended Britain's imperial prerogatives, yet the Holmes stories are notable for their ambivalence concerning matters of empire.[20] Openly jingoistic, Doyle in his fiction nonetheless cannot prevent even his overt defenses of empire from sounding like critiques. Jonathan Small is a veteran of 1857, and his account of the "torture and murder and outrage" perpetrated by "mutinous black devils" (*SF* 116, 115) upon innocent English bodies fits squarely within the xenophobic tradition of late-Victorian narratives of the Mutiny. At the height of the conflict Small watches "black fiends" (*SF* 116) burn the home of his employer, a plantation owner named Abel White. The message seems clear: Indians benefit from the rule of benevolent and "able whites," which they repay with treachery. Yet for readers who recall Collins's novel – and by this point in Doyle's tale the similarities to *The Moonstone* have long been apparent – the name Ablewhite has other resonances, namely those associated with

Godfrey's deceit and misconduct. Collins's villain becomes Doyle's victim, but the former's moral taint still faintly lingers.

This odd echo is telling, yet we need not rely solely on it to establish the novel's conflicted response to the ethics of empire. For one thing, the theft of the Agra treasure is a considerably more complicated and morally ambiguous affair than Herncastle's crime. Whereas the moonstone derives much of its value from its status within a system of religious beliefs, the Agra treasure is never more than loot. However far back its history is traced, the treasure has always comprised the spoils of the unscrupulous. Thus, where the moonstone's rightful owners are never in doubt, the Agra treasure's are always doubtful. Watson insists the treasure belongs to Mary Morstan, but her claim is if anything shakier than most. Small, Captain Morstan, Sholto, his sons Thaddeus and Bartholomew, Singh, Khan, Akbar, Achmet, not to mention the governments in Britain and India and the anonymous rajah can all claim similar rights.

In the absence of clear ownership, identifying a criminal also proves difficult. Guilt in *The Moonstone* is rigorously localized in the persons of Herncastle and Ablewhite, but in *The Sign of Four* it is anxiously dispersed until nearly everyone is enveloped. As Small's experience underscores, the problems of empire prove to be endemic to the system and not the result of the immoral acts of individuals. In Doyle's empire, everyone is a thief and no one can easily be blamed. The novel in fact fails to accomplish one of detective fiction's prime functions: affixing ultimate guilt. Tonga is demonized and shot, and Small is incarcerated, but these men are, it is clear, thoroughly victimized as well. "Justice may originally [have] been on your side," Holmes admits to his prisoner (*SF* 113), to which we can only add that justice comes to seem an inadequate measure by which to evaluate the events of the story.

Such indeterminacy can make for discomfort, and so we find Doyle working to contain his tale of imperial crime within more manageable frameworks. The weakly imagined courtship of John Watson and Mary Morstan is one sign of this attempted containment. Yet the force of the novel remains centrifugal: whereas *The Moonstone* quickly moves us from the fringes of empire into "the secret theatre of home," *The Sign of Four* continually turns our attention outward.[21] Doyle reverses the movement from public to private that characterizes Collins's narrative. In each of the first two Holmes tales, what originally look like domestic mysteries eventually expand to encompass the labyrinthine workings of large political systems. Mary Morstan first approaches Sherlock Holmes with a set of puzzles involving her father's disappearance, a newspaper advertisement, six pearls, and an anonymous letter – puzzles which affect her personally but hint at nothing beyond her family sphere. When, however, these domestic mysteries are rapidly solved, they leave in their place a second set of problems which turn out to have little to do with Mary or her situation but instead force attention on to problems of empire. By the time Small offers the "strange story" (*SF* 111) which closes the novel, *The Sign of Four* has moved away entirely from the Morstans' domestic troubles and squarely on to the imperial intrigue. Significantly, neither Mary nor her father plays more than a minor role in Small's tale.

A Study in Scarlet enacts this same troubled movement between private and public spheres. Holmes solves the mystery of Enoch Drebber's murder only after he decides whether it was a domestic or a political crime. "Was it politics, then, or was it a woman? That was the question which confronted me" (*SS* 132). When Lestrade discovers the word "RACHE" written on the wall beside Drebber's body, he immediately pronounces the crime a domestic one. "You mark my words, when this case comes to be cleared up you will find that a woman named Rachel has something to do with it" (*SS* 35). (I leave aside the question of whether Doyle is once again recalling Collins's novel and Miss Verinder.) Holmes quickly explodes the inspector's theory with the news that "Rache" is German for "revenge," implying that the murder was politically motivated. Yet though Holmes dismisses Rachel from the case, he comes to share Lestrade's conviction that "a woman" is behind all the troubles. Calling the scrawled inscription "too evidently a blind," he concludes that "it must have been a private wrong, and not a political one, which called for such a methodical revenge" (*SS* 132–33). In doing so he dismisses as claptrap newspaper reports situating the murder in the context of "sinister…political refugees and revolutionaries." "The *Daily News* observed that there was no doubt as to the crime being a political one" (*SS* 52–53).

Yet, though Holmes never acknowledges the fact, the papers are correct. Behind Jefferson Hope's vendetta stand the crimes committed by the Mormon community against Lucy and John Ferrier. In this novel Doyle draws extensively on popular conceptions of the Mormons which aligned them with secret political societies on the Continent.[22] "Not the inquisition of Seville, nor the German Vehmgericht, nor the Secret Societies of Italy" (*SS* 92) are more dangerous than the Mormons' Danite Band, we are told. As more information concerning Drebber's murder comes to light, we find that it is enmeshed in a web of political sins and crimes. As in *The Sign of Four*, the trail of detection leads ultimately to the indictment not of a guilty individual – like Small, Jefferson Hope considers himself "an officer of justice" (*SS* 128) – but of an entire community.[23] Both Small and Hope are presented as dark avengers, victims of injustice who end by capturing the imaginations and sympathies of their persecutors. In each case the arrest of a single individual turns out to be oddly irrelevant to the larger pattern of criminality revealed in the narrative.

STRANGE EVENTS AND EXTRAORDINARY COMBINATIONS

As a genre, the detective story is wholly unsuited to addressing systemic problems in any sustained way. At best, it only translates them into problems of *individual* deviance and transgression. As students of the genre often note, detective fiction offers precisely this comfort: it gives guilt an individual's name.[24] *A Study in Scarlet* and *The Sign of Four* struggle to effect this translation, to transform the sins of a community into the crimes of a person. One can argue that Doyle moves the action of these novels to the heart of London precisely in order to make criminal deviance visible by placing it against a backdrop of "normal" English life. (It helps to have a villain like the astonishingly repulsive Tonga who fits so perfectly the paradigm of the criminal atavist.) In both novels England is the scene but not – at least not directly – the source of crime.

Yet the tension between individual guilt and systemic wrong is felt even in the tales that focus solely on English life. Like *Jekyll and Hyde*, the collections of Holmes short stories that immediately follow the two novels – *The Adventures of Sherlock Holmes* (1891) and *The Memoirs of Sherlock Holmes* (1893) – are best described as anatomies of the pathology of bourgeois life. It is a pathology, moreover, that the detective proves surprisingly powerless to address.

At the beginning of his first case Holmes articulates what is ostensibly his guiding metaphor as a detective. He tells Watson that a "scarlet thread" of crime runs through "the colourless skein of life, and our duty is to unravel it, and isolate it, and expose every inch of it" (*SS* 44). In the context of normative, "colorless" behavior, Holmes suggests, crime necessarily stands out. Conversely, in best Foucauldian fashion the identification – or, as Foucault argues, the production – of deviance is instrumental in the construction of "normal" bourgeois identities. In this view the detective functions as the very embodiment of society's power of surveillance and discipline.[25] Through his agency threats to normality are localized and named; criminals are apprehended; deviance is (for the moment) halted and harmony (for the moment) restored. In addition, the genre offers psychological comfort by showing the world to be thoroughly accessible to reason and thus thoroughly knowable. As Catherine Belsey notes, detective fiction works "to dispel magic and mystery, to make everything explicit, accountable, subject to scientific analysis."[26]

Yet the first Holmes tales signally fail to accomplish these, their seemingly defining tasks. In practice, the skein of life is hardly colorless, while pulling at one thread, scarlet or no, inevitably unravels the whole. Whatever he may *say*, Holmes *acts* on the assumption that crime is not separate from everyday life, not an isolated thread in life's fabric. Rather, the criminal *is* the quotidian. "Depend upon it," Holmes says, "there is nothing so unnatural as the commonplace."[27] In a similar vein the detective admits that "where there is room for doubt that any positive crime has been committed" great wrongs most often occur ("The Red-Headed League," *A* 52). The early Holmes stories in fact portray a world in which "strange effects and extraordinary combinations" are generated out of the "normal" arrangements of bourgeois life: a world in which weddings make brides disappear, ladies' suitors are their fathers, successful businessmen maximize their profits by becoming beggars, job offers become occasions for humiliation, and even Christmas geese turn witness for the prosecution.[28] And in which detectives and their friends routinely perform criminal acts. "You don't mind breaking the law?" Holmes asks his accomplice. "Not in the least," Watson replies ("A Scandal in Bohemia," *A* 23). Far from being the celebrations of middle-class mores they are often taken for, the Holmes stories comprise a series of startling indictments of "everyday life." In them criminality is seldom portrayed as deviance. Instead it is shown to be systemic, a byproduct of the way we live now.

If the pathology of everyday life is the obverse of these stories, their reverse reveals Holmes's own well-known array of "deviant" characterological traits. Ever charitable, Watson may prefer to think of them as harmless eccentricities, but as Lawrence Rothfield points out, Doyle's tales invoke "a panoply of what in the 1880s were quite recently invented categories of deviant individuality to try to identify Holmes."[29] The detective's frequent surrenders to ennui, his boasted misanthropy and abhorrence of society, his passion for aesthetic stimulation through music or language (Holmes plays the violin, drags Watson to hear Sarasate in recital, carries a pocket Petrarch, and quotes Hafiz and Flaubert from memory), and his notorious addiction to cocaine all situate him within the familiar bounds of late-Victorian decadence. We may plausibly read these eccentricities, then, as so many rejections on Holmes's part of bourgeois norms. The detective's affinities to Oscar Wilde have often been noted; we recall too that Doyle was among the few to defend Wilde after his imprisonment.[30]

Yet as we have seen, in the Holmes tales the line between deviance and norm is surprisingly permeable. To think of Holmes simply as a cross between Dorian Gray and Jacques Collin is finally to miss how his "deviant" behavior merges with a social background in which, as the detective himself recognizes, nothing is more commonplace than the unnatural.

Given such circumstances, it should not surprise us – though somehow the fact *is* surprising – that Doyle's master detective accomplishes very little in the way of righting wrongs.[31] Despite the great confidence he inspires, throughout these early tales Holmes seldom gets his man. Odd though it sounds, of the first dozen Holmes short stories Doyle wrote, only one ("The Red-Headed League") ends the way detective stories are "supposed" to end: with the arrest of the criminal. In some instances, Holmes uncovers villainies that are not technically crimes ("The Man with the Twisted Lip") or that fall outside the jurisdiction of the British legal system ("The Five Orange Pips" and "The Noble Bachelor"), and so he cannot act. In the majority of cases, though, Holmes solves the mystery but fails to apprehend any "criminal." He thus allows blackmailers to escape ("A Scandal in Bohemia"), murderers to go unpunished ("The Boscombe Valley Mystery"), tyrannous fathers to prolong their tyranny, ("A Case of Identity" and "The Speckled Band"), thieves to flee ("The Beryl Coronet" and "The Blue Carbuncle"), and foreign revolutionaries to vanish into the night ("The Engineer's Thumb"). To be sure, there are extenuating circumstances in each case, yet their cumulative effect is to make us ask: what possible pleasure can be found in such tales?

MALE ROMANCE AND THE EROTICS OF INTERPRETATION

For pleasure is just what detective fiction promises. And, to judge from Holmes's now century-old celebrity, pleasure is just what many readers find. Yet if Doyle's detective signally fails to make much difference in the world he inhabits, and if detective fiction as a genre seems peculiarly unsuited to address the large systemic problems Doyle's tales continually gesture toward, why do readers like them? By situating the Holmes stories in the context of late-Victorian male romance, we can begin to give more specificity to the pleasures they offer. Those pleasures in turn help further illuminate the anxieties entwined with them.

"Pleasure" is the appropriate word to use in this context, for the Holmes tales are charged with various kinds of erotic energy. To point out the homosocial elements of the Holmes–Watson relationship, for instance, is not to be perverse but simply to do justice to the intensity of the ties uniting these two men. Eve Sedgwick has argued that such bonds are integral to the functioning of modern patriarchal societies in the West, even as the eroticism inherent in this bonding is disavowed.[32] In the male romance such disavowal is, as it were, foregrounded. No other genre is at once so invested in relations between men and so conspicuously – one is tempted to say, so self-consciously – naive about them. *The Adventures of Sherlock Holmes*, for example, opens with the newly married Watson passing wistfully by his old bachelor quarters in Baker Street, a site which, he tells us, "must always be associated in my mind with my wooing." Though he is presumably referring to his wife, Watson does not name the object of his affection, and his train of thought ends when he is "seized with a keen desire to see Holmes" ("A Scandal in Bohemia," *A* 10).

Such libidinal investments can coexist with, even reinforce, ideological commitments to more traditional erotic configurations. Male homosocial desire is usually mediated through women, while the institutional articulations of that desire – schools, clubs, the military, the professions – undergird rather than undermine familiar patriarchal structures, including the family. In "A Scandal in Bohemia," for instance, which opens with Watson sighing over his lost bachelor life, homosocial desire is routed through the person of "*the* woman" (*A* 9), as Holmes insists on calling Irene Adler, whose considerable attractions lead to a brief rivalry between the two men.[33] Appropriately, the "scandal" Adler provokes arises from her decision to marry "an English lawyer named Norton" (*A* 30) rather than pursue the King of Bohemia. As Holmes's ironic dismissal of the King indicates ("the lady…seems, indeed, to be on a very different level to your Majesty" [*A* 31]), this is no scandal at all but a strong endorsement of middle-class family life. Such endorsements are rare, however. Irene Adler notwithstanding, Doyle offers few positive examples of bourgeois family life. Irene herself must flee England "never to return" (*A* 30) before she can set up house with Mr. Norton unharassed by paranoid royalty or duplicitous private investigators.

Doyle's tales nevertheless do present us with one sanctified domestic space, namely those famous bachelor quarters at 221–B. Over the long course of the Holmes oeuvre the Baker Street rooms come to take on a life of their own, and they of course continue to be fetishized by the detective's many devotees. We can say that Doyle does not so much reject bourgeois notions of domesticity as reimagine them along homosocial lines. Stevenson's bachelors may sit lonely by their hearths, but Holmes and Watson quickly assume the air of an old married couple. Unsurprisingly,

Holmes responds sourly to the news of Watson's betrothal at the close of *The Sign of Four.* "I really cannot congratulate you," he says with "a most dismal groan" (*SF* 137). As the doctor's notoriously cavalier later treatment of Mary makes clear, he need not have worried. If the detective finds that "having [Watson] with me...makes a considerable difference" ("The Boscombe Valley Mystery," *A* 75), the doctor discovers that he feels "no keener pleasure than in following Holmes" ("The Speckled Band," *A* 166). Together they make 221–B Baker Street a version of that "safe and secret place" which Haggard called the romance's special domain.

Haggard's phrase refers not to the exotic locales that form the male romance's typical settings but rather to the romance form itself, to those textual spaces in which male readers are encouraged to indulge their nominally subversive fantasies. The London "criminal underworld" of the Holmes tales is a fantasy realm of exotica, titillation, and adventure similar to those offered by Haggard or Kipling, while Holmes and Watson are domestic versions of the romance form's stereotypical man of action. Yet it is also the case that the Baker Street rooms symbolically function for Holmes and Watson in exactly the way that the romance form functioned for Doyle's male readers. Like those readers, Holmes and Watson can if they wish remain in their comfortable quarters and still be endlessly stimulated and entertained. "I beg that you will draw your chair up to the fire, and favour me with some details" of your story, the detective tells one client ("The Five Orange Pips," *A* 102). A large portion of nearly every case involves just that – telling tales around the hearth. "You have come to tell me your story, have you not?" ("The Beryl Coronet," *A* 236). Holmes's typical posture during these recitations – buried in an easy chair, pipe lit, feet up, gaze abstracted – likewise suggests that of Doyle's ideal reader. One need not light out for the territories in fact, just surrender to the vicarious pleasures such narratives afford. If nothing substantial comes of such enjoyment – if thieves escape or single women remain terrorized – we can at least savor the satisfactions of close reading. "I am all attention," Holmes says ("The Speckled Band," *A* 168).

Here we touch on a further source of readerly pleasure. If one source is located in Doyle's manipulations of the erotics of homosocial bonding, another is found in what we called in Chapter 3 the erotics of reading: of being "all attention." In the Holmes stories social problems are "solved" only after they have been transformed into problems of hermeneutics (meaning, as we have seen, that as social problems they are not solved at all). Holmes himself repeatedly insists that the interest of his cases rests solely in their status as hermeneutic puzzles to be decoded through acts of detection. Of course, Holmes does not link detection to erotics but rather to the negation of erotics, or logic. On numerous occasions the detective chastises Watson for his "romanticism": "Logic is rare," he admonishes.

> Therefore it is upon the logic rather than upon the crime that you should dwell. You have degraded what should have been a course of lectures into a series of tales...You have erred...in attempting to put colour and life into each of your statements, instead of confining yourself to the task of placing upon record that severe reasoning from cause to effect which is really the only notable feature about the thing. ("The Copper Beeches," *A* 260–61)

Watson may protest weakly that "the romance was there" (*SF* 9), but the reception history of Doyle's tales suggests that most readers have been inclined to follow Holmes's directive. If, as Jameson suggests, the detective story represents itself as a "form without ideological content," that representation has also governed the critical response to the genre. By and large, readers of Holmes conspicuously ignore the "romantic" aspects of Watson's stories in order scrupulously to measure the "severe reasoning" of detection against various scientific or philosophical standards – logical positivism (Bertrand Russell), Peircian abduction (Thomas Sebeok), Freudian psychoanalysis (Carlo Ginzburg), and games theory (Jaakko Hintikka), to name only a few, in the process abstracting the tales from their historical contexts.[34]

Yet the very intensity of such interest suggests that detection generates its own libidinal gratifications. Holmes may present detection as coldly impersonal and himself as a "perfect reasoning and observing machine" ("A Scandal in Bohemia," *A* 9), but most readers can attest to the *frisson* that invariably accompanies the exercise of Holmes's interpretive skills. For the detective himself such pleasures can verge on the sadistic. Rothfield has shown how detection as practiced by Holmes is inseparable from the infliction of pain: clients and suspects alike are routinely humiliated, exposed, betrayed, or rendered helpless and bewildered as they come under the detective's pitiless scrutiny.[35] It is the very nature of Holmes's power to be able to lay bare what one might prefer to keep private. Nor do such secrets need to be "criminal" to attract Holmes's attention, as his frequent embarrassment of Watson makes clear. Victims of the detective's attention "start," "exclaim," "jump up," "swear," "stare," or like Watson stomp around the room "with considerable bitterness in [their] heart[s]" (*SF* 14) after Holmes's revelations, which are invariably violations as well. That the detective derives pleasure from these responses is apparent from his delighted laughter at provoking the perfectly harmless Mary Sutherland to give "a violent start, and [look] up with fear and astonishment upon her broad, good-humoured face" ("A Case of Identity," *A* 36) after being subjected to a particularly thorough act of Holmesian detection. If such moments yield Holmes a bonus of unalloyed pleasure, they are apt to produce more conflicted responses for readers. Like Watson, we are continually bewildered by these displays of hermeneutic prowess, and so earn our share of the general humiliation Holmes inflicts. But in so far as we are encouraged to identify with the detective, we participate in his power and bask in its effects. Either way, whether viewed from the perspective of Holmesian sadism or Watsonian masochism, detection is hardly an abstract or merely "logical" procedure. Instead it is thoroughly cathected with libidinal energy.

If what I am terming the erotics of interpretation forms the basis of much of the pleasure offered by the Holmes stories, we can also recognize that this erotics is itself historically determined. It is one example of the "perpetual spirals of power and pleasure" that Foucault has associated with the disciplinary technologies of the modern era. "The medical examination, the psychiatric investigation, the pedagogical report" – and to this list we can add the detective's examination – all "function as mechanisms" for producing "the pleasure that comes of exercising a power that questions, monitors, watches, spies, searches out, palpates, brings to light."[36] Mindful of the dangers of reduction, we can yet draw reasonably firm lines of historical connection among these bourgeois professionals – pathologists, psychiatrists, social workers, educators, and detectives – and the similar kinds of pleasure their activities produce. These are peculiarly modern pleasures: arising not from movements of the body but from exercises of the intellect, they are pleasures associated with the practice of professional interpretation in its different guises.

Such hermeneutic acts are of course never disinterested, but instead serve the more or less practical ends of social control. Yet as Foucault reminds us, a strictly functionalist view cannot account for the surplus of enjoyment generated by the various institutional mechanisms he examines. It is worth emphasizing his point that the pleasure inheres in the exercise of power, not in the fulfillment of its goals. It finally matters little, in other words, whether Holmes accomplishes anything of social value so long as he produces the distinctive *frisson* that accompanies each act of successful detection. Lost in delight at Holmes's ability to tell at a glance that Mary Sutherland is a shortsighted typist who left home in a hurry, we the more readily overlook his utter failure to prevent her continued victimization at the hands of James Windibank ("A Case of Identity," *A* 35–36, 50).

Windibank's scam may continue unhindered, but at least we know now how it works. In like manner Holmes repeatedly offers such hermeneutic pleasures as compensation for his more substantial failures. The seduction of these tales continues to be tied up with their celebrations of the value of being "all attention."

CHAPTER 7

A universal foreignness: Kipling, race, and the great tradition

How, asked T. S. Eliot as long ago as 1941, are we to read Kipling? The difficulty arises in large part from the relation between tradition and this particular, to Eliot's mind this peculiar, individual talent. "I confess," Eliot writes, "that the critical tools which we are accustomed to use...do not seem to work" in Kipling's case. Despite his importance to late-Victorian culture, Kipling strikes Eliot as "the most inscrutable of authors," a "unique" figure without literary ancestors or heirs. He is distinguished by what Eliot thinks of as a "universal foreignness," as well as by a "peculiar detachment and remoteness" from his audience, his material, and his milieu. All of which makes him a writer "impossible wholly to understand."[1]

Eliot's is not the Kipling we are likely to be familiar with. It is certainly not the Kipling of contemporary criticism, which invariably places this author at the untroubled center of an era whose most interesting activities occurred almost exclusively on the margins. Studies of the period, including the present one, have always stressed the transgressive quality of fin-de-siècle writing, its calculated and often spectacular deviances. Deviances require norms, however, and Kipling traditionally has been invoked as their most visible embodiment. He is taken as "a spokesman for the age," a "profoundly representative consciousness" who gave "expression to a whole range of national experience."[2] He is made to stand for that gallery of crumbling certainties – aesthetic, moral, political, sexual – which others triumphantly rejected or else despairingly renounced.

This familiar image of Kipling as popular apologist for the dominant ideology has obscured our view of the turbulence which his initial appearance on the literary scene provoked. The response in England to Kipling's early work in fact betrayed a deep ambivalence. Kipling reciprocated the feeling, never quite losing the sense that Great Britain, as he wrote to Rider Haggard in 1902, was merely "the most wonderful foreign land I have ever been in."[3] For the India-born author, it never felt entirely like home.

Recovering the terms of this mutual ambivalence can help us to relocate Kipling in the field of our critical perception – to dislodge him from the stagnant center. Doing so also allows us to see him more clearly in relation to the issues we have been discussing, issues involving cultural and racial decay, imperial guilt, and the decline of the "great tradition" of English letters. In many ways Eliot's response repeats that of Kipling's contemporaries, who like Eliot tried without much success to fit the young writer into established categories of literary production. The notion that Kipling could at any time have been considered eccentric from late Victorian culture is likely to strike us as counterintuitive. In fact, though, the initial responses to Kipling were every bit as fraught, as contradictory, as revelatory, as the more celebrated "trials" of many of his contemporaries.

THE NEW DICKENS

Some facts to recall. Kipling arrived in London in October 1889, aged 24, with seven years as a journalist in India behind him. His short fiction and verse, first published in colonial newspapers and then collected in inexpensive "railway editions," had won him a moderate success within a rather restricted circle of Anglo-Indian readers. His reputation in England was slight at best. By mid-1890, however, he was being hailed as "a new star out of the East," the rejuvenator of English fiction, the slayer, in Henry James's ironic phrasing, of spurious "immortals" among the London literati.[4]

> I spent an afternoon reading *Soldiers Three* [wrote Sidney Low, the editor of the *St. James's Gazette*] and when I went out to a dinner-party that evening I could talk of nothing but this marvelous youth...My host, a well-known journalist and critic of those days, laughed at my enthusiasm which he said would hardly be justified by the appearance of another Dickens. "It may be," I answered hotly, "that a greater than Dickens is here."[5]

The Kipling Boom, as it was called, was nearly unprecedented in English letters. The sheer volume of Kipling's production during this period is staggering: in 1890 alone he published or republished 78 stories, 86 poems, 12 essays and periodical pieces, and a novel – 177 items in twelve months.[6] "I was plentifully assured," Kipling wrote in his autobiography, "*vive voce* and in the press cuttings...that 'nothing since Dickens' compared with my 'meteoric rise to fame'."[7]

As both Kipling and Low indicate, comparisons with Dickens were frequent during the first months of 1890. We may be unlikely without prompting to couple the two writers, but for Kipling's contemporaries Dickens's name became a kind of critical shorthand. By invoking the great novelist, reviewers conveyed at a stroke their many-faceted sense of Kipling as a literary savior, as one who could cure the accumulated ills of a moribund English art. For these reviewers, the ties linking Kipling to Dickens were striking and various. (Even the fact that Kipling was 24 in 1890, the age at which Dickens began serializing *Pickwick*, was taken as a sign.) The two writers were made to perform similar cultural functions: each was considered to stand for what was best in the English character. Kipling's fiction, like Dickens's, struck his admirers as "English" in ways that the works of other contemporary writers, with their French or American or Russian biases, somehow did not. His books, they suggested, recaptured qualities – vigor, humor, a confident and clear-sighted practicality – that had seemed missing from fiction for a generation. "Mr. Kipling was English to the core," wrote the critic Cyril Falls, "and we were surfeited with un-English art."[8]

Among Kipling's early and most ardent champions was Andrew Lang, who found in his fiction the kind of visceral impact he associated with primitive art and with the "pure romance of adventure." What Lang and other reviewers responded to in Kipling had little to do with the thematics of his fiction, just as comparisons with Dickens were seldom at the level of content. Kipling's interest lay less in his unusual subject matter than in the forms of his stories, their peculiar rhythms, their characteristic effects and modes of perception, their "style." At this level, a level considered more in touch with fundamental energies, Kipling's difference from his contemporaries seemed most evident. His stories, said an anonymous reviewer for the *Bookman*, evinced a "savage energy"; his narrative style expressed a "native force and beauty" that was like "a caged wild beast asleep."[9] "He is vehement, and sweeps us away with him," wrote the normally phlegmatic Edmund Gosse. "It is the strength of this new story-teller that he re-awakens in us the primitive emotions of curiosity, mystery, and romance in action."[10]

From Dickens to caged beasts is a long step, and it suggests the range of cultural anxieties and desires that Kipling's arrival mobilized. With the last of the Victorian giants gone, in an artistic milieu now "surfeited" with "unEnglish" productions, Kipling seemed a survival from a more assured era. In him, many readers imagined, English fiction returned to itself after a long arid spell, recovered its true nature. Critics situated Kipling in an English literary genealogy whose most prominent member was Dickens, and his fiction was taken as evidence that the line had not, as was feared, died out. In this same period, Dickens's own reputation was being revised to make him more resolutely and comfortably "English." Important revaluations by George Gissing and G. K. Chesterton had this much in common: both writers placed Dickens's early novels firmly at the center of their studies, and marginalized the later, darker works. While acknowledging the moral complexity of the post-*Dombey* Dickens, Chesterton professed "real doubt…that it made his books better." Gissing found *The Old Curiosity Shop* "one of the most delightful [stories] in the language" and *Martin Chuzzlewit* "in some respects the greatest of his works." *Little Dorrit* by contrast shows that "the hand of the master is plainly weary," while *Our Mutual Friend* is full of "tedious superfluidity." Critics worked hard to remake Dickens into the type of the genial, pragmatic, self-assured Englishman. By the 1890s he had become, in Gissing's words, "an expression of [our] national life and sentiment." Said Chesterton: "Dickens was really doing something…that no one but an Englishman could do."[11]

At this moment of crisis in Great Britain, then, Dickens was being remodeled into a figure of English solidity, with Kipling as his avatar. At the same time, however, Kipling's work was considered to embody deeply alien tendencies. He may have been the new Dickens, but he was so, paradoxically, because of his distance from the culture. Kipling was able to embody – his fiction was able to embody – traditional English qualities because he himself was alienated from England, where such embodiment was no longer possible. His work, argued reviewers, was on this level *sui generis*, despite its connections with either established or emerging literary traditions.

Thus, while his early stories have clear affinities with the male romance, there are good reasons for distinguishing Kipling from other practitioners of the form, if only because of differences in the way he was received and read by his contemporaries. To annex Kipling entirely to the kingdom of male romance is to miss significant cultural functions he was asked to perform. The fantasies his work provoked had to do not only with masculine and racial empowerment, but also with their ultimate impossibility, at least for Kipling's English readers. It is certainly the case that Kipling's India was read as an enchanted realm, isolated from the disabling constrictions of modernity. Yet this magic space was consistently represented as *inaccessible* to members of the domestic audience. Alan Sandison among others has remarked on the "astonishing capacity" of imperialism "for fulfilling fantasies" by making romance and adventure imaginatively available to a domestic audience, but a significant qualification obtains in Kipling's case.[12]

His texts explicitly rebuffed the English reader. Male romance fantasies were played out in his stories, but in such a way as to exclude the domestic reader from any but the remotest vicarious participation. Barriers were erected in the form of the untranslated phrase, the unglossed allusion, the in-joke, the unapologetic gesture toward structures of feeling and experience which had no counterpart outside the enclosed world of Anglo-India. Even the oft-reiterated catchphrase – "But that's another story" – worked to divide Kipling's audience into those who already knew and those who would never know such stories.

He wants to go *jildi* to the Padsahi *Jhil*...to shoot snipe – *chirria*. You dhrive *Jehannum ke marfik, mallum* – like Hell?...Av he *bolos* anything, just you *choop* and *chel. Dekker*? Go *arsty* for the first *arder* mile from cantonmints. Thin *chel, Shaitan ke marfik*, an' the *chooper* you *choops* an' the *jildier* you *chels* the better *kooshy* will that *Sahib* be; an' here's a rupee for ye! ("The Three Musketeers," *ST* 4)

A passage like this, not uncommon in Kipling's early stories, is on the one hand clearly trading on the low comedy of dialect fiction. On the other hand, Kipling conspicuously refuses, here as elsewhere, to decode his character's utterances. They remain at some level opaque to anyone not already in the know. A common strategy of Kipling's early fiction is to emphasize the vast gulfs separating the small, tightly knit coterie of Anglo-Indians from those who are, as he often says, "out of it."[13] Under pressure from English publishers, Kipling glossed obscure phrases for later editions of his texts, but a work as late as *Kim* (1901) still requires an extensive textual apparatus to be wholly intelligible to uninitiated readers. (By my count, the Penguin edition of the novel contains 545 endnotes for 289 pages of text.) If dialect fiction has traditionally worked to reinscribe the superiority of the reader's norms – norms of language, ethics, cultural literacy, and so on – in Kipling's case the positions are usually reversed. It is the domestic reader who is made to feel, as Andrew Lang did, "baffled" and ultimately inadequate in the face of "*jhairuns*, and *khitmatgars*, and the rest of it."[14] Unlike most male romance texts of the fin de siècle, Kipling's fictions tend not to represent the exotic as imaginatively available for the domestic reader. Instead, what his stories repeatedly show are the circumstances under which the exotic might become available, but only for a select coterie of Anglo-Indians.

ANGLO-INDIA AND GREATER BRITAIN

We can easily miss the complex resonances heard by Kipling's contemporaries in that label, "Anglo-Indian." To recover its meanings and suggest its relevance for the reception of Kipling's work, we need to move along two historical axes. The first takes in the myths of Oceana or Greater Britain in their myriad nineteenth-century articulations. The second leads us through various post-Darwinian pseudo-sciences of race. The two axes intersect at the concept of an Anglo-India that – like the Kipling of the early reviews – recovered a properly "English" racial heritage at the periphery of empire.

The idea of a "Greater Britain" o'erspreading the globe in Anglo-Saxon solidarity received its most influential formulation in Charles Dilke's 1868 book of that title. "In 1866 and 1867 I followed England round the world," is Dilke's exuberant opening sentence, and as he traces the migrations of English-speaking peoples throughout the hemispheres he is continually struck by "the grandeur of our race, already girdling the earth."[15] For Dilke, Greater Britain referred not to a political union of Anglo-Saxon nations but rather to the saturation of the globe with English culture, English commerce, English ideals. (In fact, like many at mid-century, Dilke argued that administering formal colonies was too expensive and ought to be abandoned.) In his view, the world would inevitably come to bear an Anglo-Saxon stamp. As emigrants continued to pour forth, more and more of the globe would become simply extensions of Great Britain. "English countries [are] now the mother-lands of energy and adventure throughout the world," and thus "our race seems marching westward to universal rule" (198).

Universal English hegemony was threatened by one factor, however. Could the English people, Dilke wondered, maintain their racial identity in new climates and conditions of existence? "Whether the Englishman can live out of England" was for him a highly pertinent question. "Can he thrive except where mist and damp preserve the juices of his frame?" (378). Dilke's answer was a qualified no. The movement of any race outside its native environment led to physical and moral degeneration. In India, in Australia, in America, the English have begun to succumb to "the common fate of all migrating races" (221): a slow decay. Nevertheless, Dilke argues, strong races continue to express a core identity that cannot be wholly corrupted. If "climate, soil, manners of life,... [and] mixture with other peoples had modified the blood" of expatriate Britons, yet "in essentials the race was always one" (ix).

In making these arguments, Dilke works in the mainstream of Victorian race theory.[16] Like most nineteenth-century thinkers he imagines race not as a biological but as a biocultural category. His paradigms nonetheless come from the natural sciences, though Dilke – and here again he is representative in his thinking – draws on two incompatible traditions. The first, associated with Cuvier and later with physical anthropology, considered races as immutable types. The second, associated largely with Darwinism, saw races as subject to the same forces of evolution that shaped all organic life.[17] The tension between these two paradigms is evident in Dilke's uneasy claim that the British "race" was altered by new environments yet remained "in essentials...always one."

The effects of climate on racial character was in fact one of the century's more hotly debated topics, in large part because it bore so directly on the question of imperial expansion. If, as many claimed, northern Europeans could not survive in the tropics, then the colonial enterprise would necessarily fail.[18] Carl Vogt's influential *Lectures on Man* (1864) listed the dire consequences of transplanting Europeans to equatorial regions: disease, dilerium, anemia, infertility, and high mortality rates. The "non-adaptation of constitution to conditions," in Herbert Spencer's well-known phrase, could result in debilitations both physical and moral. In the infamous "Terminal Essay" to his translation of the *Thousand and One Nights*, Richard Burton argued that the inclination toward paederasty to be found in the "Sotadic Zone" was the result of "geographical and climatic, not racial" conditions.[19] At the turn of the century, popular ethnologists like A.H. Keane, Alfred Haddon, and William Z. Ripley reiterated the cautions of Vogt and Burton. In his compendious work, *The Races of Europe* (1899), Ripley asserted that "true colonization in the tropics by the white race is impossible" since "Teutonic peoples are exceedingly unelastic in power of adaptation to tropical climates." Such inelasticity, he concluded, "appears to be rooted in race."[20] Dilke, for instance, was alarmed by what he considered the degradation of colonial officers in India, and he therefore urged that the administration of the empire be kept in London hands (519–25).

By the end of the century, however, opinion on the possibility of acclimatization had become decidedly mixed.[21] This was not because of advances in knowledge – despite all the activity, little new was learned about race in the first decades after Darwin – but because of a growing cultural investment in the colonies as an antidote to an enfeebled modernity. Ripley noted the "curious complication" that it was "precisely those people who need the colonies most, and who are bending all their political energies to that end," who were most unsuited racially for the task.[22] Those needs were economic, of course, but they were also increasingly psychological. Casting about in 1864 for an example of English complacency, Matthew Arnold had lighted on Sir Charles Adderley's confident assertion that "the old Anglo-Saxon race are the best breed in the whole world" precisely because of the suitability of British weather. "The absence of a too enervating climate, too unclouded skies...has rendered us superior to all the world."[23]In 1891 Edward Carpenter, diagnosing the "disease of civilization," came to just the opposite conclusion:

> That this climate...at its best may not be suited to the highest developments of human life is quite possible. Because Britain has been the scene of some of the greatest episodes of Civilization, it does not follow that she will keep the lead in the period that is to come; and the Higher Communities of the future will perhaps take their rise in warmer lands, where life is richer and fuller, more spontaneous and more generous, than it can be here.[24]

Carpenter enthused over the "superabundant health" of native races and argued that a "similar physical health and power of life are also developed among Europeans who have lived for long periods in more native conditions." By century's close Darwin's work was being invoked to support the claim that a change of locale might reinvigorate a species or race,[25] just as it had earlier been used, under the pressure of different cultural needs, to back the opposite conclusion.

During this same period the concept of Greater Britain was undergoing significant transformations. On the one hand, in works like J. R. Seeley's *The Expansion of England* (1883), the notion of a federation of English-speaking peoples begins to take on a distinctly militarist cast as British hegemony was threatened by other industrial nations. On the other hand, the colonies come to be invested with therapeutic value. Where Dilke saw the English race declining as it moved further from its island home, later writers contend that the outposts of empire offer the only sure tonic for a dying people. In his paean to British imperialism, *Oceana* (1886), J. A. Froude argues that the colonies provide an arena "where the race might for ages renew its mighty youth." At the periphery of empire, "the race is thriving with all its ancient characteristics." Given the conditions prevailing in England itself, writes Froude, "it is simply impossible that the English men and women of the future generations can equal or approach the famous race that has overspread the globe."[26] Twenty years later Lord Curzon likewise aligns himself with those who hold that "on the outskirts of Empire...is to be found an ennobling and invigorating stimulus for our youth, saving them alike from the corroding ease and the morbid excitements of Western civilization."[27]

The Anglo-Indian became the type of this new, reinvigorated Briton. "A window is opened on the future," wrote Lang of Kipling's stories, "and we have a glimpse of what our race may become when our descendants have lived long in alien lands, in changed conditions... There will be new and passionate types of character."[28] According to Lang, in Anglo-India the very processes of evolution were made visible. There, one could witness the British race, altered by environment and by extended contact with alien peoples, slowly being transformed into something radically different. Freed from what Carpenter called the "enfeeblement, obscuration, duplicity,...division, discord, possession by devils" of modernity, the Anglo-Indian managed to combine the intellectual maturity of the Westerner with a physical and emotional vigor no longer found in the aging West. He combined, in Lionel Johnson's phrase, "mind and muscle."[29]

In the popular imagination, the colonies were no longer the dumping ground for second sons, social outcasts, and the chronically underemployed. Part of the developing myth of Anglo-India was that the work of empire attracted the sturdiest of domestic stock, leaving only the dregs behind. The fitness of the Anglo-Indian to rule was an inheritance of "his forefathers," wrote John Strachey in 1888, "who have transmitted to him not only their physical courage, but the powers of independent judgement, the decision of character, the habits of thought," and other qualities needed for "the discharge of the various duties of civilised life."[30] Having emptied England of its best, Anglo-India could provide a space for the exercise and propagation of virtues which had been desiccated by modern life in the West. Anglo-India was what England had been.

Anglo-Indians themselves, as Lewis Wurgaft suggests, "came to regard themselves as the incarnation of austerity, courage, and self-control."[31] If such eminently Victorian virtues were conspicuous in the colonies, that was largely because of their perceived absence at home. According to K. Bhaskara Rao, "the Anglo-Indian was the image of the perfect Anglo-Saxon."[32] Kipling contributed heavily to this myth of the indefatigable colonial administrator on whose shoulders the empire rested. No theme appears more often in his early stories than the disastrous consequences of sending a modern Englishman to do an Anglo-Indian's job. The Pluffles, Pagetts, McGoggins, Garrons, and Faizannes of his fiction – all "queer exports" ("The Conversion of Aurelian McGoggin," *PT* 126) from home who bungle their chances abroad – underscore Kipling's conviction regarding the unfitness of the typical Briton to perform the work of empire.

Though writers like Lang and Carpenter (and occasionally Kipling himself) talk of the Anglo-Indian as a "hybrid" race, miscegenation is not the issue. Thanks to its elasticity, Victorian race theory allowed for the idea that racial identities could be altered solely by contact with alien cultural and physical environments. At this level, the fantasy of a healthy "mixing of bloods" could be entertained without awakening sexual taboos. Despite Hannah Arendt's claim that modern race theory originates in a concern for "purity," the British have always found the notion of symbolic hybridization congenial. Victorian anthropologists routinely argued that the British "race," an amalgam of Celtic, Norse, Teutonic, Norman, and Roman cultures, was the stronger for its disparate elements.[33] In an 1893 essay titled "The Ancestry of Genius," Havelock Ellis argued that great writers in Britain are almost invariably of "mixed blood," by which he means simply that their ancestry contains traces of both Nordic and Celtic elements.[34] By the close of the century, though, influxes of fresh blood were no longer forthcoming. "Where are the untried races," cried Arthur Balfour, "competent to construct out of the ruined fragments of our civilisation a new and better habitation for the spirit of man?"[35]

Into this cultural climate Kipling arrived with his stories of competent, strong-willed, occasionally violent, even savage Anglo-Indians. His fictions held out the promise of a new and better habitation abroad for the race's spirit, but they just as surely intensified existing anxieties about domestic decay. The Anglo-Indian pointed backward to a lost racial heritage and forward to an uncertain, to some unnerving, Darwinian future. Not surprisingly, Kipling himself was often described in terms that made his racial heritage problematic. Reminiscing about their early friendship, George Charles Beresford remarked on a certain donnishness in Kipling's bearing, an impression of "extreme seriousness and crabbed age." But the effect was offset by a physical appearance that, to Beresford's mind at least, could only be described via the vocabulary of contemporary anthropology.

> The modelling of his head was peculiar. His skull appeared of moderate size in relation to his rather large face; his forehead retreated sharply from a heavy browline – in fact, so sharp was the set-back from the massive eyebrow ridges that he appeared almost "cave-boy". His lower jaw was massive, protruding and strong; the chin had a deep central cleft that at once attracted attention. Owing to its width, his face appeared rather Mongolian.[36]

In descriptions such as this, the heir to Dickens is remade into a progenitor of Wells's Morlocks.

RACE AND NARRATIVE AUTHORITY

I have thus far been speaking as if Kipling's texts existed only as occasions for critics to vent their collective hopes and anxieties. To a large extent this was the case. Kipling's first readers projected onto his work a map of the culture's psychic landscape. Yet it is also the case that, in oblique ways, Kipling joined the discussion. Oblique, because such issues seldom push their way into the thematic texture of his stories. In Kipling's early fiction the narrative message is often slight enough and confidently delivered. Its "secrets," to use Frank Kermode's formulation, are less securely but no less insistently offered to our attention.[37] Taken as a whole, Kipling's India stories betray an obsession with writing, narrative authority, and the dissemination of texts; and with the ways in which these issues become enmeshed with questions of race and race degeneration.

At the beginning of "His Chance in Life," Kipling's narrator takes us, as he often does, "straight away from" the enclosed world of Anglo-India, landing us "far beyond everything and everybody you ever knew in your respectable life" at that psycho-geographical "Borderline where the last drop of White blood ends and the full tide of Black sets in" (*PT* 84). Such borders recur throughout Kipling's fictions, and much narrative energy is expended in their simultaneous maintenance and transgression. In this case, however, the narrator pauses to consider the possibility that he may not be qualified to enter imaginatively into the lives of "the Borderline folk": "One of these days, this people…will turn out a writer or a poet; and then we shall know how they live and what they feel. In the meantime, any stories about them cannot be absolutely correct in fact or inference" (*PT* 85).

On one level, this is a clear instance of Orientalist discourse such as Edward Said has taught us to see. "They" are incapable of speaking for themselves, so "we" must speak for them. What I want to point out, though, is the passage's overt claim, namely that racial identity and narrative authority are somehow entwined. The ability to write accurately about the Borderline folk, it is suggested, depends on being of them. Authority inheres in blood. We might then read Kipling's disclaimer as in part a defensive gesture, an attempt to ward off the notion that he himself could be the writer or poet he speaks of. That this possibility troubled Kipling is evident, I will argue, throughout his early volumes. While his narratives repeatedly violate racial borderlines to bring back reports from "across the river, which was the end of all the Earth" ("Wee Willie Winkie," *WWW* 295), they also betray deep-rooted misgivings about the implications of that move.

More precisely, the passage from "His Chance in Life" is less concerned with crossing borders than with being on the Border. Kipling's narrative personae often find themselves in such liminal areas, where blood is mixed and racial identity becomes fluid or problematic. Miscegenation occasionally occurs in Kipling's early fiction – "Beyond the Pale," "Without Benefit of Clergy," and "The Man Who Would be King" contain the best-known instances – but what I am concerned with here are the literary equivalents of such transgressions. In Kipling's fiction narrative authority is everywhere predicated on racial authority, but the strategies used to establish such authority are, more often than not, troubled and insecure. We can begin to define these strategies by looking at two characters – both of them, not coincidently, failed writers – who appear several times in Kipling's early fiction and who provide models for his narrative practice. One is the police officer Strickland, the other the drunken classics scholar McIntosh Jellaludin.

Strickland is Kipling's Anglo-Indian *par excellence*. He is also a potential writer and, we quickly suspect, a surrogate for Kipling himself. "One of these days, Strickland is going to write a little book on his experiences. That book will be worth buying" ("Miss Youghal's Sais," *PT* 36). Strickland's qualifications as the policeman he is and the writer he might be rest on "his outlandish custom of prying into native life" (*PT* 33). Strickland, we are told, thoroughly understands the native mind "from the inside" because he has penetrated where few Englishmen have gone:

> He held the extraordinary theory that a Policeman in India should try to know as much about the natives as the natives themselves...He was initiated into the *Sat Bhai* at Allahabad once, when he was on leave; he knew the Lizzard-Song of the Sansis, and the *Halli-Hukk* dance, which is a religious can-can of a startling kind... He had helped once, at Jagadhri, at the Painting of the Death Bull, which no Englishman must ever look upon; had mastered the thieves'-patter of the *changars*, had taken an Eusufzai horse-thief alone near Attock; and had stood under the sounding-board of a Border mosque and conducted service in the manner of a Sunni Mollah. (*PT* 31–32)

A close connection is established between Strickland's knowledge and the power he wields. By "perpetually 'going Fantee'" (*PT* 31) Strickland acquires information which would be inaccessible otherwise. Such information is figured as racial knowledge: "getting inside" the native mind means penetrating a surface individuality to uncover the racial essence beneath. Within the context of the stories, Strickland can impersonate natives because he recognizes that they think and act only within certain knowable boundaries. The information elicited is of course put to the practical and coercive ends of empire: greater law and order, a more efficient control. The policeman is, moreover, never allowed to be tainted by his forays into Indian life. Indeed, both his knowledge and his authority are validated by his detachment, his perfect objectivity. Despite his continual interaction with "natives," Strickland's racial identity is never troubled. He may impersonate a Sunni mollah or a Eusufzai horse-thief, but he is never in danger of becoming one. Strickland arranges and controls, classifies and evaluates, turning random information into useful knowledge.

Strickland also provides a model for a form of narrative authority, one Kipling often employs in his stories. Kipling implicitly links Strickland's techniques with his own. Both men transform chaotic experience to make it useable, consumable. As a journalist, Kipling quickly acquired a reputation for knowing more about the colonial underworld than the police did. "I would wander till dawn in all manner of odd places," he wrote in his autobiography, "liquor shops, gambling- and opium-dens...wayside entertainments such as puppet-shows, native dances; or in and about the narrow gullies under the Mosque of Wazir Khan for the sheer sake of looking."[38] Like Strickland, Kipling was celebrated among Anglo-Indians for, as his friend E. Kay Robinson put it, "his insight into the strangely mixed manners of life and thought of the natives of India." Robinson thought "most wonderful" Kipling's thorough understanding of Indian racial and cultural signs: "Show him a native, and he would tell you his rank, caste, race, origin, habitat, creed, and calling."[39] We discover in fact that Strickland models himself on an unnamed predecessor, a man who can "pass for Hindu or Mahommedan, hidedresser or priest, as he pleases" ("Miss Youghal's Sais," *PT* 31). While Strickland's mentor is never identified, we can without much strain speculate that Kipling had himself in mind. Kipling called an early volume *In Black and White*, a title which points both to the ability to move easily between two worlds and to the journalistic accuracy – he has got it down in black and white – of what is represented.

Like Strickland, Kipling confidently ventriloquizes native voices while remaining himself unaffected. His narrators roam freely, minutely recording what they see. They plunge into urban deserts ("'The City of Dreadful Night'"), venture into forbidden districts ("Dray Wara Yow Dee"), attend outlandish ceremonies ("In the House of Suddho"), help unravel criminal mysteries ("The Return of Imray"), and routinely penetrate dangerous liminal spaces ("Bubbling Well Road"). Yet they remain aloof, untouched by what they encounter, ostensibly there "for the sheer sake of looking." Kipling's always unnamed first-person narrators are shadowy presences, hovering around the edges of stories until the important moment comes to step forward and make sense of what has occurred. "Then there is Me, of course; but I am only the chorus that comes in at the end to explain things" ("In the House of Suddho," *PT* 160). Climbing to the top of a great mosque in "'The City of Dreadful Night'," one narrator "gazes intently" at the "spectacle of sleeping thousands" spread out beneath him and, unlike Christ in the Wilderness, does not hesitate to claim it for his imaginative kingdom (*BW* 40–41).

This kind of narrative practice has its clear advantages, not to mention a firm, readily apparent ideological backbone. Kipling establishes a continuity between the policeman and the writer, both of whom engage in dispassionate observation.[40] The image of the privileged watcher atop the Minar, above the unaware city yet prying into its secret heart, captures succinctly the role each man plays and the duty he performs. Just as Strickland enforces the law so that the machinery of colonial exploitation may run more smoothly, so Kipling's imperial narrators impose aesthetic order on their material so that it may be more readily consumed. India is transformed via narrative into useable information. "To have made India a real place to dwellers in Great Britain is itself an imperial conquest," wrote an admiring Gleeson White in 1890.[41] To remain credible, these narrators continually iterate their psychological distance from their material and revel in their physical proximity. Like Strickland, Kipling's personae must be able to move easily and without danger of contamination through opium den ("The Gate of the Hundred Sorrows"), royal court ("The Amir's Homily"), and Buddhist monastery ("The Finances of the Gods"), in order to reproduce, as E. Kay Robinson put it, every "horizontal division of rank" and every "vertical division of caste" in a complex Indian society.[42] Cyril Falls would later write that Kipling's achievement lay in the fact that he "feels" and "understands" India yet "writes...as an Englishman."[43]

Such narrative authority operates in several registers. It is most noticeable perhaps in the clean, sharp rhythms of Kipling's prose – a journalist's fine prose, which Kipling self-consciously honed in his newspaper work. Its sparseness and precision, its studied commitment to "just plain facts about who is doing what" ("William the Conqueror," *DW* 230), its eschewal of ambiguity, are meant to induce readerly confidence in Kipling's accuracy and objectivity. And so they did: Henry James was not alone in praising Kipling's ability to produce the real thing, unmediated by "any bookish associations." He "has been put up to the whole thing directly by life," James marvelled, "and not by the communication of others."[44]

Kipling's prose continually calls attention to its seeming transparency. The plain style reinforced Kipling's assertion of control, his ability to convey the truth. "Book learning" is scorned in favor of direct experience, unmediated by "intellectually 'beany'" systems of thought or philosophy ("The Conversion of Aurelian McGoggin," *PT* 128). "Theory killed him dead," we are told of one unfortunate character ("Thrown Away," *PT* 18).

Paradoxically, however, Kipling's imperial narrators also rely for their authority on the same bookish associations they so loudly reject. Far from being transparent representations, these stories continually read India through the lenses of previous stories. When Kipling's narrator looks out from the Minar, he immediately frames the scene in terms familiar to a Western reader. "Dore might have drawn it! Zola could describe it" ("'The City of Dreadful Night'," *BW* 40).[45] When he unveils a mysterious native ceremony as a fraud, he uses Poe as a reference point ("In the House of Suddho"). While describing the world of the half-caste, he rests on the authority of the Anglo-Indian poet Henry Derozio ("His Chance in Life"). Shakespeare is often invoked, as is the Bible. Kipling's texts in fact deploy an extraordinarily dense field of literary and cultural allusion (despite contrary assertions, Kipling was remarkably well-read), which permeates his fictions and mediates our experience of them. Readers' encounters with India thus become resolutely *textual* experiences. "For all practical purposes" in India, one narrator tells us, "the old *Arabian Nights* are good guides" ("Beyond the Pale," *PT* 190).

This textualization of India is not necessarily incompatible with Kipling's opposing insistence on unmediated experience. Both are strategies for establishing authorial mastery. The invocations of familiar artists serve to reduce the chaotic and alien, the potentially threatening world of native India, to the comfortably known. Kipling's narrators often lend authority to their visions by showing us how to understand and interpret them. What might otherwise seem unaccountable, uncanny, inherently "Other" in these visions is rendered harmless by being brought within the purlieu of Western reason.

There is considerable evidence in Kipling's autobiography to suggest that his personal relation to India was, from its beginnings, textual. When he returned to Lahore in 1882, he brought with him an extensive "knowledge" of the Orient derived from boys' adventure stories, the popular literature of the exotic, and a wide variety of travel narratives and personal accounts. A long list could be compiled from the autobiography alone, from *The Arabian Nights* and *Robinson Crusoe* to Wellington's India Despatches and G. W. Trevelyan's *Competition Wallah*. Just as pertinent was

Kipling's fascination with London's South Kensington Museum, to which he acquired a season's pass as a child. Here the East was packaged and condensed for easy consumption ("the labels alone were an education," he said), and its truths revealed in a systematic manner.[46] Kipling's father, Lockwood, was himself curator of the Lahore Museum from 1874 to 1895. Kipling was thus immersed in an Orientalist, textualized vision of the East.

I am not suggesting that the intellectual baggage Kipling carried into India was unusual; the point is precisely how ordinary it was. Yet the remarkable thing is that Kipling's "imperial narrators" do not rule all his early fiction. Interwoven among them are stories marked by an absence of distance and objectivity, a loss of control, the breakdown of the conventions on which both racial and narrative authority rest. It is in these stories that the myth of Kipling as untroubled apologist for empire collapses.[47]

Strickland's authority is directly challenged in the very last of the *Plain Tales*, through the character of McIntosh Jellaludin. "He [Jellaludin] used actually to laugh at Strickland as an ignorant man – 'ignorant West and East' – he said" ("To Be Filed for Reference," *PT* 346). Like Strickland, Jellaludin has "his hand on the pulse of native life" (*PT* 347). Unlike the police officer, however, Jellaludin has not maintained a position of detached observation, but has instead "gone native." Strickland impersonates Indians; Jellaludin, his friends fear, has become one.

> When a man begins to sink in India, and he is not sent Home by his friends as soon as may be, he falls very low from a respectable point of view. By the time that he changes his creed, as did McIntosh, he is past redemption. In most big cities natives will tell you of two or three *Sahibs*, generally low-caste, who have turned Hindu or Mussulman, and who live more or less as such. But it is not often that you can get to know them. (*PT* 340–41)

Kipling signals the difference between Strickland and Jellaludin through the label he assigns to each. While Strickland is called an Anglo-Indian, McIntosh falls under the very different heading of "Eurasian." The hyphen is in this instance telling. While both terms denote a hybridization of Englishman and Indian, they connote different things for Kipling. Through successful acclimatization, the Anglo-Indian has recovered the Englishman's "innate" racial qualities of vigor and purpose, adding them to a civilized rationality and insight. The Eurasian, on the other hand, has seen his racial identity undermined through extended contact, physical and emotional, with the racial Other.

Such undermining produces its own kind of authority, as Jellaludin is quick to point out. Because he has changed his name and creed, taken a Muslim wife, and lives "more or less" as a native, McIntosh, in Kipling's view, possesses the kind of intimate, unmediated knowledge denied to the policeman or the imperial narrator. The narrator of "To Be Filed for Reference" knows Jellaludin's potential value for a writer – "he was all that I wanted for my own ends" – and cultivates his acquaintance "after dark," but is rebuffed by McIntosh for being "painfully ignorant" (*PT* 347, 342). "[O]f the people of the country," Jellaludin tells him, "you know nothing" (*PT* 343).

Jellaludin's most notable feature is his drunken erudition. He is the only character in all of Kipling's Indian stories who is learned – the only character, in other words, whose literary education matches Kipling's own. Yet in his perpetually drunken discourse, Western culture splinters into disconnected fragments, becomes a meaningless bricolage. "The man's mind was a perfect rag-bag of useless things" (*PT* 344). "To Be Filed for Reference" opens with Jellaludin singing Rossetti's "Song of the Bower," which is interrupted in mid-verse as he stumbles into a camel, and continues through a long series of fragmented, misremembered, and jumbled-together quotations, few of which have any apparent relevance. He quotes Ovid, Virgil, Horace, Dante, Browning, Rossetti, Swinburne, and even Kipling himself, but the effect is finally to parody the kind of textualized knowledge of India that Kipling's imperial narrators routinely invoke. Jellaludin's quotations lack the explanatory power possessed by the allusions to Dore or the *Arabian Nights*. We are not permitted to mediate our experience of India through an authoritative Western tradition, since that tradition has itself broken down into Jellaludin's "ravings in Greek and German." These are the languages, we recall, of nineteenth-century philology, whose centrality in shaping Victorian Orientalism has long been recognized.[48] His racial identity made problematic, Jellaludin also, and causally, makes problematic the western discourses which derive from and underwrite that identity.

Having done so, McIntosh Jellaludin produces a text of his own. Its contents, derived from Jellaludin's personal experiences, are said to constitute the definitive work on Indian life, far surpassing in true knowledge anything Strickland might write. The manuscript is a mess, however, "a hopeless muddle" of fragments "full of...nonsense," "a big bundle...of old sheets of miscellaneous notepaper, all numbered and covered over with fine cramped writing," in places indecipherable (*PT* 348). Jellaludin bequeaths his treasure to the narrator with a request that he take charge of its publication. The narrator accepts the manuscript with reluctance and, anxious to distance himself from its author, professes not to understand it. If Jellaludin provides a second model of narrative authority, one in which knowledge of India is mediated not through texts but through one's own body, it is a model Kipling's narrative persona is loath to embrace. He appeals for help to Strickland, who suspects "the writer was either an extreme liar or a most wonderful person. He thought the former." Together they edit the manuscript ("the bundle needed much expurgation") and file it away – for reference but not, it seems, for publication (*PT* 350).

Jellaludin names his text *The Book of Mother Maturin*, the title of Kipling's own long-planned, never-finished magnum opus of Indian life. Begun in 1885, this work occupied Kipling for the better part of two decades but was left, like Jellaludin's manuscript, a mass of fragments.[49] The pain its composition caused seems often to have been intense. Almost from the beginning, Kipling suspected that the book would ultimately overwhelm him, that the "queer jumble" of his experiences in India would not cohere into some recognizable literary shape. *Mother Maturin* is the sign of a crisis of representation for Kipling. He wanted, he said, "to deal with the unutterable horrors of lower class Eurasian and native life" in a way that would not replicate official "reports and reports and reports."[50] To do so meant abandoning traditional representational practices of the kind I have associated with Kipling's imperial narrators. The need for alternative narrative strategies seems to have weighed heavily on Kipling, without his being able finally to imagine what such practices might look like.

Thus, rather than a Jellaludin-like counterpart to Kipling's imperial narrators, we find instead a series of covert attacks on those narrators' modes of writing. "To be Filed for Reference" constitutes one such attack. One of a small handful of stories written solely with the *Plain Tales* in mind, its function as the last of those tales is primarily a disruptive one. It compels us to read back through what has preceded it, but with an eye skeptical to Stricklandesque pieties and certainties. Once alerted, we become aware of alternate energies in the stories, currents which seldom surface as manifest theme or symbol but which nevertheless trouble the narrative stream. Writing is associated not with truth but with distortion, deception, bad faith. "'Can you lie?' 'You know best,' I answered. 'It's my profession'" ("Thrown Away," *PT* 23).

Such lies are inseparable from the generic forms that clothe them: the journalistic account, the Orientalist treatise, the official report, the realist tale. Journalists are revealed as double agents ("The Man Who Was"). Would-be ethnologists are ridiculed and humiliated ("Wressley of the

Foreign Office"). Colonial officers consciously mask the truth in their reports ("The Head of the District"). Fiction writers are coerced into "the concoction of...big, written lie[s], bolstered by evidence, to soothe...[the] people at Home" in England ("Thrown Away," *PT* 26). Kipling's Indian tales as a whole are shot through with a kind of self-lacerating irony, as the familiar narrative forms for representing the exotic – forms Kipling himself habitually employs – are all shown to be corrupt. As often as writing is associated with truth, clarity, sanity in these stories, it is just as often linked with madness, hallucination, loss of control, death. Aurelian McGoggin is struck down by aphasia as he reaches for a copy of the *Pioneer*, Kipling's own newspaper. The disorder is an appropriate one. Once confident in his assertions, McGoggin is left unable to do more than string together meaningless words. "Perfectly conceivable – dictionary – red oak – amenable – cause" ("The Conversion of Aurelian McGoggin," *PT* 131). He eventually recovers, yet lives "in fear and trembling, wondering whether he would be permitted to reach the end of any sentence he began" (*PT* 133).

We continually find Kipling establishing troubled, clandestine affiliations with the McGoggins and Jellaludins of his fiction, with those who, as he says in one of his earliest stories, have only "a sick man's command of language" ("The Phantom Rickshaw," *PR* 4). When he gathered together his Indian tales for publication in America, Kipling called the collection *Mine Own People.* The title phrase appears twice within the volume. Both instances occur in stories of miscegenation ("Beyond the Pale" and "Namgay Doola") and refer us not to the English or Anglo-Indian communities, but to the Eurasian. Finally it was there that Kipling covertly located himself, there that he proffered his uneasy loyalties.

Such details as I have been foregrounding are dispersed throughout Kipling's texts. They seldom coalesce into pattern or coherent argument, but instead mark nodes of disruption. They "interrupt," to employ Ed Cohen's useful term, the thrust of Kipling's narratives, momentarily disturbing the normally tight fit of ideology and representational practice.[51] One of the few sustained explorations of these links appears in "The Mark of the Beast." Kipling's emotional investment in this story was evidently great. As the first tale he tried to publish in England, it was to be Kipling's introduction to a domestic audience. He sent "The Mark of the Beast" anonymously to Andrew Lang in 1886, but Lang – later of course Kipling's staunch admirer – rejected the story with vehemence, claiming he would have paid five pounds not to have read such "poisonous stuff."[52]

In the tale, a weak but arrogant Englishman named Fleete desecrates a Hindu temple during a drunken spree. An outraged Hindu priest, naked, leprous, his body shining "like frosted silver," embraces Fleete, pressing his faceless head onto the Englishman's breast. Over the next twenty-four hours Fleete is transformed into a wolf, whose writhings and howlings Kipling's narrator finds "loathsome." Racial degradation is presented as a communicable disease, passed from flesh to flesh and afflicting those whose constitutions are less than sturdy. Kipling's narrative surrogate distances himself from the action only to establish oblique affiliations with Fleete. (Fleete's very name connects him with Kipling's trade, since it invites us to remember that the center of London journalism is in Fleet Street.)

The narrator turns to Strickland for support, but the policeman admits the situation "baffled him completely" (*PR* 175). He is for once quite clearly not in control of events. Strickland does not understand what is happening, nor is he able to explain Fleete's transformation in any rational way. Nothing he knows can account for what has occurred. The narrator is similarly at a loss. In contrast to Kipling's imperial narrators, he is unable to assuage readerly anxiety by demystifying events, by showing native magic to be in reality a trick or sham. He is unable, in other words, to textualize the event, to reduce it to a comfortable version of the already-known. Driven to desperation, Strickland and the narrator finally capture the offending Hindu priest and torture him, thereby "convincing" him to lift the spell on Fleete.

The narrator's complicity in the torture is foregrounded as much by his initial reluctance as by his ultimate acquiescence. He continues to identify with Strickland, recoiling from the knowledge of the racial Other which Fleete quite literally embodies. Such identification is strained, however, and becomes increasingly marked by a wilful blindness to how thoroughly Strickland's methods have been discredited. The distance the policeman so assiduously cultivates between himself and native life breaks down as he is forced into direct physical contact with the Silver Man, whose "flesh was not the flesh of a clean man" (*PR* 187). When, unable to triumph in any other way, Strickland resorts to torture, the narrator signals his complicity not simply by assisting in the act but also by refusing to represent it: "This part is not to be printed" (*PR* 187). The mark of the beast is erased from Fleete's breast, and that effacement is answered by another: the erasure of the writer's marks.

Order is restored and a happy ending achieved, but at the cost of remarkable brutality. The narrative turns away from this brutality, since to represent it would be to reveal how firmly Strickland's authority rests on violence and coercion, on the strong arm of the imperialist. The narrator's own authority is also shown to be grounded in a form of violence, a wrenching of events to force them into some familiar shape. At one point he attempts to reduce the story to an illustration of conventional wisdom. The gesture is cut short, however: "I said, 'There are more things...'" (*PR* 190), but he cannot finish the cliché. "[T]he word wouldn't come" that would soothe his anxieties, the narrator acknowledges, "because I knew that I was lying" (*PR* 183). Altogether, he admits of himself and Strickland, we "had disgraced ourselves as Englishmen" (*PR* 190).

THE NOVELIST WHO FAILED

"The Mark of the Beast" was not published until July 1890, at the height of the Kipling Boom in London. Kipling was by this time in the midst of his first novel, *The Light that Failed*. Despite the success of his short fiction, more was required of Kipling. As reviewers seldom tired of reiterating, only a novel would determine whether he belonged permanently in the first rank of British writers. Many of the same reviewers who responded most forcefully to Kipling's "difference" were also loudest in demanding that he now take up that most English of literary forms, the long social novel. No other rite of passage would suffice. If Kipling was to be the new Dickens, he must demonstrate his command of the master's tools.

Such demands must be seen as part of a general fin-de-siècle anxiety over the decline of the novel – by which we should understand simply the decline of a certain kind of novel and its attendant cultural manifestations: the lending library, the monthly magazine, the multi-volume hardcover text, and so on. The disappearance from the domestic scene of robust, multi-plotted, serialized narratives was much remarked on, and it was often linked to the perceived decline in British racial puissance. Kipling was undoubtedly puissant, but needed now to express that power in a more culturally meaningful form than the short story. That Kipling had hitherto clung to the brief narrative as his preferred genre (an adherence originating in the space limitations imposed by newspaper publication) was considered by contemporaries as an accident of place rather than of temperament or material conditions. The short sketch, Lionel Johnson suggested, was suited to the necessarily constricted life of Anglo-India, but "for literary purposes" it was "impossible to take English life of all kinds by storm" except by way of the novel.[53] Only the novel, the argument goes, had sufficient generic heft to subdue the complexities of modern civilization. Kipling himself thought a lasting reputation could be secured only in this way. As early as 1885 his letters are full of schemes to produce a work suitable for weekly serialization in Britain.[54]

The novel he dutifully produced in 1890 was a critical disaster, the one unmitigated failure of Kipling's early career. (Indeed, it continues to embarrass even sturdy Kipling apologists today.[55]) The novel is at once a botched Dickensian narrative and a confused, often bitter denunciation of such narratives. It is marked by an emotional and generic schizophrenia: as a work of art, it attempts to be the very thing it professes to despise. Similarly, Kipling's hero, the painter Dick Heldar, exists in a number of contradictory registers. He is an amalgam of Strickland and Jellaludin, an artist whose success – whose life – is seen alternately in the very different terms generated by those irreconcilable figures. Ultimately *The Light that Failed* is a *kunstlerroman* distinguished by an utter confusion regarding the proper cultural functions of either *das kunstwerk* or *der kunstler.*[56]

The poles between which Heldar oscillates as an artist are best signified by the two publications he draws for. The first, despised and belittled by Heldar, is a well-paying mass market periodical specializing in the derivative, the trite, the unoffending. It is called *Dickenson's Weekly*. To be Dickens's Son, in other words, Heldar – whose own Christian name is of course a truncated version of the novelist's surname – must sell out his talent and produce a kind of art that he considers hackneyed and insipid. Later he will label this the "watered Dickens and water" approach to representation (*LF* 154). The decline of British culture, Heldar claims, is directly linked to the feminization of its artists. This is not so much a reproach of Dickens himself as of his weak successors. The "epicene young pagans" (*LF* 53), who include both writers and painters, cannot reproduce in their work the vigor of their predecessors and so are content with pale imitations. As artists, they are what Andrew Lang had called the "small change" of the Victorian period.

Heldar's disdain does not, however, erase the fact that he is willing to work for *Dickenson's*. Nor does Kipling's ambivalence over being designated Dickens's heir erase the fact that he is willing to write in recognizably Dickensian modes. Many readers have noted Kipling's indebtedness to the Victorian novelist in the opening chapter of *The Light that Failed*, for instance. The account of Dick's and Maisie's orphaned childhood reads, thanks to the literary shorthand Kipling was so adept at, like a mightily condensed *David Copperfield*. Similar echoes can be heard throughout Kipling's early writings. One could argue that Kipling did not need the prompting of English critics to think of his life and career in terms of Dickens, since he had done so from the beginning. He seems to have regarded his own childhood experiences, in particular his exile to Southsea at age six, as uncannily reenacting the familiar Dickensian narrative of abandonment and recovery. Kipling's memories of the Southsea "House of Desolation," recounted most famously in "Baa Baa Black Sheep" and in his autobiography (as well as in *Light*), are so heavily mediated by Dickensian paradigms that Kipling's biographers discount their veracity, though Kipling himself swore they were true. More telling perhaps is the testimony of Kipling's sister Alice, who remembered repeated readings of Dickens during the Southsea years.[57] Though the fact has not been remarked on, Kipling's first fictions continually invoke Dickens as a kind of guardian angel, one who for instance watches over the Anglo-Indian writer's nocturnal city prowlings. (When Kipling left India for England, he wrote a farewell tale in which he imagines himself, in dreamy reverie, surrounded by all his characters. "The Last of the Tales" gestures both toward *A Christmas Carol* and to those well-known posthumous drawings of Dickens seated among his hovering fictional children.)

Having suggested how thoroughly Kipling internalized this model, we must make the corollary point: that it is a model often so disfigured in his fiction as to be almost unrecognizable. This is especially the case with his work of 1889–90. The violence with which Kipling wrenches Dickensian tropes from their accustomed moorings is everywhere evident in *The Light that Failed*. Familiar generic signals are emitted only to be uncomfortably distorted. Dick and Maisie are children in a recognizably Victorian world, but they themselves are far from being the descendants of Little Dorrit or Paul Dombey. The brutality of their natures ("when the spirit moved him he would hit…cunningly and with science" [*LF* 5]) is matched only by the skill with which they lie and plot to achieve their goals. These are children maimed by their experiences, just as Kipling himself felt maimed. They do not respond to unChristian behavior by becoming paradigms of Christian virtue, as Paul Dombey does for example, but instead learn to retaliate secretly and with cunning. Kipling learned the same trick. *The Light that Failed* is itself an instance of such "hitting back."

The second publication Heldar works for takes us to the opposite extreme from *Dickenson's*, to art that is "brutal and coarse and violent" (*LF* 55). Dick calls it the Nungapunga Book, and it circulates only among his friends. This is a secret text, one Heldar works at in moments of irritation, and it becomes the repository of his, and Kipling's, subterranean anxieties about the racialized body. "Nungapunga" means "naked," according to Heldar, and thus the book's hero – a British war journalist nicknamed the Nilghai – is always drawn without clothes.

In it Dick had drawn all manner of moving incidents, experienced by himself or related to him by the others, of all the four corners of the earth. But the wider range of the Nilghai's body and life attracted him most... [He] represented incidents in the Nilghai's career that were unseemly, – his marriages with many African princesses, his shameless betrayal, for Arab wives, of an army corps to the Madhi, his tattooment by skilled operators in Burmah, his interview (and fears) with the yellow headsmen in the blood-stained execution-ground of Canton, and finally, the passings of his spirit into the bodies of whales, elephants, and toucans. (*LF* 144)

Among the extraordinary aspects of this extraordinary passage, we can note how Dick's fascination with "the wider range of the Nilghai's body" leads him immediately to a consideration of "unseemly incidents"; and further, how these unseemly incidents (which are nonetheless also "moving") all involve the breaking down of the racial distance separating the Westerner from various manifestations of the racial Other. Later Dick will draw a "procession" of the Nilghai's wives, "Medes, Parthians, Edomites," overrunning Trafalgar Square (*LF* 147). Fascination with and fear of the exotic (particularly of the feminine exotic) is here combined with anxiety concerning the consequences of extended contact. A variety of physical "intimacies" – sexual intercourse, combat, tattooing, execution, transmigration of souls – are courted, but always with the proviso that they finally be acknowledged as both brutal violations of self and "shameless betrayals" of one's caste or race. Misogyny, homophobia, race hatred, and self-loathing characterize this text, which takes up a central position within Kipling's own text: the Nungapunga Book appears at the dead middle of *The Light that Failed*, and its energies and anxieties radiate through the rest of Kipling's narrative.

Heldar's portrayal of the Nilghai is clearly meant to humiliate. Like McIntosh Jellaludin, the Nilghai of the Nungapunga Book has become an "unutterable horror." Yet Heldar's humiliation of him is equally a form of self-humiliation, since the events related in the Book are, in some sense, Dick's own. The "moving incidents" were "experienced by himself," if only in fantasy. It is Dick Heldar, we recall, whose physical integrity is violated by a knife wound at the hands of an Arab soldier. It is Heldar, too, who is continually associated imagistically with racial Others, who is called "savage in soul," "utterly lawless," a "beast," "sick and savage," a "heathen," a "cold-blooded barbarian" (*LF* 5, 62, 64, 89, 136, 179), and so on. His obsession with the Nungapunga Book is largely an obsession with racial integrity, displaced onto art. The Nilghai's naked body becomes in turn a sign of Heldar's own racial vulnerability and degradation. As his friend Torpenhow points out, Dick does his best or at least his most characteristic work in the Book, where few will see it. While he is most himself there, he is unwilling to acknowledge that self publicly. Just as Kipling refused to embrace Jellaludin or the Book of Mother Maturin openly, so too does Heldar dissociate himself from the Nilghai.

The divisions and tensions of *The Light that Failed*, its angers and anxieties and violences, can make for unpleasant reading, but the novel's interest may lie finally in that very unpleasantness. This is after all the work Kipling produced at the moment of his greatest celebrity, and it may seem an odd response to fame. Yet its anger is an index of the personal and professional contradictions that were forced to the surface of Kipling's life at this moment. (In October 1890, the novel finished, Kipling suffered a nervous breakdown and left the country.) The writer who posted a notice on the door of his first London flat – "To Publishers, A Classic While You Wait" – was also the writer who distrusted what he called "Literature (*with* the L)" as "immoral and degrading and futile," and who deeply resented the burden placed on him to revive a moribund tradition of "classic" English novels.[58] Likewise, the writer who routinely invoked Dickens as his model was also the one who with self-conscious savagery mauled Dickens in his fiction. And the writer whose literary persona came increasingly to be grounded in affirmations of racial solidarity with his English public was also the writer whose own fears about racial vulnerability were most publicly on display.

Not surprisingly given such contradictions, Kipling wrote two conclusions for *The Light that Failed*. (Even here, comparisons with *Great Expectations* intrude themselves.) A single ending could not contain all Kipling's, or the culture's, contradictions. The first version, which appeared in *Lippincott's Monthly Magazine* in January 1891, is shamelessly sentimental. Heldar, now blind and penniless, nevertheless wins the love of Maisie, the childhood friend who had previously scorned him. Love reigns; domesticity prevails. Allusions to *Jane Eyre* accumulate thickly. The treacly quality of the magazine ending puzzles Kipling enthusiasts today, just as it discomfited even the most well-disposed of late-Victorian readers. Yet that may be its point: the conclusion bludgeons with its pathos. Rather than indicating his surrender to the conventions of the Victorian novel, which is how it is usually read,[59] such a transparently artificial ending may as easily indicate Kipling's disdain for that tradition. Taken seriously, it makes nonsense of what comes before. The *Lippincott's* ending can be read as an angry, bitter parody of, and finally dismissal of, novelistic conventions of closure. The fin-de-siècle novelist, no longer able in good conscience to provide what is expected of him, instead offers his audience a conventional ending as an act of bad faith.

The bound novel offered an alternate conclusion. It ostensibly rejects the sentimentality of the magazine version, but in one respect it remains solidly traditional. Dick – blind, dirty, unemployed, restless, lonely, bitter, disruptive – is banished from England back to the colonies, where he can do no harm. The problems he raises for the culture are "solved" in a time-honored way. He is removed from the scene, and then he dies. Heldar is thus, as one of his friends says in a telling pun, put "out of the race" (*LF* 223). Yet Kipling manages one final image which encapsulates the novel's unresolved tensions. Dozing as he rides camelback across the desert to his death, Heldar imagines painting himself as part of an Oriental tableau.

> From the safe distance of London he was watching himself thus employed, – watching critically. Yet whenever he put out his hand to the canvas that he might paint the tawny yellow desert under the glare of the sinking moon, the black shadow of the camel and the two bowed figures atop, that hand held a revolver and the arm was numbed from wrist to collar-bone. Moreover, he was in the dark, and could see no canvas of any kind whatever. (*LF* 326)

In a novel often unaware of its deepest obsessions, this is a moment of extraordinary clarity for Kipling. It makes literal Heldar's divided consciousness, and by extension Kipling's own. Kipling imagines himself as observer and observed, his identifications uneasily split between the debilitated Heldar and a London audience critically watching. He is Strickland, separated by a "safe distance" from the picturesque but alien landscape he attempts to record, and he is also Jellaludin, degraded and now inescapably part of that landscape. As an artist, he is deeply attracted to the tawny yellow desert and its inhabitants, finds them worth recording, yet recognizes the homologous relation of colonial artist and imperialist. The hand that ought to hold a paintbrush holds a gun instead. The entire tableau is defined by darkness and paralysis, an artistic numbness running from wrist to collar-bone.

This, rather than Heldar's death a few paragraphs on, is the novel's climax. It underscores that "universal foreignness" which Eliot suggested was Kipling's most salient attribute. Yet Eliot finally has in mind only that sense of spiritual homelessness familiar to the Modernist in exile. Kipling's sense of foreignness – racial, cultural, emotional, artistic – cut deeper. It was felt in the viscera rather than the psyche. It sat uneasily with the culture's demands on him, the tasks he was encouraged to perform. Kipling was asked to compensate for all manner of losses. It is difficult otherwise to account adequately for the fervor with which he was embraced by the British literati in the early 1890s, a fervor out of all proportion to his relatively slight output. To a greater degree than any of his contemporaries, Kipling was made to feel the weight of the traditions, literary and social, he was expected to sustain. To identify him as the new Dickens was to invoke a quite specific notion of authorship, a notion that was increasingly at odds with the ways most writers – James, Wilde, Shaw, Conrad, Hardy, Gissing, and others – conceived of their roles. If theirs was an ethos of self-conscious opposition to the social mainstream, his was to involve an equally self-conscious integration into that current. Kipling was expected to revive, among other things, the recently deceased conception of the artist as public voice, as spokesman for a bourgeois ruling class threatened from every side.

He was willing enough to try. And by the turn of the century, after the publication of the *Jungle Books*, the Stalky stories, *Kim*, and the series of important public poems culminating in "Recessional" and "The Islanders," he had largely succeeded in the task. This is the Kipling who has come down to us. But the Kipling of 1890 is in many ways a more complex and compelling figure. This is the Kipling of "The Mark of the Beast," the Kipling who suffered a nervous breakdown while writing *The Light that Failed* and then published incompatible endings for that novel simultaneously, the Kipling who, less than eighteen months after arriving, fled Britain, not returning to settle there permanently until 1896. The deep, often anguished divisions within his early life and work arose from his ambivalent attempt to fill what Edmund Gosse had termed the "void" at the center of British literary culture.[60] That Kipling was in many respects ill-suited for the job constitutes much of his interest. He tried to shoulder the authorial mantle left by the Victorian giants – a mantle others were eagerly shedding – and the weight at first disabled him.

CONCLUSION

Modernist empires and the rise of English

In 1941, with Kipling five years dead, Eliot could remake him into a kind of Modernist fellow traveler, a writer whose "peculiar detachment and remoteness" from late-Victorian readers sat uneasily with the kinds of demands made on him by the public. In 1919 Eliot had imagined a quite different Kipling. Reviewing his latest volume of verse, Eliot had written disparagingly of Kipling as a mere "public speaker," an "orator or preacher" to the masses, and therefore not a serious artist. The unsurprising corollary to this claim is that Kipling's popularity ensures that he will remain *unheard* by those whom Eliot calls "discerning critics." "The arrival of a new book of his verses is not likely to stir the slightest ripple on the surface of our conversational intelligentsia." He is, Eliot claims oxymoronically, "a neglected celebrity." The very title of the review, "Kipling Redivivus," implies that the older writer has been utterly forgotten, yet he is forgotten – by discerning readers – precisely because he is the most well-known of contemporary writers. The piece closes with an exhortation. "It is wrong, of course, of Mr. Kipling to address a large audience; but it is a better thing than to address a small one. The only better thing is to address the one hypothetical Intelligent Man who does not exist and who is the audience of the Artist."[1]

The ideology of High Modernism is audible enough here, but there is more to be said about the essay. For one thing, Eliot spends the bulk of it attempting to show that Kipling's verse has "an affinity...even a likeness" to that of one other poet: Swinburne. We may not think to couple them, he says, but their weaknesses as writers are identical. "Both are men of a few simple ideas, both are preachers, both have marked their styles by an abuse of the English Bible." This likeness supersedes the manifest unlikeness of their respective "ideas." Kipling's have to do with Empire and a public school ethos, Swinburne's with "Liberty," by which Eliot means a facile and sentimental attachment (in keeping with "the model of Shelley") to untenable notions of personal freedom and indulgence. Both writers "throw themselves" into their poems, "gesturing the emotion of the moment" in a manner that Eliot considers "to be, frankly, immature." Such abandon is the source of their power as preachers to sway the masses, yet it leads to an abuse of language that Eliot deplores. True artists by contrast stand "simply, coldly independent" of their materials and their audiences.

Without much straining, we can hear beneath Eliot's own simple, cold rhetoric the more heated tones of Robert Buchanan. Eliot does not speak of hooligans and fleshly poets, but his criticisms have clear affinities to those of the earlier writer. Likewise, his insistence that, despite their apparent differences, Kipling and Swinburne are aspects of the same phenomena echoes fin-de-siècle claims that jingoism and aestheticism were upwellings of a single underlying decadence. And neither Buchanan nor his contemporaries would have found anything unfamiliar in Eliot's intertwined fears concerning "softness," sensuality, mass culture, and the decay of linguistic purity.

At such moments Modernism's continuities with the fin de siècle are quite discernible. For Eliot, as for Pound, Lawrence, Hulme, and others, Modernism was a regenerative project, an attempt to overcome the deleterious effects of a "frankly immature" but nevertheless widespread decadence. The task could be couched in narrowly literary terms – the embrace of Classical restraint over Romantic excess, for instance – but as the last twenty years of scholarship have amply shown, it takes very little critical pressure to make politics stand forth.

> Who are those hooded hordes swarming
> Over endless plains, stumbling in cracked earth
> Ringed by the flat horizon only
> What is the city over the mountains
> Cracks and reforms and bursts in the violet air
> Falling towers
> Jerusalem Athens Alexandria
> Vienna London
> Unreal (lines 369–77)

Eliot may have insisted that *The Waste Land* (1922) was not social criticism but simply "rhythmical grumbling," but it is difficult not to see the above lines as rehearsing, in however etiolated or displaced a fashion, the same anxieties that exercised an earlier generation concerning the threat of "alien" masses (whether foreign or lower-class domestic) and the resulting collapse of imperial civilization. Similarly, though Eliot carefully directs our attention to Baudelaire and Dante as glosses on the Unreal City (lines 60–76), we can easily broaden the perspective to take in late-Victorian and Edwardian discourses on urban degeneration. Even the truncated story of Lil and Albert in "A Game of Chess" (lines 139–67) derives some of its edgy energy from widespread fears about the "unfit" but still fecund lower classes. "She's had five already" (line 160).[2]

"I am all for empires," Eliot once wrote to Ford Madox Ford, but he meant by this something quite other than Kipling would have. The empire Eliot refers to was no temporal entity but instead comprised the Western tradition as it flowed from Virgil to the present.[3] That tradition, that empire, he reiterated throughout his career, was continually being modified in its details without being affected in its essence. As Frank Kermode phrases it, Eliot saw "the mind of Europe as changing, but superannuating nothing;...the present joining and altering the past in some modality beyond chronological time."[4] To translate the imperial order from a temporal to a transcendent realm, and from a political to an aesthetic mode, had its clear advantages. One could pledge fealty to such an empire without fear that it would decay, upheave, or otherwise betray one's loyalty. We note, too, that Eliot's anointing of Virgil as the *origo et fons* of culture constitutes a firm rejection of late-Victorian Hellenism. By the time Eliot embarked on his important critical essays of the 10s and 20s, Hellenism had long since seemed inseparable from effeminate decadence. It would be an exaggeration to say that Eliot (or Pound or Lewis) strove to inject a new martial spirit into English thought and writing, yet the value they placed on qualities like austerity, restraint, discipline, "hardness," bears more than a passing resemblance to the masculinist ideal of the previous generation.

A shift has occurred, though. Where late-Victorian critiques of softness were invariably made in the name of an embattled middle class, for Eliot the bourgeoisie are at the heart of the problem. Charges of degeneracy and irreversible weakness are now being leveled *at* the middle classes rather than *by* them. Another way to put this is to say that the definition of what constitutes "the masses" has migrated upward. For turn-of-the-century social critics like Arnold White or C. F. G. Masterman, the term is in most respects still synonymous with the "mob": lower class, urban, politically disaffected, potentially violent. "It is in the city Crowd," wrote Masterman in 1909, "where...the impression (from a distance) is of little white blobs of faces borne upon little black twisted or misshapen bodies, that the scorn of the philosopher for the mob, the cynic for humanity, becomes for the first time intelligible."[5] For Masterman, the crowd is defined precisely by its ideological remoteness from his own position. By the 1920s and 30s, however, the notion of "the masses" has taken on its more contemporary connotations, so that "mass society" is now seen to overlap at key points with middle-class culture and ideology. "A crowd flowed over London Bridge, so many,/I had not thought death had undone so many" (lines 62–63): Eliot's urban crowd is unquestionably middle class. This is the sense of "the masses" as it is used, for instance, in W. R. Inge's "Democracy" (1926) or Ortega y Gasset's *Revolt of the Masses* (1930) or W. B. Yeats's *On the Boiler* (1938). We need not assent to John Carey's extreme formulation – Carey argues that "the principle around which modernist literature and culture fashioned themselves was the exclusion of the masses... [and] the denial of their humanity" – in order to see that, by aligning themselves with what Ortega y Gasset called "the clerisy," writers such as Eliot or Yeats sought to carve out a space apart from the degenerate bourgeois masses, the same masses for whom, as Eliot complained in his 1919 essay, Kipling spoke.[6]

This is not to say that the bourgeoisie did not themselves continue to deploy the rhetoric of degeneracy in the old ways. Degenerationist tropes permeated middle-class thought long after the "scientific" basis of Lombroso's or Nordau's arguments had been debunked.[7] Moreover, as the vigorous history of the eugenicist movement in Britain indicates, fears of racial decay and of the unfit hordes continued to motivate scientific research far into the twentieth century. "National efficiency" and its relation to the tasks of empire remained pressing issues as well.[8] Yet by the 1920s invocations of degenerationist paradigms tended less to be commonsensical than openly ideological. It was less possible to invoke degeneration naively, without some awareness of the political commitments it entailed. Indeed, efforts to strip degenerationism of its commonsensicality can be found in much middle-brow fiction of the period. (I use the term "middle-brow" unpejoratively.) In the works of writers like E. M. Forster, Aldous Huxley, and Christopher Isherwood, tropes of degeneration are effectively "denaturalized," their underlying ideologies laid bare.[9]

Yet if old "solutions" to the problem of national decay were beginning, in some quarters anyway, to seem untenable, the problem itself remained. An interest in rejuvenating the national character continued to be near the heart of a broad range of cultural institutions and discourses. I want to conclude by briefly touching on one such discourse, that of English Studies, since it has important affinities with Eliot's notion of an "imperial" canon immune from decay. Indeed, the relatively rapid rise and consolidation between 1880 and 1920 of English as an autonomous intellectual discipline is one of the most striking features of the period, and it can be fully explained only in relation to the anxieties of national decline we have been considering. Among the diverse factors that went into the making of English, "the need to arrest cultural degeneration and to preserve the national heritage," according to Brian Doyle, "was overridingly in evidence."[10]

English Studies takes it place among many related cultural expressions of the same desire: the desire to define, promulgate, and sustain a distinct national identity, one that would be proof against the ravages of history or circumstance. As Peter Brooker and Peter Widdowson point out, it is no accident that this is the moment when Shakespeare is raised to the status of national poet.[11] The idea of a National Theatre was seriously broached for the first time.[12] A short span of time saw the founding of the National Trust (1895), the National Portrait Gallery (1896), and the Tate Gallery (1897), as well as the publication of the *Oxford English Dictionary* (1884–1928), the *Dictionary of National Biography* (1885–1900), the *Oxford Book of English Verse* (1900), and the *Cambridge History of English Literature* (1907–1916). To this list we can also add the many and varied practices and rituals celebrating "Englishness" that make up what Eric Hobsbawm and Terence Ranger call the "invention of tradition" during this period.[13]

The proponents of English sought to distinguish it from other disciplines by insisting that its study required more than the absorption of a body of knowledge. To live intimately with English literature was to engage in a process of spiritual and moral growth and to awaken to a sense of the national character in its very essence. The study of English, said F. W. Moorman, Professor of English at Leeds University, led to "the cultivation of the mind, the training of the imagination, and the quickening of the whole spiritual nature."[14] The great works of the canon, it was argued, made students aware of their special identity as Englishmen while also lifting them above the accidents of time or place. English literature was "a conning tower," said C. H. Herford, Professor of English at Manchester University, "with a view beyond bounds of class, locality, time or country," yet it also "deepened our sense of the import of nationality."[15] The national character was, in this view, unchanging, though its essential elements may, on occasion, be hidden from view.

Just as in the fin de siècle, then, literature is considered to be inextricably entangled with the health of the polis and the individuals who comprise it. The difference is that now literature, in the form of a stable canon, has been "secured," made safe, sequestered from the contamination of history and politics. Fears about the decline of English letters could thus be allayed, since the canon was by definition immune from change. It was, as Eliot argued, ever-new, ever-relevant, ever-*present*. At the same time, the institutionalizing of English Studies helped to regulate access to literature. Canons entail apocrypha; works considered heretical or otherwise unsafe could more easily be removed from sight in an institutional setting.

Canons also entail hermeneutics, and a clerisy to practice it. From its inception English Studies was defined by conflicting impulses that its proponents struggled to reconcile. On the one hand, there was a low-church faith in the power of literature to speak directly to all who approached; on the other, a decidedly Romish tendency to assert that the laity was incompetent to perform unassisted the acts of interpretation required. Thus the 1921 Newbolt Report on "The Teaching of English in England" could assert that "the Professor of literature in a university should be – and sometimes is, as we gladly recognize – a missionary in a more real and active sense than any of his colleagues."[16]

As the Newbolt Report as a whole indicated, by 1921 the battle between low- and high-church factions for the control of English had been won by the priests. The professionalizing of English Studies at the university level had in fact been halting and uneven. Early appointments to the most prestigious positions had usually gone to people like George Saintsbury, Edmund Gosse, Arthur Quiller-Couch, and Walter Raleigh – dilettantes all, if only in the sense of openly scorning the notion that the study of English literature could be done "professionally." As John Gross has noted, turn-of-the-century English departments were the last refuge of belletrists and old-fashioned men of letters.[17] Such men looked with bewilderment at someone like John Churton Collins, the cranky, scornful, vituperative Professor of English at Birmingham University who missed no opportunity to insist on the need for more professional standards within the discipline.[18]

By the 1920s those standards were the norm, and the professional reader quickly became ensconced in academies on both sides of the Atlantic. With the professionalizing of English, as Doyle points out, came the adoption of those "masculine" values traditionally associated with the professional: rationality, rigor, objectivity, a commitment to explicit standards governing the production of knowledge, and the embrace of that "clean cold detachment" counselled, in a different context, by Eliot.[19] With the triumph of the professional came the promise, too, that the institutionally guided study of literature would somehow be therapeutic, that it could sooth our ills and recoup our losses. In that sense, English Studies is the unrecognized heir of those earlier professional discourses that similarly had promised the rejuvenating value of "being all attention." Indeed, since its beginnings English Studies has been, at heart, a prospectus for cultural renewal. Needless to say, it is a legacy that we are still struggling to accommodate ourselves to.

Notes

INTRODUCTION: DECLINE AND FALL

1 See Lukács, *The Theory of the Novel*, trans. Anna Bostock (1920; rpt. Cambridge: MIT Press, 1971); also Mikhail Bakhtin, "Epic and Novel," in Michael Holquist, ed., *The Dialogic Imagination: Four Essays by M. M. Bakhtin* (Austin: University of Texas Press, 1981), 3–40; and especially Benedict Anderson's *Imagined Communities: Reflections on the Origin and Spread of Nationalism* (London: Verso, 1983), esp. 28–49. On the connections between nationalism and fiction-making, see *Nation and Narration*, ed. Homi Bhabha (London: Routledge, 1990). On the uses of epic poetry in the nineteenth century, see Stuart Curran, *Poetic Form and British Romanticism* (Oxford: Oxford University Press, 1986), 158–205, and Herbert F. Tucker, "The Epic Plight of Troth in *Idylls of the King*," *English Literary History* (hereafter *ELH*) 58 (1991), 701–20.

2 Frank Kermode, *The Sense of an Ending: Studies in the Theory of Fiction* (Oxford: Oxford University Press, 1967).

3 John Stokes, *In the Nineties* (Hemel Hempstead: Harvester Wheatsheaf, 1989), esp. 10–22. See also J. Edward Chamberlin, "Whose Spirit is This? Some Questions about Beginnings and Endings," in *Fin de Siècle/Fin du Globe: Fears and Fantasies of the Late Nineteenth Century*, ed. John Stokes (New York: St. Martin's, 1992), 220–39.

4 Daniel Pick, *Faces of Degeneration: A European Disorder c. 1848–1918* (Cambridge: Cambridge University Press, 1989); William Greenslade, *Degeneration, Culture and the Novel 1880–1940* (Cambridge: Cambridge University Press, 1994); Sander L. Gilman, *Difference and Pathology: Stereotypes of Sexuality, Race, and Madness* (Ithaca: Cornell University Press, 1985), esp. 60–67, 191–238.

5 *Evolution by Atrophy in Biology and Sociology* (1894), cited in Pick, *Faces of Degeneration*, 23.

6 Greenslade, *Degeneration, Culture and the Novel*, 2. Writing of the discourses of pathology that arose during the nineteenth century, Michel Foucault notes that their power in part resides in the way they "form objects that are in fact highly dispersed." See *The Archeology of Knowledge* (London: Tavistock, 1972), 44.

7 Says Greenslade: "So pervasive and seductive was the terminology of degeneration in this period that it was all but impossible to avoid" (*Degeneration, Culture and the Novel*, 8).

8 See David Forgacs, ed., *An Antonio Gramsci Reader: Selected Writings 1916–1935* (New York: Schocken, 1988), 327.

9 Fredric Jameson, *The Political Unconscious: Narrative as a Socially Symbolic Act* (Ithaca: Cornell University Press, 1981), 79.

10 Greenslade, *Degeneration, Culture and the Novel*, 10. A notable exception to this trend is Pick, who argues that "a certain interrogation of, or even resistance towards" dominant paradigms can be found in fin-de-siècle popular fiction (*Faces of Degeneration*, 155).

11 Holbrook Jackson, *The Eighteen Nineties* (London: Grant Richards, 1913), 62.

12 Stokes, *In the Nineties*, xviii.

13 For a reading of this period that stresses its "millenial optimism," see Tom Gibbons, *Rooms in the Darwin Hotel: Studies in English Literary Criticism and Ideas 1880–1920* (Nedlands: University of Western Australia Press, 1973). See also the essays in Stokes, ed., *Fin de Siècle, Fin du Globe*, which collectively examine not just "decline but discovery, new areas of change, of growth and healthy disturbance" (12).

14 Kenneth Burke, *The Philosophy of Literary Form: Studies in Symbolic Action*, 3rd ed. (Berkeley: University of California Press, 1973), 1.

15 *Ibid.*

16 *Ibid.*, 9. Fredric Jameson's perhaps better-known account of the relation between literary text and historical "subtext" may be taken as an elaboration of Burke's position: "The literary or aesthetic act therefore always entertains some active relationship with the Real; yet in order to do so, it cannot simply allow 'reality' to persevere inertly in its own being, outside the text and at a distance . . . The symbolic act therefore begins by generating and producing its own context in the same moment of emergence in which it steps back from it, taking its measure with a view toward its own projects of transformation. The whole paradox of what we have here called the subtext may be summed up in this, that the literary work or cultural object, as though for the first time, brings into being that very situation to which it is also, at one and the same time, a reaction." See Jameson, *Political Unconscious*, 81–82.

1 DEGENERATION AND FICTION IN THE VICTORIAN FIN DE SIÈCLE

1 Robert Buchanan, "The Voice of the Hooligan," *Contemporary Review* 26 (1899), 776–77.

2 On hooliganism, see Geoffrey Pearson, *Hooligan: A History of Respectable Fears* (New York: Schocken, 1984), esp. 69–75; William Greenslade, "Fitness and the Fin de Siècle," in *Fin de Siècle/Fin du Globe*, ed. Stokes, 42–45; and Joseph Bristow, *Empire Boys: Adventures in a Man's World* (London: HarperCollins, 1991), 78–80, 183–85. In 1885 Dr. James Cantlie of Charing Cross Hospital argued that a distinct form of degenerative illness – he proposed calling the condition "urbomorbus" – was endemic to lower-class urban life. See *Degeneration Amongst Londoners: A Lecture Delivered at the Parkes Museum of Hygiene* (London: Field & Tuer, 1885), 24. J. Milner Fothergill comes to a similar conclusion in *The Town Dweller: His Needs and Wants* (London: H. K. Lewis, 1889).

3 Buchanan, "The Voice of the Hooligan," 777.
4 Robert Buchanan, "The Fleshly School of Poetry: Mr. D. G. Rossetti," *Contemporary Review* 18 (1871), 335–37.
5 Barbara Spackman, *Decadent Genealogies: The Rhetoric of Sickness from Baudelaire to D'Annunzio* (Ithaca: Cornell University Press, 1989), 1.
6 Buchanan, "The Fleshly School of Poetry," 340, 338.
7 Buchanan, "The Voice of the Hooligan," 783.
8 Arthur Waugh, "Reticence in Literature," *The Yellow Book.* (1894), 1, 217.
9 Hugh E. M. Stutfield, "Tommyrotics," *Blackwood's Edinburgh Magazine* 157 (June 1895), 833–45.
10 William Watson, "The Fall of Fiction," *Fortnightly Review* 50 (1888), 324–36.
11 Greenslade, "Fitness and the Fin de Siècle," 43.
12 On Morel's importance, see Pick, *Faces of Degeneration,* 44–59, 189–201; and Robert A. Nye, *Crime, Madness, and Politics in Modern France: The Medical Concept of National Decline* (Princeton: Princeton University Press, 1984), 121–26.

In its reliance on the opposition between "normative" and "deviant" structures, degeneration theory takes its place alongside other life sciences in the nineteenth century. As Michel Foucault has demonstrated, the life sciences depended largely on the primacy of the body as an organizing metaphor. Foucault has argued for the emergence in the late eighteenth century of the "medicalized" body: the body as mapped by practitioners of the newly-ascendant life sciences. Where disease had once been defined in mechanical terms as a punitive attack on the body from without, it later came to be seen as a process inherent within the living organism. Disease diverted the organism from its "normal" state, meaning that the study of disease required first that the normative healthy body be identified. The binary opposition of health and sickness corresponded to an opposition of the normal and the pathological, and it was this fundamental dichotomy that came to structure thought in all the human sciences. "The prestige of the sciences of life," Foucault argues, derived in part from "the comprehensive, transferable character of biological concepts" and in part from

> the fact that these concepts were arranged in a space whose profound structure responded to the healthy/morbid opposition. When one spoke of the life of groups and societies, of the life of the race, or even of the "psychological life," one did not think first of the internal structure of *the organized being*, but of the *medical bipolarity of the normal and the pathological.* Consciousness lives because it can be altered, maimed, diverted from its course, paralyzed; societies live because there are sick, declining societies and healthy, expanding ones; the race is a living being that one can see degenerating; and civilization, whose deaths have so often been remarked on, are also, therefore, living beings.

See Foucault, *The Birth of the Clinic: An Archeology of Medical Perception*, trans. A. M. Sheridan Smith (New York: Vintage, 1975), 34–35. Also apposite are Foucault's discussion of degeneration in *The History of Sexuality*, 3 vols., trans.

Robert Hurley (New York: Vintage, 1980), I, 116–20, and Georges Canguilhem, *The Normal and the Pathological* (New York: Zone, 1991).

13 As John Stokes notes, for late-Victorian critics it "carried a burden of meaning greater than any other derogatory adjective." See Stokes, *In the Nineties*, 26. For an effective deconstruction of the term, see Oscar Wilde, "The Soul of Man Under Socialism" (1891), rpt. in *The Artist as Critic: Critical Writings of Oscar Wilde*, ed. Richard Ellmann (Chicago: University of Chicago Press, 1968), 274–76.

14 Buchanan, "The Fleshly School of Poetry," 340.

15 On the disparate uses of degeneration theory across a wide variety of late-Victorian disciplines, see the essays collected in *Degeneration*, ed. Gilman and Chamberlin

16 Nye, *Crime, Madness, and Politics*, 119.

17 Pick, *Faces of Degeneration*, 8.

18 Tom Gibbons notes how readily evolutionary and devolutionary narratives were "used to give an up-to-date and 'scientific' air to beliefs which were venerable before Darwin and Spencer had published a word"; these were not new ideologies but "old ideologies rehabilitated." See *Rooms in the Darwin Hotel*, 6.

19 Antonio Gramsci, "Notes for an Introduction and an Approach to the Study of Philosophy of the History of Culture," in *An Antonio Gramsci Reader*, ed. Forgacs, 343. Further page references to this essay are given parenthetically in the text.

20 Greenslade, *Degeneration, Culture and the Novel*, 23.

21 See *Report of the Interdepartmental Committee on Physical Deterioration* (London, 1904), esp. III, 13–14, 34–38. For discussions of the committee's formation and conclusions, see Richard A. Soloway, *Demography and Degeneration: Eugenics and the Declining Birth Rate in Twentieth-Century Britain* (Chapel Hill: University of North Carolina Press, 1990), 41–47; and Thomas E. Jordan, *The Degeneracy Crisis and Victorian Youth* (Albany: State University of New York Press, 1993), 237–39.

22 Michel Foucault, *Language, Memory, Counterpractice: Selected Essays and Interviews*, ed. Donald F. Bouchard (Ithaca: Cornell University Press, 1977), 154. In his otherwise useful *Idols of Perversity: Fantasies of Feminine Evil in Fin de Siècle Culture* (New York: Oxford University Press, 1986), for instance, Bram Dijkstra makes the unhelpful assertion that degeneration theory contributed solely to the "idealization of...white males and the concomitant assumption that somehow all others were degenerate" (160).

23 See Gibbons, *Rooms in the Darwin Hotel*, 35–38; and Greenslade, *Degeneration, Culture and the Novel*, 92–99, 122–24.

24 Arthur Symons, "The Decadent Movement in Literature" (1893), in *Aesthetes and Decadents of the 1890s: An Anthology of British Poetry and Prose*, ed. Karl Beckson, rev. ed. (Chicago: Academy Chicago, 1982), 135–36.

25 Greenslade, *Degeneration, Culture and the Novel*, 15.

26 See Allon White, *The Uses of Obscurity: The Fiction of Early Modernism* (Boston: Routledge and Kegan Paul, 1981), esp. ch. 3.

27 Eugene S. Talbot, *Degeneracy: Its Causes, Signs, and Results* (London: Walter Scott, 1898), 161–362.

28 Henry Maudsley, *Life in Mind and Conduct: Studies of Organic in Human Nature* (London: Macmillan, 1902), 54.

29 J. Simms, *Physiognomy Illustrated* (1872), quoted in Pick, *Faces of Degeneration*, 52.

30 Bram Stoker, *Dracula* (1897; rpt. Harmondsworth: Penguin, 1979), 28–29.

31 *Ibid.*, 406. Harker's descriptions also emphasize the Count's aristocratic features and bearing: aquiline nose, thin mouth and lips, domed forehead, and haughty demeanor. Even his hands initially strike Harker as "white and fine" (28). As I point out in Chapter 2, associating degenerate traits with both the upper and the lower classes is one mark of degeneration theory's status as a middle-class discourse.

32 Robert Reid Rentoul, *Race Culture; or, Race Suicide (A Plea for the Unborn)* (London: Walter Scott, 1906), ix. Rentoul was a practicing doctor as well as a vigorous proponent of negative eugenics.

33 Under the rubric of "cerebral stigmata," for instance, Talbot gathered a diverse collection of phenomena, which he subdivided into categories like sensory degeneracy (deaf-mutism, color blindness, smell abnormalities), intellectual degeneracy (paranoia, insanity, hysteria, epilepsy, idiocy, "one-sided genius"), and ethical degeneracy (crime, prostitution, sexual perversion, drunkenness, pauperism). Under the same umbrella, W. Duncan McKim listed such "vexing conditions" as "the morbid fear of pins or broken glass...the dread of very large or small places, of crowded assemblies, of the dark, of being buried alive;...the impulse to count, to buy for the sake of buying, to hoard, to steal, to burn, to kill, to take one's own life." See Talbot, *Degeneracy*, 37; and W. Duncan McKim, *Heredity and Human Progress* (New York and London: G. P. Putnam's Sons, 1900), 47.

34 Quoted in Talbot, *Degeneracy*, 23.

35 Alexander Welsh, *Strong Representations: Narrative and Circumstantial Evidence in England* (Baltimore: Johns Hopkins University Press, 1992), esp. 1–42, 152–84.

36 See Talbot, *Degeneracy*, esp. 33–37.

37 On the relation between late-Victorian realism and medical paradigms of character, see Lawrence Rothfield, *Vital Signs: Medical Realism in Nineteenth-Century Fiction* (Princeton: Princeton University Press, 1992), esp. chs. 4 and 5; and Jenny Bourne Taylor, *In the Secret Theatre of Home: Wilkie Collins, Sensation Narrative, and Nineteenth-Century Psychology* (London: Routledge, 1988).

38 Henry Maudsley, *Body and Will: Being an Essay Concerning Will in Its Metaphysical, Physiological, and Pathological Aspects* (New York: D. Appleton, 1884), 32. Compare Evadne Frayling's remark in Sarah Grand's novel, *The Heavenly Twins* (New York: Cassell, 1893): "You must know that there is no past in the matter of vice. The consequences become hereditary, and continue from generation to generation" (127).

39 Walter Bagehot, *Physics and Politics; or, Thoughts on the Application of the Principles*

of "Natural Selection" and "Inheritance" to Political Society (New York: D. Appleton, 1873), 2. Further page references to this work are given parenthetically in the text.

40 Ernest Renan, "What is a Nation?" (1882), rpt. in Homi K. Bhabha, ed., *Nation and Narration* (London: Routledge, 1990), 19.

41 Indeed, we can usefully compare Bagehot's definition with Shelley's discussion of imitation in the preface to *Prometheus Unbound* (1819) for the contrast it affords:

> It is impossible that any one who inhabits the same age with such writers as those who stand in the foremost ranks of our own, can conscientiously assure himself, that his language and tone of thought may not have been modified by the study of the productions of those extraordinary intellects. It is true, that, not the spirit of their genius, but the forms in which it has manifested itself, are due, less to the peculiarities of their own minds, than to the peculiarity of the moral and intellectual condition of the minds among which they have been produced. Thus a number of writers possess the form, whilst they want the spirit of those whom, it is alleged, they imitate; because the former is the endowment of the age in which they live, and the latter must be the uncommunicated lightning of their own mind.

It is precisely the distinction between form and spirit that Bagehot erases, claiming instead that the spirit of any individual utterance is in fact determined by the form or style in which it finds expression. For the Shelley quotation, see *Shelley's Poetry and Prose*, ed. Donald H. Reiman and Sharon B. Powers (New York: W. W. Norton, 1977), 134.

42 Christopher Herbert, *Culture and Anomie: Ethnographic Imagination in the Nineteenth Century* (Chicago: University of Chicago Press, 1991), 141. As is apparent, my discussion of Bagehot is indebted to Herbert's suggestive reading of *Physics and Politics*; see esp. 128–49.

43 Edwin Ray Lankester, *Degeneration: A Chapter in Darwinism* (London: Macmillan, 1880), 59–60.

44 *Ibid.*, 33. Unlike other crustaceans, barnacles have no organs of sight or touch; Lankester argued that they had been lost through disuse.

45 *Ibid.*, 60. On Lankester, see Gibbons, *Rooms in the Darwin Hotel*, 34; Pick, *Faces of Degeneration*, 173–74, 216–18; Greenslade, *Degeneration, Culture and the Novel*, 32–33; and R. K. R. Thornton, *The Decadent Dilemma* (London: Edward Arnold, 1983), 10–11. As Greenslade points out, Lankester's work, along with that of Francis Galton, was central to the developing fin-de-siècle notion of the "degenerate fit" – those whose very degeneracy made them better able to thrive in unhealthy environments. The collorary to this argument was, of course, that to be "healthy" was – tragically, self-pityingly – to be unfit for modern life. See "Fitness and the Fin de Siècle," 42–46; *Degeneration, Culture and the Novel*, 41–43.

46 Maudsley, *Body and Will*, 321.

47 Quoted in David C. Smith, *H. G. Wells* (New Haven: Yale University Press, 1986), 48.

48 Maudsley, *Body and Will*, 327.

49 See Linda Dowling, *Language and Decadence in the Victorian Fin de Siècle* (Princeton: Princeton University Press, 1986).
50 Stutfield, "Tommyrotics," 837.
51 James Ashcroft Noble, "The Fiction of Sexuality," *The Contemporary Review* 67 (April 1895), 490.
52 Janet E. Hogarth, "Literary Degenerates," *Fortnightly Review* n.s. 57 (1895), 586–92.
53 For a detailed, highly informative account of the reception history of *Degeneration*, see Milton P. Foster, "The Reception of Max Nordau's 'Degeneration' in England and America," Ph.D. dissertation, University of Michigan, 1954.
54 Max Nordau, *Degeneration* (1892; rpt. Lincoln: University of Nebraska Press, 1993), 17. Further page references to this work are given parenthetically in the text.
55 George Bernard Shaw, *The Sanity of Art: An Exposure of the Current Nonsense about Artists Being Degenerate* (1896; rpt. London: New Age Press, 1908), 17.
56 Cf Stutfield: "That morbid and nasty books are written is nothing: their popularity is what is disquieting" ("Tommyrotics," 836).
57 On this subject Nordau agrees with his contemporary Gustave Le Bon. In his study of crowds, Le Bon argued that groups of people "think" only through the "words and images" of others. Incapable of independent reasoning, they allow themselves to be formed by the strong rhetoric of their leaders. More often than not, however, the power of persuasion is an attribute of degenerate individuals, those "morbidly nervous, excitable, half-deranged persons who are bordering on madness." See Le Bon, *The Crowd: A Study of the Popular Mind* (London: T. Fisher Unwin, 1896), 34, 136.
58 "The Case of Wagner," in *Basic Writings of Nietzsche*, ed. Walter Kaufmann (New York: Modern Library, 1968), 626–27. The following quotations can be found on 613. Gibbons points out that Nietzsche's wording is lifted almost verbatim from Paul Bourget's 1881 essay on Baudelaire. Writes Bourget: "A style of decadence is one in which the unity of the book is decomposed to give place to the independence of the page, in which the page is decomposed to give place to the independence of the phrase, and the phrase to give place to the independence of the word." See Gibbons, *Rooms in the Darwin Hotel*, 32–33. Havelock Ellis translated this passage in his 1889 essay, "A Note on Paul Bourget"; its influence can be felt in Arthur Symons's definition of decadence as "that learned corruption of language by which style ceases to be organic." See "A Note on George Meredith," *The Fortnightly Review* 67 (November 1897), 677.
59 Stutfield, "Tommyrotics," 840.
60 In "Sex and Modern Literature," *Nineteenth Century* 37 (April 1895), B. A. Crackenthorpe crowned Nordau "the prince of graphomaniacs" (611). Even Nordau's sympathizers seldom resisted the urge to pathologize him. Stutfield thought he showed signs of nervous disease, while Hogarth dryly suggested that readers should "be grateful to Dr. Nordau for his display of

graphomania. It is not every degenerate whose passion for writing has made him so entertaining a critic" ("Literary Degenerates," 592).

61 On the professionalization of literary studies, see Gerald Graff, *Professing Literature: An Institutional History* (Chicago: University of Chicago Press, 1987) and Chris Baldick, *The Social Mission of English Criticism* (Oxford: Oxford University Press, 1983). Frank Kermode examines how the practice of hermeneutics is structured by professional protocols in "Institutional Control of Interpretation," *The Art of Telling: Essays on Fiction* (Cambridge: Harvard University Press, 1983), 168–84.

62 See W. J. Reader, *Professional Men: The Rise of the Professional Classes in Nineteenth-Century England* (New York: Basic Books, 1966), Magali Sarfatti Larson, *The Rise of Professionalism* (Berkeley: University of California Press, 1977), and Andrew Abbott, *The System of Professions* (Chicago: University of Chicago Press, 1988).

63 Stokes, *In the Nineties*, 12. As early as 1899, Edward Garnett recognized that "*Degeneration* is, strictly speaking, the *reductio ad absurdam* of the utilitarian theory in the life of the middle classes. All the ignorance, prejudice, and limitations of the average man in matters aesthetic were deified there, and set up before his delighted eyes as scientific truths." See "Nordau Reconsidered," *The Academy* (21 January 1899), 96.

2 ATAVISM, PROFESSIONALISM, AND *JEKYLL AND HYDE*

1 See *Robert Louis Stevenson: The Critical Heritage*, ed. Paul Maixner (London: Routledge & Kegan Paul, 1981), 200–01.

2 Robert Louis Stevenson, *The Strange Case of Dr. Jekyll and Mr. Hyde* (1886; rpt. Harmondsworth: Penguin, 1979), 35. Further page references to this novel are given parenthetically in the text.

3 *Criminal Man According to the Classification of Cesare Lombroso*, briefly summarized by his daughter Gina Lombroso Ferrero, with an introduction by Cesare Lombroso (New York and London: G. P. Putnam's Sons, 1911), xiv. The following quotations can be found on xiv–xv.

4 Daniel Pick usefully situates Lombroso's work both in the context of Italian class politics and in relation to opposing theories of criminality developed in mid-century France. See *Faces of Degeneration*, 109–52. On Lombroso's reception and influence in England, see 176–89, and William Greenslade, *Degeneration, Culture and the Novel*, 88–102.

5 John Addington Symonds for instance read the story as a parable of atavistic man. See his March 1886 letter to Stevenson, reprinted in *Critical Heritage*, ed. Maixner, 210–11. Recent critics who have studied the tale's indebtedness to theories of criminality, atavism, and devolution include Ed Block, Jr., "James Sully, Evolutionist Psychology, and Late Victorian Gothic Fiction," *Victorian Studies* 25 (Summer 1982), 443–67; Donald Lawler, "Reframing *Jekyll and Hyde*: Robert Louis Stevenson and the Strange Case of Gothic Science Fiction," in *Dr. Jekyll and Mr. Hyde After One Hundred Years*, ed. William

Veeder and Gordon Hirsch (Chicago: University of Chicago Press, 1988), 247–61; Martin Tropp, "*Dr. Jekyll and Mr. Hyde*, Schopenhauer, and the Power of the Will," *The Midwest Quarterly* 32 (Winter 1991), 141–55; and Marie-Christine Lepps, *Apprehending the Criminal: The Production of Deviance in Nineteenth-Century Discourse* (Durham: Duke University Press, 1992), 205–20.

6 See Gertrude Himmelfarb, *The Idea of Poverty: England in the Early Industrial Age* (London: Faber and Faber, 1984), esp. 312–400, and Gareth Stedman-Jones, *Outcast London: A Study in the Relationship Between Classes in Victorian Society* (Oxford: Clarendon Press, 1971), esp. 127–51, 281–313. Judith Walkowitz shows how degeneration, atavism, criminality, and class came together in the social discourses of the 1880s in *City of Dreadful Delight: Narratives of Sexual Danger in Late-Victorian London* (Chicago: University of Chicago Press, 1992), ch. 7.

7 Nordau, *Degeneration*, 7.

8 See Stevenson's letter of 1 March 1886 to F. W. H. Myers in *The Letters of Robert Louis Stevenson*, ed. Sidney Colvin, 4 vols. (New York: Charles Scribner's Sons, 1911), III, 326: "About the picture, I rather meant that Hyde had bought it himself; and Utterson's hypothesis of the gift an error."

9 Elaine Showalter emphasizes the class dimensions of Stevenson's tale, though she sees Hyde simply as a bourgeois fantasy of an eroticized proletariat. She argues that we should read the novel's class interests in terms of "the late-nineteenth-century upper-middle-class eroticization of working-class men as the ideal homosexual objects." Hyde's proletarian status makes him a figure both of fear and desire for Stevenson's professional gentlemen. See Showalter, *Sexual Anarchy: Gender and Culture at the Fin de Siècle* (Harmondsworth: Penguin, 1990), 111.

10 Referring to the proliferation of interpretations of Hyde within the novel, Veeder and Hirsch argue that "*Jekyll and Hyde* engages ineptly in self-analysis in order to call into question the very possibility of such analysis and to complicate comparable analytic moves by the reader." See "Introduction" to *Jekyll and Hyde After One Hundred Years*, ed. Veeder and Hirsch, xii. By arguing for such awareness, they usefully reverse a long-standing tradition of seeing Stevenson as the most innocent of writers, one whose value was separate from his intentions. The most powerful articulation of this latter position is still G. K. Chesterton's in his *Robert Louis Stevenson* (New York: Dodd, Mead, 1928): "I am by no means certain that the thing which he preached was the same as the thing which he taught. Or, to put it another way, the thing which he could teach was not quite so large as the thing which we could learn…[Stevenson] had the splendid and ringing sincerity to testify…to a truth which he did not understand" (22–23). In other words, as the professional reader whose learning is needed to make sense of an unself-conscious text, Chesterton plays Jekyll to Stevenson's Hyde.

11 Myers wrote four letters to Stevenson on the subject of *Jekyll and Hyde* (21 February, 28 February, and 17 March 1886, and 17 April 1887), which are reprinted in *Critical Heritage*, ed. Maixner, 213–22.

12 See "Collated Fractions of the Manuscript Drafts of *Strange Case of Dr. Jekyll and Mr. Hyde*," in *Jekyll and Hyde After One Hundred Years*, ed. Veeder and Hirsch, 24. For a general discussion of Stevenson's alterations from manuscript to printer's copy to first edition, see William Veeder, "The Texts in Question," *ibid.*, 3–13.

13 My reading makes few distinctions among Enfield, Utterson, Lanyon, and Jekyll, whom I take as types of the bourgeois professional rather than as individuals, and thus largely interchangeable. For readings that do make such distinctions, see Block, "James Sully," 448; Mark M. Hennelly, Jr., "Stevenson's 'Silent Symbols' of the 'Fatal Cross Roads' in *Dr. Jekyll and Mr. Hyde*," *Gothic* 1 (1979), 10–16; Irving Saposnik, *Robert Louis Stevenson* (New York: Twayne, 1974), 10; and Stephen Heath, "Psychopathia Sexualis: Stevenson's *Strange Case*," *Critical Quarterly* 28 (1986), 104. Block, Hennelly, and Saposnik single out Utterson as the novel's only "healthy" character, while Heath nominates both Utterson and Enfield for that honor. Closer to the position I take is that of Masao Miyoshi, *The Divided Self: A Perspective on the Literature of the Victorians* (New York: New York University Press, 1969), who also stresses the interchangeability of the primary male characters, noting that the "important men of the book...are all unmarried, intellectually barren, emotionally joyless, stifling" (297).

14 In "Children of the Night: Stevenson and Patriarchy," William Veeder argues for Enfield's vicarious participation in this scene and notes that "exculpation of Hyde has marked Enfield's narrative from the start." In *Jekyll and Hyde After One Hundred Years*, ed. Veeder and Hirsch, 107–60, at 117–18.

15 I owe this idea to a suggestion made by William McKelvy in an unpublished essay (1993) on *Jekyll and Hyde.*

16 Veeder suggests that when Hyde appears at Lanyon's door ludicrously engulfed in Jekyll's oversized clothes we are likely to be reminded of a little boy dressing up as daddy; see "Children of the Night," 126.

17 "Here is another lesson to say nothing" (34). "Let us make a bargain never to refer to this again" (34). "This is a private matter, and I beg of you to let it sleep" (44). "I wouldn't speak of this" (55). "I cannot tell you" (57). "You can do but one thing...and that is to respect my silence" (58). "I daren't say, sir" (63). "I would say nothing of this" (73). As Lepps points out regarding the opening conversation between Enfield and Utterson, "the novel begins with the silent recognition of an unsayable relation between an unnameable high personage and an indescribable creature" (*Apprehending the Criminal*, 210).

18 In recounting how Hyde negotiated for Lanyon's help to retrieve the chemical, Jekyll emphasizes how Hyde on this occasion "rose to the importance of the moment" and mastered himself "with a great effort of the will" (93–94). Regarding Hyde's subsequent conversation with Lanyon, both Veeder and Peter K. Garrett have noted that Hyde now speaks in the professional tones of Jekyll. See Veeder, "Children of the Night," 131, and Peter K. Garrett, "Cries and Voices: Reading *Jekyll and Hyde*," in *Jekyll and Hyde After One Hundred Years*, ed. Veeder and Hirsch, 59–72, at 66.

19 Among previous critics of the novel, only Veeder has discussed this scene, coming to conclusions quite different from mine. He reads the tableau as a projection of Utterson's unconscious, a "kind of parlor primal scene," with "Jekyll/Hyde as father/mother in cozy domesticity" ("Children of the Night," 136). Veeder's reading is richly suggestive, though it neglects what I take to be an important facet of Stevenson's description, namely that the tableau is an empty one: no one is alive to enjoy the cozy domesticity.

20 Later of course Jekyll accuses Hyde of "scrawling in my own hand blasphemies on the pages of my books" (96), though even this leaves room for doubt as to ultimate responsibility. Jekyll, had he wished to be conclusive, could have said "scrawled in *his* own hand," since the two men share the same handwriting.

21 For readings that place Hyde's weeping in the context of late-Victorian discourses on femininity, see William Patrick Day, *In the Circles of Fire and Desire: A Study of Gothic Fantasy* (Chicago: University of Chicago Press, 1985), esp. 91–92; and Janice Doane and Devon Hodges, "Demonic Disturbances of Sexual Identity: The Strange Case of Dr. Jekyll and Mr/s Hyde," *Novel* 23 (Fall 1989), 63–74.

22 Letter to Edmund Gosse dated 2 January 1886; see *Letters*, II, 313.

23 For a reading of *Jekyll and Hyde* as "an unconscious 'allegory' about the commercialization of literature and the emergence of a mass consumer society in the late-Victorian period," see Patrick Brantlinger and Richard Boyle, "The Education of Edward Hyde: Stevenson's 'Gothic Gnome' and the Mass Readership of Late-Victorian England," in *Jekyll and Hyde After One Hundred Years*, ed. Veeder and Hirsch, 265–82.

24 Lloyd Osbourne, *An Intimate Portrait of R. L. S.* (New York: Charles Scribner's Sons, 1924), 59.

25 Letter to Archer dated October 1887; see *Letters*, III, 19.

26 Letter to Gosse dated 2 January 1886; see *Letters*, II, 313.

27 See Peter Keating, *The Haunted Study: A Social History of the English Novel 1875–1914* (London: Secker & Warburg, 1989), 9–87; Nigel Cross, *The Common Writer: Life in Nineteenth-Century Grub Street* (Cambridge: Cambridge University Press, 1985), 204–23; and N. N. Feltes, *Literary Capital and the Late Victorian Novel* (Madison: University of Wisconsin Press, 1993).

28 See Keating, *Haunted Study*, 16–17. W. E. Henley negotiated with Cassell's on Stevenson's behalf for the book publication of *Treasure Island.* Cassell's offered a £100 advance on royalties covering the first 4,000 copies plus £20 for each additional 1,000 copies. Stevenson thought he had sold his copyright for £100.

29 Thomas Stevenson bought the house as a wedding present for Fanny Stevenson. She and Louis lived there between January 1885 and August 1887. Thomas died in May 1887, and Louis almost immediately insisted on moving, though Fanny by all accounts was happy at Skerryvore. Ian Bell writes that "in Samoa, Stevenson never spoke of the place. It was as though he had expunged the memory of imprisonment, despite having written

some of his most famous works while living – like a 'weevil in a biscuit' – at the house." See Bell, *Robert Louis Stevenson: Dreams of Exile* (Edinburgh: Mainstream, 1992), 179.

30 Quoted in Frank McLynn, *Robert Louis Stevenson: A Biography* (London: Hutchinson, 1993), 240.

31 Letter to Gosse dated 12 March 1885; see *Letters*, II, 271. Archer is quoted in J. A. Hammerton, ed., *Stevensoniana: An Anecdotal Life and Appreciation of Robert Louis Stevenson* (Edinburgh: John Grant, 1907), 75. Jenni Calder quotes an unpublished letter of Fanny's: "The tramp days are over, and this poor boy is now, for the rest of his life, to be dressed like a gentleman." See Calder, *Robert Louis Stevenson: A Life Study* (New York: Oxford University Press, 1980), 152.

32 Stevenson was clearly uneasy at this time about his loss of faith in socialism. Joking to Gosse that "the social revolution will probably cast me back upon my dung heap" at Skerryvore, Stevenson said his political change of heart was sure to bring upon him the wrath of H. M. Hyndman, the socialist politician. "There is a person Hyndman whose eye is upon me; his step is beHynd me as I go." (Letter dated 12 March 1885; see *Letters*, II, 271.) Readers who feel Edward Hyde lurking in that "beHynd" might also recall the emphasis given in the tale to Hyde's sinister footsteps and disconcerting gaze. Equating Hyde with Hyndman (and thus with socialism) gives additional weight to readings that focus on the class issues raised in the novel. For an opposing view, see Christopher Harvie's argument for Stevenson's lifelong, thoroughgoing Toryism in "The Politics of Stevenson," in *Stevenson and Victorian Scotland*, ed. Jenni Calder (Edinburgh: University of Edinburgh Press, 1981), 107–25.

33 See Walter Besant, *The Art of Fiction* (Boston: Cupples, Upham, 1884), 4–6.

34 Useful discussions of the Besant–James–Stevenson debate can be found in Feltes, *Literary Capital*, 65–102; John Goode, "The Art of Fiction: Walter Besant and Henry James," in *Tradition and Tolerance in Nineteenth-Century Fiction*, ed. D. Howard, J. Lucas, and J. Goode (London: Routledge and Kegan Paul, 1966); and Mark Spilka, "Henry James and Walter Besant: 'The Art of Fiction' Controversy," *Novel* 6 (Winter 1973).

35 See Keating, *Haunted Study*, 9–15, for the furor Trollope caused, particularly by his insistence that novelists were no different than shoemakers or tallow-chandlers.

36 See Henry James, "The Art of Fiction," in *Essays on Literature; American Writers; English Writers*, ed. Leon Edel and Mark Wilson (New York: Library of America, 1984), esp. 49–53. James had reason to be worried, since the late 1880s and the 90s saw a boom in "how-to" manuals for writers, many of which were written under the unofficial auspices of The Society of Authors. See Keating, *Haunted Study*, 71–73; and Cross, *Common Writer*, 211–12.

37 "On Some Technical Elements of Style in Literature" (1885), in *The Works of Robert Louis Stevenson*, ed. Sidney Colvin, 25 vols. (London: Chatto and Windus, 1911), XVI, 242.

38 "A Humble Remonstrance" (1885), *Works*, IX, 152–53.

39 "Books Which Have Influenced Me" (1887), *Works*, XVI, 274.

40 The first quotation is from "The Morality of the Profession of Letters" (1881), *Works*, XVI, 266, the second from "On Some Technical Elements of Style in Literature," *Works*, XVI, 243.

41 Jonathan Freedman, *Professions of Taste: Henry James, British Aestheticism, and Commodity Culture* (Stanford: Stanford University Press, 1990).

42 George Saintsbury, "The Present State of the English Novel" (1888), in *The Collected Essays and Papers of George Saintsbury 1874–1920*, 4 vols. (London: Dent, 1923), III, 126. On Stevenson and adventure, see Edwin M. Eigner, *Robert Louis Stevenson and Romantic Tradition* (Princeton: Princeton University Press, 1966). On Stevenson as an aesthete and consummate stylist, see Vladimir Nabokov, *Lectures on Literature*, ed. Fredson Bowers (New York: HBJ, 1980), 179–205.

43 *Works*, XVI, 187. Further page references to this essay are given parenthetically in the text.

44 Stevenson wrote to Myers that *Jekyll and Hyde* was written to ward off "Byles the Butcher." Letter to Myers dated 1 March 1886; see *Letters*, II, 325.

45 Letter to T. Watts-Dunton dated September 1886; see *Letters*, II, 348.

46 Stevenson's version of the novel's genesis agrees in outline with the stories told by Fanny Stevenson and Lloyd Osbourne while significantly altering the emotional and moral valences of their accounts. According to both Fanny and Lloyd, Fanny found Louis's first, dream-inspired draft of the novel unsuitable. Louis, she said, "had treated it simply as a story, whereas it was in reality an allegory." After a heated argument, Louis burned the manuscript and started over to produce a version more in keeping with Fanny's moral vision of the story. Both Fanny and Lloyd report that Louis agreed that his second, Fanny-inspired draft of the tale was more marketable. In "A Chapter on Dreams" the two stages are collapsed together: the Brownies both produce the original tale and simultaneously revise it into a marketable story. The censor, rather than being outside the author (in this case in the person of Fanny), is instead thoroughly internalized. For Lloyd's account of *Jekyll and Hyde*'s writing, see *Intimate Portrait*, 62–67; for Fanny's, see Nellie van de Grift Sanchez, *The Life of Mrs. Robert Louis Stevenson* (New York: Charles Scribner's Sons, 1920), 118–19.

47 It can of course be argued with some justice that "A Chapter on Dreams" simply rationalizes Stevenson's failure to be the subversive he sometimes claimed he was. As Veeder points out, the successive drafts of *Jekyll and Hyde* show him toning down and in some cases deleting potentially objectionable material. See "The Texts in Question," 11–12.

48 Unpublished letter quoted in Calder, *A Life Study*, 291. We might in turn connect the letter's invocation of the "amusements of the fireside" to *Jekyll and Hyde*'s portrayal of the hearth as the site of bourgeois isolation and solipsism.

49 Letter to Gosse dated 2 January 1886; see *Letters*, II, 313.

50 Ronald Thomas convincingly argues that Hyde is "the product of Jekyll's pen." See "The Strange Voices in the Strange Case: Dr. Jekyll, Mr. Hyde, and the Voices of Modern Fiction," in *Jekyll and Hyde After One Hundred Years*, ed. Veeder and Hirsch, 78.

51 *Critical Heritage*, ed. Maixner, 215.

52 The objections of Haggard and Cook are reprinted in *Critical Heritage*, ed. Maixner, 202–03.

53 Leonard Woolf, "The Fall of Stevenson," in *Essays on Literature, History, Politics, Etc.* (London: Hogarth, 1927), 41.

54 See William Archer, "Robert Louis Stevenson: His Style and Thought" (1885), rpt. in *Critical Heritage*, ed. Maixner, 160–69; and George Moore, *Confessions of a Young Man* (1886; rpt. Swan Sonnenschein, 1892), 284–87.

55 "A College Magazine," *Works*, IX, 37.

56 Thomas, "Strange Voices," 79.

57 Most recent studies of the novel have stressed what can be called the heteroglossia of the "Full Statement," its deployment of a multitude of conflicting voices and perspectives. A notable exception to this critical trend is Garrett, who argues for the formal and ideological conservatism of Jekyll's narrative while acknowledging the "factors that resist" the novel's drive toward monovocality. See Garrett, "Cries and Voices," 59–61.

3 READING EROTICS AND THE EROTICS OF READING

1 Quoted in Ed Cohen, *Talk on the Wilde Side: Toward a Genealogy of a Discourse on Male Sexualities* (New York: Routledge, 1993), 255.

2 Nordau criticizes Wilde for his aestheticism, dandyism, and decadence. As Alan Sinfield notes, the association of these terms with male same-sex love was far from inevitable in the 1880s and early 90s. At no point does Nordau accuse Wilde of being homosexual; indeed, he seems to have written *Degeneration* in ignorance of the rumors of Wilde's sexual practices. In a revised 1896 edition of the work, Nordau briefly comments on Wilde's trials and imprisonment yet, as Sinfield writes, "it is plain that he does not consider homosexuality to be a central aspect of his theme, decadence." See Sinfield, *The Wilde Century: Effeminacy, Oscar Wilde and the Queer Moment* (London: Cassell, 1994), 89–98.

3 See Cohen, *Talk on the Wilde Side*, esp. 121–98, for a discussion of the ways journalistic accounts of the trial shaped public perceptions of Wilde.

4 Nordau, *Degeneration*, 317–18.

5 Cohen, *Talk on the Wilde Side*, 1–2. A number of recent critics have made this claim, including Sinfield, *Wilde Century*, 109–29; Eve Kosofsky Sedgwick, *Between Men: English Literature and Male Homosocial Desire* (New York: Columbia University Press, 1985), 216–17; Martin Green, *Children of the Sun: A Narrative of Decadence in England after 1918* (New York: Basic Books, 1976), 23–40; and Linda Dowling, *Hellenism and Homosexuality in Victorian Oxford* (Ithaca: Cornell University Press, 1994), 132–54.

6 Cohen, *Talk on the Wilde Side*, 131.

7 The statute makes no mention of intimacies between women. Jeffrey Weeks argues that this silence resulted from the belief that women, as mere receptacles of male seed, played no active role in conception. They therefore could not "sin against nature" in the way that men could. See Weeks, *Coming Out: Homosexual Politics in Britain, from the Nineteenth Century to the Present* (London: Quartet, 1977), 5.

8 Foucault, *The History of Sexuality*, I, 43.

9 Oscar Wilde, *The Picture of Dorian Gray* (1891; rpt. Harmondsworth: Penguin, 1985), 231. Further page references are given parenthetically in the text.

10 Weeks notes that "in terms of social obliquy" the bill ensured that "all homosexual males as a class were equated with female prostitutes." See Jeffrey Weeks, "Inverts, Perverts, and Mary-Annes: Male Prostitution and the Regulation of Homosexuality in the Nineteenth and Early Twentieth Centuries," *Journal of Homosexuality* 2 (Winter 1981), 118. On the regulation of prostitution, see also Judith Walkowitz, "Male Vice and Female Virtue: Feminism and the Politics of Prostitution in Nineteenth-Century Britain," in *Powers of Desire: The Politics of Sexuality*, ed. Ann Snitow, Christine Stansell, and Sharon Thompson (New York: Monthly Review Press, 1983). In *City of Dreadful Delight*, 81–134, Walkowitz gives a detailed account of Stead's exposé and its political and social after-effects. "The Maiden Tribute of Modern Babylon" appeared in the *Pall Mall Gazette* 6, 7, 8, and 10 July 1885.

11 Quoted in Walkowitz, *City of Dreadful Delight*, 103. On the relation between the Labouchère amendment and "purity" campaigns, see Richard Dellamora, *Masculine Desire: The Sexual Politics of Victorian Aestheticism* (Chapel Hill: University of North Carolina Press, 1990), 198–201; and Joseph Bristow, "Wilde, *Dorian Gray*, and Gross Indecency," in *Sexual Sameness: Textual Differences in Lesbian and Gay Writing*, ed. Bristow (London: Routledge, 1992), 48–51.

12 See Weeks, *Coming Out*, 18.

13 As Cohen, Weeks, Dellamora, Sinfield, Bristow, and others have pointed out, in the years leading up to Wilde's arrest middle-class hysteria over the "threat" posed by the homosexual man had been further intensified, most notably by the Cleveland Street Scandal of 1889 with its revelations of male prostitution rings involving working-class boys and their aristocratic clients. See H. Montgomery Hyde, *The Cleveland Street Scandal* (New York: Cowards, McCann, and Geoghegan, 1976), and Colin Simpson, Lewis Chester, and David Leitch, *The Cleveland Street Affair* (Boston: Little, Brown, 1976). Oblique and not so oblique allusions to Cleveland Street were a staple both of the critical response to *Dorian Gray* and of the press accounts of Wilde's trials. "Mr. Wilde has brains, and art, and style," wrote Charles Whibley in the *Scots Observer*, "but if he can write for none but outlawed noblemen and perverted telegraph boys, the sooner he takes to tailoring (or some other decent trade) the better for his own reputation and the public morals." See *Oscar Wilde: The Critical Heritage*, ed. Karl E. Beckson (New York: Barnes & Noble, 1970), 75.

14 Carson's first victory involved the message on Queensberry's calling card, which Carson insisted read "To Oscar Wilde, posing as a Sodomite." In fact Queensberry's handwriting resisted confident decoding. An alternate reading – one that Richard Ellmann says Wilde at first adopted – was "To Oscar Wilde, ponce and Sodomite." In either case an insult was intended, but "ponce and Sodomite" would have made Carson's task much more difficult, since it meant proving that Wilde had committed the acts of a ponce (a pimp) and a sodomist. By enforcing the "posing as" reading of the card, Carson ensured that the trial became an extended inquiry into Wilde's character. To pose as a sodomite required only that one appear to be the kind of person who would perform indecent acts. Wilde's counsel, Sir Edward Clarke, never contested Carson's reading of the calling card. For his biography of Wilde, Ellmann engaged a handwriting expert who deciphered the message as "To Oscar Wilde Posing Somdomite." See Ellmann, *Oscar Wilde* (New York: Alfred A. Knopf, 1988), 438, 613.

15 As Lee Edelman notes, while late-Victorian science considered "the gay body as inescapably textual," nevertheless "the textual significance…attributed to homosexuality [was] dauntingly overdetermined." By the 1880s and 90s, it was no longer sufficient to match physical stigmata with spiritual essence. See Edelman, "Homographesis," *The Yale Journal of Criticism* 3 (1989), 191. Cohen, *Talk on the Wilde Side*, 181–98, points out how Wilde's body became the object of much attention in press accounts of the trials.

16 H. Montgomery Hyde, *The Trials of Oscar Wilde* (London: William Hodge, 1948), 122. Queensberry himself seemed not to make any distinction between these two senses of "posing." To him, even pretending to be a "somdomite" was criminal. During questioning by Sir Edward Clarke, Wilde reported that he had confronted his accuser thus: "Then I asked, 'Lord Queensberry, do you seriously accuse your son and me of improper conduct?' He said, 'I do not say you are it, but you look it. You look it, and you pose as it, which is just as bad.'" See Hyde, *Trials*, 119.

17 *Ibid.*, 166.

18 *Ibid.*, 124, 167.

19 *Ibid.*, 124. In "Oscar Wilde, W. H., and the Unspoken Name of Love," *ELH* 58 (1991), 982–84, Lawrence Danson discusses Carson's invocation of the "ordinary reader" and argues that Wilde rejected common sense constructions of language in order to affirm "the power of *his* language to name *his* desire, precisely in its evasions, its silences, its refusals of determinate meaning" (984).

20 Hyde, *Trials*, 124.

21 Later in the novel Lord Henry dismisses "sound English common sense" as "the inherited stupidity of the race" (216).

22 Regenia Gagnier, *Idylls of the Marketplace: Oscar Wilde and the Victorian Public* (Stanford: Stanford University Press, 1986), 7–8.

23 Quoted in Gagnier, *Idylls of the Marketplace*, 8.

24 This aspect of Wilde's thought has received much fine critical attention over

the past decade. See especially Jonathan Dollimore, *Sexual Dissidence: Augustine to Wilde, Freud to Foucault* (Oxford: Clarendon, 1993), 8–23, 64–67; and Rita Felski, "The Counterdiscourse of the Feminine in Three Texts by Wilde, Husymans, and Sacher-Masoch," *Proceedings of the Modern Language Association* (hereafter *PMLA*) 106 (October 1991), esp. 1096–97.

25 See *Critical Heritage*, ed. Beckson, 73.

26 Rachel Bowlby, "Promoting Dorian Gray," *Oxford Literary Review* 9 (1987), 150.

27 On Spencer's influence, see Bruce Haley, "Wilde's 'Decadence' and the Positivist Tradition," *Victorian Studies* 28 (Winter 1985), 215–20. On Wilde's assimilation of Victorian evolutionist paradigms, see J. E. Chamberlin, *Ripe Was the Drowsy Hour: The Age of Oscar Wilde* (New York: Seabury Press, 1977), 48–52, 65–67; Michael S. Helfand and Philip E. Smith II, "Anarchy and Culture: The Evolutionary Turn of Cultural Criticism in the Work of Oscar Wilde," *Texas Studies in Language and Literature* 20 (1978), 199–215; and Helfand and Smith, *Oscar Wilde's Oxford Notebooks: A Portrait of Mind in the Making* (Oxford: Oxford University Press, 1989), 1–106.

28 "The Critic as Artist, with Some Remarks upon the Importance of Doing Nothing," in *The Artist as Critic*, ed. Ellmann, 314–408, at 383, 393. Rodney Shewan has argued for W. K. Clifford's influence on Wilde's notion of development. Wilde took notes in his commonplace book on Clifford's posthumously published lectures (1879), where he would have read: "To become crystallized, fixed in opinion and mode of thought, is to lose the great characteristic of life, by which it is distinguished from inanimate nature: the power of adapting itself to circumstances." The residual Lamarckianism of Clifford's position would not have appealed to Wilde, though (as Shewan notes) its Paterian qualities would. See Shewan, *Oscar Wilde: Art and Egotism* (London: Macmillan, 1977), 106–08.

29 "A map of the world that does not include Utopia is not worth glancing at, for it leaves out the one country at which Humanity is always landing." See "The Soul of Man Under Socialism," in *Artist as Critic*, ed. Ellmann, 269–70.

30 Quoted in Shewan, *Art and Egotism*, 108.

31 See "The Decay of Lying: An Observation," in *Artist as Critic*, ed. Ellmann, 297.

32 Cf Clifford's argument in "Conditions of Mental Development" (1868) concerning "the immense importance to a nation of checking the growth of conventionalities. It is quite possible for conventional values to get such power that progress is impossible...In the face of such a danger, *it is not right to be proper*" (Clifford's italics). Quoted in Shewan, *Art and Egotism*, 107.

33 *Critical Heritage*, ed. Beckson, 72.

34 Rupert Hart-Davis, ed., *The Letters of Oscar Wilde* (London: Rupert Hart-Davis, 1962), 259.

35 *Ibid.*

36 *Ibid.*, 263. Cf. Sinfield, *Wilde Century*: "Dorian arrives at disaster not because he abjures conventional moral principles but because he remains under their sway" (100).

37 "The Soul of Man Under Socialism," in *Artist as Critic*, ed. Ellmann, 270; Wilde's italics.

38 "The Portrait of Mr. W. H.," in *Artist as Critic*, ed. Ellmann, 152. Subsequent references are given parenthetically in the text.

39 On the tradition of the fatal book in the nineteenth century, see Dowling, *Language and Decadence*, 103–74. On the witness stand Wilde named *A Rebours* as the original of the book Lord Henry lends Dorian. See Hyde, *Trials*, 130–31. As Donald Lawler points out, however, Wilde elsewhere discounted Huysman's influence. See Lawler, *An Inquiry into Oscar Wilde's Revisions of* The Picture of Dorian Gray (New York: Garland, 1988), 67–75, for a discussion of other possible sources.

40 *Letters*, ed. Hart-Davis, 266. Reviewing *Dorian Gray* in the *St. James's Gazette*, Samuel Henry Jeyes deplored the fact that the novel "constantly hints, not obscurely, at disgusting sins and abominable crimes." See *Critical Heritage*, ed. Beckson, 68.

41 As D. A. Miller puts it, the function of an open secret "is not to conceal knowledge, so much as to conceal the knowledge of the knowledge." See *The Novel and the Police* (Berkeley: University of California Press, 1988), 205–06.

As will be clear, I am arguing that *Dorian Gray* is decidedly not what Peter J. Rabinowitz calls a "fragile text," though it is often treated as one. In "'Betraying the Sender': The Rhetoric and Ethics of Fragile Texts," *Narrative* 2 (October 1994), 201–13, Rabinowitz posits a corpus of texts whose value resides in their ability to "pass" as "straight" (in the sense of conforming to dominant ideologies) while also offering subversive messages to those able to understand them. Such a text requires "*two* audiences: one audience that's ignorant and another that knows the truth *and remains silent about it*" (205; emphasis in original). Rabinowitz further claims that the "performative success" of these works is irretrievably compromised once the "ignorant" portion of the audience is clued in; hence their status as "fragile" texts. Thus "those who know what the work is doing need to refrain from speaking about it if the work is to fulfill its rhetorical aims" (205). My point is that while critics often implicitly treat *Dorian Gray* as if it "performed" in this way, in fact at no time was there an audience that was not already "in the know."

42 Hyde, *Trials*, 229.

43 *Ibid.*, 344.

44 *The Importance of Being Earnest*, in Oscar Wilde, *The Complete Plays*, ed. H. Montgomery Hyde (London: Methuen, 1988), 229. It can of course be argued that decoding the homosexuality in *Dorian Gray* has usually involved no more than reading Wilde's life into his work. Certainly, Wilde's antagonists in court were often guilty of circular reasoning: they knew that Wilde was a sodomist because his novel endorsed sodomy, just as they knew that the novel endorsed sodomy because Wilde was himself a sodomist. Yet the persuasiveness of much of the finest recent criticism – Dollimore, Sedgwick, Danson, Cohen among others – is grounded in the refusal of biographical

readings of the novel. Implicit in all these works is the claim that the homoeroticism in *Dorian* would be discernible even if we knew nothing of its author. In "Writing Gone Wilde: Homoerotic Desire in the Closet of Representation," *PMLA* 102 (October 1987), for instance, Ed Cohen strives "to understand how 'everyone knows' what lurks behind Wilde's manifestly straight language" (805). Correctly rejecting the "crude biographical explanation," Cohen argues that homosexual desire is discernible in the novel's "aesthetic ideology," which "foregrounds representation with a eroticized milieu that inscribes the male body within circuits of male desire" (805).

45 W. Graham Robertson, *Time Was* (London, 1931), 135. We may suspect that Wilde is simply being disingenuous here, since he would have known that the carnation did in fact signify as a code for at least some in the audience. Still, as Sinfield points out (*Wilde Century*, 118, 128), the link between green carnations and male love was by no means as unproblematic in 1892 as has sometimes been assumed. Only with the publication of Robert Hichens's 1894 novel *The Green Carnation* was the connection cemented in the popular consciousness.

46 "Lord Arthur Savile's Crime," in Oscar Wilde, *Complete Shorter Fiction*, ed. Isobel Murray (Oxford: Oxford University Press, 1979), 27.

47 "The Sphinx without a Secret," in *Complete Shorter Fiction*, ed Murray, 55. The following quotation is on 58.

48 Needless to say, this trajectory of skepticism–belief–certainty–indifference inscribes a male model of sexual passion and activity.

49 William A. Cohen, "Willie and Wilde: Reading *The Portrait of Mr. W. H.*," *South Atlantic Quarterly* 88 (Winter 1989), 228–30.

50 On Wilde's use of pornographic puns, see Christopher Craft, "Alias Bunbury," *Representations* 31 (Summer 1990), 19–46. On sexual metaphors in "The Portrait of Mr. W. H." and their relation to Wildean aesthetics, see Kevin Kopelson, "Wilde, Barthes, and the Orgasmics of Truth," *Genders* 7 (Spring 1990), 22–31.

51 The spurt of blood does not appear in the revised 1893 version of the tale.

52 Dollimore, *Sexual Dissidence*, 67.

53 *Critical Heritage*, ed. Beckson, 72, 74–75, 76–77.

54 "The Decay of Lying," in *Artist as Critic*, ed. Ellmann, 305.

55 *Complete Plays*, ed. Hyde, 41.

56 Bristow, "Wilde, *Dorian Gray*, and Gross Indecency," 54.

57 Mosse, "Introduction" to Nordau, *Degeneration*, xv.

58 George Eliot, "The Natural History of German Life" (1856), in *Essays of George Eliot*, ed. Thomas Pinney (London: Routledge and Kegan Paul, 1963), 270.

59 Besant, *The Art of Fiction*, 13–14.

60 "The Soul of Man Under Socialism," in *Artist as Critic*, ed. Ellmann, 286.

4 FROM HEROIC FRIENDSHIP TO MALE ROMANCE

1 Wilde, *The Picture of Dorian Gray*, 133.

2 See Sedgwick, *Between Men.*

3 David Trotter, *The English Novel in History 1895–1920* (London: Routledge, 1993), 152.

4 See John Mackenzie, *Propaganda and Empire* (Manchester: Manchester University Press, 1984), and John Mackenzie, ed., *Imperialism and Popular Culture* (Manchester: Manchester University Press, 1986).

5 George Curzon, Marquess of Kedleston, *Frontiers* (Oxford: Oxford University Press, 1907), 58.

6 Phyllis Grosskurth, ed., *The Memoirs of John Addington Symonds: The Secret Homosexual Life of a Nineteenth-Century Man of Letters* (Chicago: University of Chicago Press, 1984), 99. Further references to this work, abbreviated *M*, are given parenthetically in the text.

7 Letter dated 1 February 1889, in *The Letters of John Addington Symonds*, ed. Herbert M. Schueller and Robert L. Peters, 3 vols. (Detroit: Wayne State University Press, 1967–69), III, 345–47.

8 *Letters*, ed. Schueller and Peters, III, 345, 347.

9 John Addington Symonds, "A Problem in Modern Ethics" (1890), rpt. in *Homosexuality: A Cross Cultural Approach*, ed. Donald Webster Cory (New York: Julian Press, 1956), 3, 53, 60. Further references to this work, abbreviated *ME*, are given parenthetically in the text.

10 The most notable examples are Whitman's "Calamus" poems, which Symonds says "became for me a sort of Bible" (189). Symonds engaged in a decades-long correspondence with Whitman, and eventually wrote a book on him. On the influence of Whitman's homoerotic poetry on late-Victorian English writers, see Sedgwick, *Between Men*, 201–17.

11 In her biography of Symonds, Phyllis Grosskurth quotes numerous letters to this effect. In 1864 Symonds wrote to Graham Dakyns: "I find it wholly impossible to say anything that is not grossly autobiographical." The following year Symonds confided to Dakyns that he could do no other than "write Essays upon the matter of [my] own heart." Again to Dakyns, this time in 1872, he wrote: "I cannot write in verse to any purpose except upon the old Subject." See Grosskurth, *John Addington Symonds: A Biography* (London: Longmans, Green, 1964), 80, 102, 151.

12 See Symonds, *A Problem in Greek Ethics* (1883), rpt. in *Studies in Sexual Inversion* (n.p., 1928), 72–73. Further references to this work, abbreviated *GE*, are given parenthetically in the text.

13 Letter dated 13 January 1880, in *Letters*, ed. Schueller and Peters, II, 621. Of *Vagabunduli Libelles* (1884) Symonds wrote to Dakyns (10 April 1882): "The key to the whole I may not publish." (*Letters*, ed. Schueller and Peters, II, 743.) As these quotations suggest, Symonds, unlike Wilde, proceeded on the assumption that homoerotic desire could be "encoded" within texts. Indeed, Timothy d'Arch Smith argues that Symonds's practice of indirec-

tion and evasion provided a model for the Uranian poets of the fin de siècle. See *Love in Earnest: Some Notes on the Lives and Writings of English Uranian Poets from 1889 to 1930* (London: Routledge and Kegan Paul, 1970), 12: "The most important lesson taught in Symonds's published writings was 'the ways of evasion'."

14 Wayne Koestenbaum, *Double Talk: The Erotics of Male Literary Collaboration* (London: Routledge, 1989), 5.

15 For the history of Symonds's manuscript, see the foreword to Grosskurth's edition of the *Memoirs*, 9–12.

16 Letter dated 6 December 1890, in *Letters*, ed. Schueller and Peters, III, 476.

17 Letter dated November 1870, in *Letters*, ed. Schueller and Peters, II, 118. Like Rossetti, Symonds eventually disinterred his poems. Earlier still, in July 1869, he had allowed Sidgwick to hurl the key to the desolation box into the river Avon, though again the poems were quickly returned from exile. See Grosskurth, *John Addington Symonds*, 128.

18 Letter dated 3 March 1886, in *Letters*, ed. Schueller and Peters, III, 120–21.

19 Asked by Charles Frederick Gill, "What is the 'Love that dare not speak its name'?" Wilde replied:

> "The Love that dare not speak its name" in this century is such a great affection of an elder for a younger man as there was between David and Jonathan, such as Plato made the very basis of philosophy, and such as you find in the sonnets of Michelangelo and Shakespeare. It is that deep, spiritual affection that is as pure as it is perfect. It dictates and pervades great works of art...It is in this century misunderstood, so much misunderstood that it may be described as the "Love that dare not speak its name," and on account of it I am placed where I am now. It is beautiful, it is fine, it is the noblest form of affection. There is nothing unnatural about it. It is intellectual, and it repeatedly exists between an elder and a younger man, when the elder man has intellect, and the younger man has all the joy, hope and glamour of life before him. That it should be so the world does not understand. The world mocks at it and sometimes puts one in the pillory for it.

See Hyde, *Trials*, 236.

20 Cohen, *Talk on the Wilde Side*, 200–01.

21 Dowling, *Hellenism and Homosexuality*, xv; see also 27–92.

22 John Addington Symonds, *Studies in the Greek Poets*, 2 vols. (1875; rpt. New York: Harper & Bros., 1880), II, 382.

23 On the relation of physical and mental health in Victorian culture, see Bruce Haley, *The Healthy Body and Victorian Culture* (Cambridge: Harvard University Press, 1978), esp. 3–45.

24 At one point in his *Memoirs* Symonds writes that it is "an article in my creed of social duty" that those suffering from hereditary "abnormalities" like inversion "ought to refrain from procreation" (260), for the moment apparently forgetting his four daughters. Their names were Janet, Lotta, Margaret, and Katherine.

25 Letter dated 22 July 1890 to Horatio Forbes Brown, in *Letters*, ed. Schueller and Peters, III, 477.

26 Sedgwick, *Between Men*, 210. Sedgwick usefully situates Symonds within the "new configurations of male homosexuality" that opened up in the last quarter of the century for middle-class men. As opposed to the effeminacy associated with aristocratic homosexual behavior, middle-class men "who explored a range of forms and intensities of male homosocial bonds tried to do so without admitting culturally defined 'femininity' into them as a structuring term. Even when men of this class formed overt sexual liaisons with other men, they seem to have perceived the exclusion of women from their intimate lives as virilizing them, more than they perceived the choice of a male object as feminizing them" (207).

27 William Watson, "The Fall of Fiction," *Fortnightly Review* 50 (1888), 324.

28 Watson's concerns were echoed a decade later by Edmund Gosse. Throughout the nineteenth century, Gosse writes, "English fiction had been straying further and further from the peculiarly national type of Ben Jonson and Smollett." Though the early Dickens had briefly "resuscitated" the form, Gosse like Watson worries that the future of the novel, and by extension the nation, will be one of increasing enervation. See Gosse, *A Short History of Modern English Literature* (1897; rpt. New York: D. Appleton, 1905), 392.

29 Andrew Lang, "A Dip in Criticism," *Contemporary Review* 54 (1888), 502. Watson fired a last salvo in "Mr. Haggard and His Henchmen," *Fortnightly Review* 50 (1888), 684–88.

30 "The Present State of the English Novel," in *Collected Essays and Papers*, III, 121. For his collected works, Saintsbury combined two essays with this title, one written in 1888, the other in 1892. The passages I quote originated in the 1888 essay.

31 Lang, "Realism and Romance," *Contemporary Review* 52 (November 1887).

32 Maudsley, *Body and Will*, 321.

33 See *Degeneration*, ed. Gilman and Chamberlin.

34 E. B. Tylor, *Primitive Culture*, 2 vols. (1871; rpt. New York: Harper & Row, 1970), II, 533.

35 Andrew Lang, *Adventures Among Books* (London: Longmans, Green, 1905), 37.

36 Lang, "Realism and Romance," 689.

37 Saintsbury, "The Present State of the English Novel," III, 126.

38 Andrew Lang, *Essays in Little* (New York: Charles Scribner's Sons, 1894), 141.

39 Rider Haggard, "About Fiction," *Contemporary Review* 51 (1887), 175.

40 Sandra Siegel, "Literature and Degeneration: The Representation of 'Decadence'," in *Degeneration*, ed. Gilman and Chamberlin, 199–219.

41 Showalter, *Sexual Anarchy*, 79. Other recent examinations of late-Victorian romance and adventure novels include Patrick Brantlinger, *Rule of Darkness: British Literature and Imperialism 1830–1914* (Ithaca: Cornell University Press, 1988), esp. 227–53, and Sandra M. Gilbert and Susan Gubar, *Sexchanges*, vol. 2 of their *No Man's Land: The Place of the Woman Writer in the Twentieth Century* (New Haven: Yale University Press, 1989), 3–46.

42 Rider Haggard, "Elephant Smashing and Lion Shooting" (1894), quoted in Norman Etherington, *Rider Haggard* (Boston: Twayne, 1984), 66.

43 Frederic Harrison, "The Decadence of Romance," *Forum* 17 (1894), 223–24.
44 For an informative account of the relation of nineteenth-century publishing practices to the status of female authors, see Gaye Tuchman with Nina E. Fortin, *Edging Women Out: Victorian Novelists, Publishers, and Social Change* (New Haven: Yale University Press, 1989). More general accounts of the changes in publishing practices over the last quarter of the century that led to the collapse of the three-decker are Richard D. Altick, *The English Common Reader: A Social History of the Mass Reading Public, 1800–1900* (Chicago: University of Chicago Press, 1957), 294–318; John Gross, *The Rise and Fall of the Man of Letters: Aspects of English Literary Life Since 1800* (London: Weidenfeld, 1969), 204–40; Guinevere L. Griest, *Mudie's Circulating Library and the Victorian Novel* (Bloomington: University of Indiana Press, 1970), 120–212; and Keating, *Haunted Study*, 22–27.
45 "About Fiction," 175. The best known expression of male hysteria at the "feminization" of fiction is George Moore's *Literature at Nurse* (London: Vizetelly, 1885).
46 Lang, "Realism and Romance," 693, 692.
47 Quoted in Bell, *Robert Louis Stevenson*, 19. Even Saintsbury, despite his affection for romance fiction, thought that the "purity, simplicity, and...strength" of traditional English writing had suffered "permanent or at least lasting damage" in modern fiction. Examining the stylistic mannerisms of "our younger writers," Saintsbury calls them "symptoms...[or] signs of decadence or transition." He then adds: "Whether it is to be decadence or transition, that is the question." See *A History of Nineteenth Century Literature* (London: Macmillan, 1896), 461, 464–67.
48 Quoted in Cross, *The Common Writer*, 214. An irked Thomas Hardy no doubt spoke for the many writers in Balfour's audience when he noted in his diary later: "We hid our diminished heads."
49 In this context see Chris Bonge's analysis of the nostalgia inherent in late-Victorian imperialism in *Exotic Memories: Literature, Colonialism, and the Fin de Siècle* (Stanford: Stanford University Press, 1991).
50 Bernard Porter, *The Lion's Share: A Short History of British Imperialism 1850–1983*, 2nd ed. (London: Longman, 1984), xi.
51 J. A. Hobson, *Imperialism: A Study* (London: George Allen & Unwin, 1902). The use of imperialism as a palliative for domestic ills was straightforwardly urged by Cecil Rhodes in 1895. Attending a meeting of unemployed workers in London's East End, Rhodes was alarmed by the "wild speeches" he heard and "became more than ever convinced of the importance of imperialism." The acceleration of the imperialist agenda was the "solution to the social problem" and the only way to prevent revolution. "The Empire, as I have always said, is a bread and butter question. If you want to avoid civil war, you must become imperialists." Lenin made Rhodes's statement into one of the cornerstones of his critique of imperialism. See V. I. Lenin, *Imperialism: The Highest Stage of Capitalism* (New York: International Publishers, 1939), 79. For useful accounts of imperialism's compensatory

aspects, see Elie Halevy, *Imperialism and the Rise of Labour* (1927; rpt. New York: Barnes and Noble, 1961); A. P. Thornton, *The Imperial Idea and Its Enemies* (London: Macmillan, 1959); Ronald Hyam, *Britain's Imperial Century 1815–1914* (New York: Barnes and Noble, 1976); John M. MacKenzie, *Propaganda and Empire: The Manipulation of British Public Opinion 1880–1960* (Manchester: Manchester University Press, 1984); Eric Hobsbawm, *The Age of Empire 1875–1914* (New York: Vintage, 1989).

52 Two years after Hobson's *Imperialism* was published, a memorandum from the Director-General of the Army Medical Service suggested that the Boer War had been lost because British men were shorter, smaller, weaker, and more sickly than their immediate ancestors. This widely publicized report provoked a scandal, quickly prompting a series of Parliamentary hearings to determine "the causes and indications of degeneracy" among the nation's adult male population. Taylor's memorandum is reprinted as Appendix I in Parliament's *Report of the Interdepartmental Committee on Physical Deterioration* (London, 1904), 95–97. Taylor drew on an earlier article by General Sir Frederick Maurice, who claimed that sixty percent of the male population of Britain were physically unfit for military service. See Maurice, "Where to Get Men," *Contemporary Review* 81 (1902), 78–86. To modern ears, the homoerotic overtones of Maurice's title are audible enough, and they indicate once again the continuities between the male love idealized by Wilde and Symonds and the homosocial bonds that structure "straight" culture. After noting such continuities, Alan Sinfield reminds us that "various celebrated imperialists, including Cecil Rhodes and General Gordon, married late, were accompanied by boys, and wrote in praise of them. Lord Kitchener, whose World War I poster told British boys that their country needed them, found his own peace with an aide-de-camp." See Sinfield, *The Wilde Century*, 67.

53 Bristow, *Empire Boys*, 20.

54 "Recent reports on the deterioration of our race ought to be taken in time before it is too late," Baden-Powell darkly warns in the first edition of his handbook for the Scouts, adding that British men had become "wishy-washy slackers without any go in them." See R. S. S. Baden-Powell, *Scouting for Boys* (London: Horace Cox, 1908). On the history of the scouts, see Michael Rosenthal, *The Character Factory: Baden-Powell and the Origins of the Boy Scout Movement* (New York: Pantheon, 1986). On the relation between scouting and empire, see Bristow, *Empire Boys*, 170–94; on the relation between scouting and manliness, see Allen Warren, "Popular Manliness: Baden Powell, Scouting and Development of Manly Character," in *Manliness and Morality: Middle-Class Masculinity in Britain and America 1800–1940*, ed. J. A. Mangan and James Walvin (New York: St. Martin's Press, 1987), 199–219. Baden-Powell used Rome as an object lesson of the dangers of falling away from "the standards of [one's] forefathers," a common rhetorical move of the period. The title of Thomas Hodgkin's 1898 essay, "The Fall of the Roman Empire and its Lessons for Us," describes the subject matter of

numerous polemics. Though Hodgkin concludes that England's empire would endure because its hegemony was based on moral rather than military might (an argument first adumbrated by Macauley seventy-five years earlier), others were not so sure. See Hodgkin, "The Fall of the Roman Empire and its Lessons for Us," *Contemporary Review* 73 (1898), 51–70. See also Raymond F. Betts, "The Allusion to Rome in British Imperialist Thought of the Late Nineteenth and Early Twentieth Centuries," *Victorian Studies* 15 (December 1971), 149–59.

55 As Bristow writes, "by the end of the century, then, tenets of imperialism were shaping the ideological dimensions of subjects studied in school. Yet these new rulings...were not imposed by fiat on the world that schoolchildren were learning to appreciate. Instead they reinforced already established imperial assumptions that had for many years acted as the main precepts guiding the production of adventure fiction for children" (*Empire Boys*, 20).

56 Haggard, "About Fiction," 172.

57 Martin Green, *Dreams of Adventure, Deeds of Empire* (New York: Basic Books, 1979).

58 Sigmund Freud, *The Interpretation of Dreams*, trans. James Strachey (New York: Avon, 1965), 490–91. Further page references are given parenthetically in the text.

59 Quoted in Showalter, *Sexual Anarchy*, 88.

60 Henry Miller, *The Books in My Life* (London: Peter Owen, 1952), 96.

61 Rider Haggard, *She* (1887; rpt. Oxford: Oxford University Press, 1991), 19. Further page references are given parenthetically in the text.

62 John Goode argues that fin-de-siècle representations of *femmes fatale* like Ayesha differ from earlier portrayals in their (usually occluded) awareness of them as engaged in "feminist" rewritings of female subjectivity and sexuality. These are women "whose sexuality is a critical, self-realizing (and therefore within the ideology, unnatural) mode of knowledge. At the same time, it is a category in which the subjectivity of the woman becomes an object of man's ordeal, a force which disorients the given, hegemonic world-view." Goode sees this kind of "disorienting" operating most forcefully in *She*. See "Woman and the Literary Text," in *The Rights and Wrongs of Women*, ed. Juliet Mitchell and Ann Oakley (Harmondsworth: Penguin, 1976), 231, 235–37.

63 Gilbert and Gubar, *Sexchanges*, 35.

64 Neither Ayesha's body nor her speech has been deformed by the pressures of history. Though Holly, "a learned man" (147), has with long study mastered Arabic, Greek, Latin, and Hebrew, he cannot speak them with "the music of the sweet tongue" (146) that Ayesha commands. She knows these languages in the original "purity" associated with speech, before they were "debased and defiled" into writing (146). Later, overcome by Ayesha's beauty, Holly falls on his knees and begins to babble "in a sad mixture of languages" (190).

65 For a discussion of Haggard's revisions, see Norman Etherington, *The Annotated* She*: A Critical Edition of H. Rider Haggard's Victorian Romance* (Bloomington: Indiana University Press, 1991), xix–xxxiii.

66 Sir Henry Rider Haggard, *The Days of My Life*, 2 vols. (London: Longmans, Green, 1926), I, 248. Haggard biographer Morton Cohen notes that "Haggard was very particular about the map [for *King Solomon's Mines*], insisting that it be drawn on linen with real blood." See Cohen, *Rider Haggard: His Life and Works* (London: Hutchinson, 1948), 91. In 1893 Harry How visited Haggard's home for a celebrity interview with the now-famous author, who showed him the map and the Sherd and recounted the anecdotes connected with them as if they were, by this time, old familiar stories. See Harry How, *Illustrated Interviews* (London: George Newnes, 1893), 62–64. According to Peter Beresford Ellis in *Henry Rider Haggard: A Voice From the Infinite* (London: Routledge and Kegan Paul, 1978), 117, the Sherd of Amenartas was eventually donated to the collection of the Norwich Museum, where it still resides.

67 The connection between writing and the male body is made even more explicit in *King Solomon's Mines* (1885), where Jose da Silvestra uses his own blood to produce his map. For his writing utensil he uses a cleft bone taken from a male corpse; Allan Quartermain takes this bone away with him and continues to use it as a pen.

68 Laura Chrisman, "The Imperial Unconscious? Representations of Imperial Discourse," *Critical Quarterly* 32 (1990), 45.

69 In this context we should also note Haggard's personal conviction that he had lived through at least five previous incarnations. See *Days of My Life*, II, 167–72.

70 Alan Sandison notes that Haggard's "consuming preoccupation is with time" and calls attention to a passage in the introduction to *Allan Quartermain* (1885): "Out of the soil of barbarism has [civilization] grown like a tree, and as I believe, into the soil like a tree it will once more, sooner or later, fall again, as the Egyptian civilisation fell, as the Hellenic civilisation fell, and as the Roman civilisation fell." See Sandison, "A Matter of Vision: Rudyard Kipling and Rider Haggard," in *The Age of Kipling*, ed. John Gross (New York: Simon and Schuster, 1972), 127–34, at 129–30.

71 The novel also makes clear that the people of Kor did not simply "fall" but rather "degenerated" into the Amahagger, who are explicitly offered as object lessons in the dangers of race mixing. Having intermarried with other peoples, the survivors of Kor find their racial integrity fatally compromised. Ayesha tells Holly, "the race of the Amahagger that is now is a bastard brood of the mighty sons of Kor" (181). Like Kipling, Haggard portrays such "curious mingling" of bloods (181) as leading inevitably to race decay.

72 Ella Haggard published an epic poem, *Myra, or the Rose of the East*, in 1857. A second long poem, *Life and Its Author*, was published posthumously in 1890. Rider's sense of his mother is perhaps best revealed by his decision to dedicate his 1889 novel about Cleopatra to her.

73 See Koestenbaum, *Double Talk*, 143–61.

74 Gilbert and Gubar argue that "it is surely significant that Leo's quest is not

only *for* a woman, it is in behalf of a woman. Both his goal and impetus, therefore, suggest his secondariness and instrumentality" (*Sexchanges*, 12).

75 See Showalter, *Sexual Anarchy*, 59–75, for a discussion of Eliot's reputation in the fin de siècle.

5 STOKER AND REVERSE COLONIZATION

1 See Charles Dilke, *Greater Britain: A Record of Travel in English-Speaking Countries during 1866 and 1867* (New York: Harper & Brothers, 1868).

2 Indeed, throughout Haggard's novel Ayesha is shown to be a more committed and thoroughgoing imperialist than either Holly or Vincey. *She* was written between January and March 1886, and two events from those months – Gladstone's return to office and the Irish Home Rule debate – surface briefly in the *Graphic* magazine version of the text. (Haggard loathed Gladstone and the Irish with equal fervor.) Apprised by her guests of the general political situation in England, Ayesha takes a firm line: the prime minister is to be hotpotted, the Irish exterminated. Andrew Lang persuaded Haggard to excise these passages from the first edition of *She*, along with Holly's praise of Ayesha as "a kind of glorified Bismarck." As Ayesha's highhanded treatment of the Amahagger indicates, the worst excesses of imperial brutality are projected onto her, where they can be both repudiated and, at the novel's end, atoned for through her sacrificial immolation.

3 Quoted in Bernard Bergonzi, *The Early H. G. Wells: A Study of the Scientific Romances* (Manchester: Manchester University Press, 1961), 124.

4 H. G. Wells, *The War of the Worlds* (1898; rpt. New York: Pocket Books, 1962), 292. Subsequent page references are given parenthetically in the text.

5 For a richly suggestive account of the centrality of pain and punishment in Wells's fiction, see V. S. Pritchett, "The Scientific Romances" (1946), reprinted in *H. G. Wells: A Collection of Critical Essays*, ed. Bernard Bergonzi (Englewood Cliffs, NJ: Prentice-Hall, 1976), 32–38.

6 Frank McConnell notes that "the Martians are not, after all, aliens. They are ourselves, mutated beyond sympathy, though not beyond recognition." See *The Science Fiction of H. G. Wells* (New York: Oxford University Press, 1981), 130.

7 The artilleryman does not appear in Wells's first version of the tale, which was serialized in 1897 in *Pearson's Weekly*. Wells added the episodes when he revised the story for book publication the following year.

8 On eugenics, see G. R. Searle, *The Quest for National Efficiency: A Study in British Politics and Political Thought 1899–1914* (Berkeley: University of California Press, 1971); Searle, *Eugenics and Politics in Britain 1900–1914* (Leyden: Noordhoff International Publishers, 1976); Bernard Semmell, *Imperialism and Social Reform: English Social-Imperial Thought 1895–1914* (Cambridge: Harvard University Press, 1960); and Lindsay Farrall, *The Origins and Growth of the English Eugenics Movement, 1865–1925* (New York: Garland, 1985). Wells's proto-Fascistic vision of the samurai can be found in *A Modern Utopia* (1905).

9 An instructive contrast can be drawn between Wells's cautionary tale and a sequel rushed into print later that same year in the United States. Garrett P. Serviss's *Edison's Conquest of Mars* claimed to pick up the story where Wells left off. In it an American space fleet, armed and outfitted by a patriotic band of scientist-inventors led by, yes, Thomas Edison, successfully invades Mars in retaliation for the earlier attack. On the basis of Serviss's straightforwardly imperialist novel, which was apparently a financial success, it would seem that America – young, brash, clear-conscienced – did not yet share Britain's anxiety over imperial decay. For an account of Serviss's novel, see Philip Klass, "Wells, Welles, and the Martians," *New York Times Book Review*, 28 February 1988.

10 In his exhaustive survey, I. F. Clarke identifies 165 invasion tales published between 1871 and 1900, including 25 sequels or responses to Chesney's novel in 1871 alone. See *Voices Prophesying War 1763–1984* (London: Oxford University Press, 1966), 228–33. For other discussions of invasion scare novels, see Samuel Hynes, *The Edwardian Turn of Mind* (Princeton: Princeton University Press, 1967), 34–53; and Cecil D. Eby, *The Road to Armageddon: The Martial Spirit in English Popular Fiction, 1870–1914* (Durham: Duke University Press, 1988), 1–37.

11 Daniel Pick, *War Machine: The Rationalization of Slaughter in the Modern Age* (New Haven: Yale University Press, 1993), 115–35. On the relation between immigration and English fears of race-mixing in the fin de siècle, see David Feldman, "The Importance of Being English: Jewish Immigration and the Decay of Liberal England," in *Metropolis: London Histories and Representations*, ed. David Feldman and Gareth Stedman Jones (London: Routledge, 1989), 56–84.

12 Barbara Arnett Melchiori provides summaries of many dynamite novels in her *Terrorism in the Late Victorian Novel* (London: Croom Helm, 1985).

13 See Brantlinger, *Rule of Darkness: British Literature and Imperialism 1830–1914* (Ithaca: Cornell University Press, 1988), 228–29. For a somewhat different account of the conjunction of Gothic and imperialism, see Judith Wilt, "The Imperial Mouth: Imperialism, the Gothic, and Science Fiction," *Journal of Popular Culture* 14 (Spring 1981), 618–28. Wilt sees Britain's "imperial anxieties" summoning up "the great gothic and science fiction tales of the 80s and 90s" (620), which in turn do the cultural work of "subverting" imperial ideology.

14 David Punter, *Literature of Terror: A History of Gothic Fictions from 1765 to the Present Day* (London: Longmans, 1980), 62. Recently, Gothic fiction has benefited from the general turn within the academy to historicist studies. A number of critics have begun to place *Dracula* in the context of late-Victorian culture. Carol A. Senf sees Stoker reacting to the phenomenon of the "New Woman" of 1890s fiction; Ernest Fontana reads most of the novel's characters, including the Count himself, as types of Lombroso's criminal man; Christopher Craft relates the novel's "anxiety over the potential fluidity of gender roles" to Victorian discourses on sexual "inversion";

Jennifer Wicke delineates the novel's participation in emerging technologies of consumption and mass culture; Franco Moretti sees Dracula as a "metaphor" for monopoly capitalism that late-Victorian bourgeois culture refuses to recognize in itself; and Kathleen Spencer situates the novel within a host of fin-de-siècle discourses including degeneration, materialist medicine, and parapsychology. See Senf, "*Dracula*: Stoker's Response to the New Woman," *Victorian Studies* 26 (1982), 33–49; Fontana, "Lombroso's Criminal Man and Stoker's *Dracula*," *Victorian Newsletter* 66 (1984), 25–27; Craft, "'Kiss Me With Those Red Lips': Gender and Inversion in Bram Stoker's *Dracula*," *Representations* 8 (1984), 107–33; Wicke, "Vampiric Typewriting: *Dracula* and its Media," *ELH* 59 (1992), 467–93; Moretti, "The Dialectic of Fear," *New Left Review* 136 (1982), 67–85; Spencer, "Purity and Danger: *Dracula*, the Urban Gothic, and the Late Victorian Degeneracy Crisis," *ELH* 59 (1992), 197–225.

15 John Allen Stevenson, "A Vampire in the Mirror: The Sexuality of *Dracula*," *PMLA* 103 (1988), 139–49. Stevenson's remark is surprising, since his essay convincingly places *Dracula* in the context of late-century thought on marriage, race, and exogamy. Convincing psychoanalytic readings of *Dracula* include C. F. Bentley, "The Monster in the Bedroom: Sexual Symbolism in Bram Stoker's *Dracula*," *Literature and Psychology* 22 (1972), 27–32; Stephanie Demetrakapoulous, "Feminism, Sex-Role Exchanges, and Other Subliminal Fantasies in Bram Stoker's *Dracula*," *Frontiers* 2 (1977), 104–13; Carrol L. Fry, "Fictional Conventions and Sexuality in *Dracula*," *Victorian Newsletter* 42 (1972), 20–22; Gail Griffin, "'Your Girls That You All Love Are Mine': *Dracula* and the Victorian Male Sexual Imagination," *International Journal of Women's Studies* 3 (1980), 454–65; Maurice Richardson, "The Psychoanalysis of Ghost Stories," *Twentieth Century* 166 (1959), 419–31; Phyllis Roth, "Suddenly Sexual Women in Bram Stoker's *Dracula*," *Literature and Psychology* 27 (1977), 113–21. I am not suggesting that there is a single psychoanalytic paradigm that these writers all follow, only each considers psychoanalysis as the critical approach best suited to Stoker's novel.

16 *The Spectator* 79 (31 July 1897), 151.

17 A concern with questions of empire and colonization can in fact be found in nearly all of Stoker's tales. In works such as "Under the Sunset" (1882), *The Snake's Pass* (1890), *The Mystery of the Sea* (1902), and *The Man* (1905) narratives of invasion, while not central to the plot, intrude continually upon the main action of the story. Legends of French invasions of Ireland in *The Snake's Pass*; attacks by the Children of Death on the Land Under the Sunset in the fairy tales; accounts of the Spanish Armada, Sir Francis Drake, and, in a more contemporary vein, the Spanish-American War of 1898 in *The Mystery of the Sea*; allusions to the Norman invasion of Saxon England in *The Man* – in each work, seemingly unrelated narratives of imperial expansion and disruption themselves disrupt the primary story, as if Stoker were grappling with issues he could not wholly articulate through his main plot. And, as his references to the Armada and to Norman and French invasions suggest,

Stoker is everywhere concerned with attacks directed specifically against the British Isles.

Stoker's more overtly Gothic fictions – *The Jewel of Seven Stars* (1903), *The Lady of the Shroud* (1909), and *The Lair of the White Worm* (1911) – fit Patrick Brantlinger's paradigm of imperial Gothic (see note 13 above), with its emphasis on atavism, the supernatural, and psychic regression. Each of the "heroines" in these novels – Queen Tera, Princess Teuta, Lady Arabella – represents the eruption of archaic and ultimately dangerous forces in modern life. (That Stoker associates these eruptions with women is hardly coincidental. Fear of women is never far from the surface of his novels.) Equally important is the fact that each of these Gothic fantasies intersects with narratives of imperial decline and fall: the decay of the Egyptian dynasties in *Jewel*, the defeat of the Turkish empire in *Shroud*, the collapse of the Roman empire in *Lair*. The conjunction of Gothic and empire brings Stoker's later novels thematically closer to *Dracula*. If they cannot match *Dracula*'s power and sophistication, this is in part because Stoker became increasingly unwilling or simply unable to address the complex connections between his fictions and the late-Victorian crisis of empire.

18 Carol Senf, "*Dracula*: The Unseen Face in the Mirror," *Journal of Narrative Technique* 9 (1979), 160–70; Burton Hatlen, "The Return of the Repressed/Oppressed in Bram Stoker's *Dracula*," *Minnesota Review* 15 (1980), 80–97; Judith Wilt, *Ghosts of the Gothic* (Princeton: Princeton University Press, 1980). See also Richard Wasson's "The Politics of *Dracula*," *English Literature in Transition* 9 (1960), 24–27.

19 See Joseph Bierman, "The Genesis and Dating of *Dracula* from Bram Stoker's Working Notes," *Notes and Queries* 24 (1977), 39–41. For a brief description of Stoker's manuscripts and notes for *Dracula*, including a "List of Sources" that Stoker drew up, see Phyllis Roth, *Bram Stoker* (Boston: Twayne, 1982), 145–46. Stoker gleaned his version of Carpathian history and culture entirely from travel narratives, guidebooks, and various works on Eastern European superstitions, legends, and folktales. Daniel Farson, one of Stoker's biographers, mentions his "genius for research" (*The Man Who Wrote* Dracula: *A Biography of Bram Stoker* [London: Michael Joseph, 1975], 148). Stoker's debt to Le Fanu is most immediately evident in a chapter deleted from *Dracula*, in which Harker, traveling to Castle Dracula, discovers the mausoleum of a "Countess Dolingen of Gratz in Styria." The chapter was later reprinted separately as "Dracula's Guest." See *The Bram Stoker Bedside Companion: Ten Stories by the Author of* Dracula," ed. Charles Osborne (New York: Taplinger, 1973).

20 Bram Stoker, *Dracula* (1897; rpt. Harmondsworth: Penguin, 1984), 286. Further page references to the novel are given in the text.

21 I have based my observations on standard Victorian and Edwardian works in English on the region, which include John Paget, *Hungary and Transylvania* (London: Murray, 1855); James O. Noyes, *Roumania* (New York: Rudd & Carlton, 1857); Charles Boner, *Transylvania: Its Products and Its People* (London:

Longmans, 1865); Andrew W. Crosse, *Round About the Carpathians* (Edinburgh and London: William Blackwood and Sons, 1878); C. Johnson, *On the Track of the Crescent* (London: Hurst & Blackett, 1885); M. Edith Durham, *The Burden of the Balkans* (London: Edward Arnold, 1905); Jean Victor Bates, *Our Allies and Enemies in the Near East* (New York: E. P. Dutton, n.d.); and especially Emily Gerard, *The Land Beyond the Forest: Facts, Figures, and Fancies from Transylvania*, 2 vols. (Edinburgh and London: William Blackwood and Sons, 1888).

22 Bates, *Allies and Enemies*, 3.

23 Boner, *Transylvania*, 1–2.

24 Stevenson, "Vampire in the Mirror," 144.

25 Gerard, *Land Beyond the Forest*, I, 304–05. Scholars have long recognized Stoker's reliance on Gerard's book. See Roth, *Bram Stoker*, 13–14, and Leonard Wolf, *The Annotated Dracula* (New York: Clarkson Potter, 1975), xiii–xiv and references in his annotations throughout.

26 Daniel Pick makes this point in *Faces of Degeneration*, 167–68.

27 A full discussion of the gender issues raised by Dracula is outside the scope of this essay. Many critics have discussed the thinly disguised fear of women evident in the novel. In addition to Craft, Demetrakapoulous, Fry, Griffin, Roth, and Weissman, see Marjorie Howes, "The Mediation of the Feminine: Bisexuality, Homoerotic Desire, and Self-Expression in Bram Stoker's *Dracula*," *Texas Studies in Language and Literature* 30 (Spring 1988), 104–19; and Ann Williams, "Si(g)ns of the Fathers," *Texas Studies in Language and Literature* 33 (Winter 1991), 445–63.

28 See L. P. Curtis, *Anglo-Saxons and Celts: A Study of Anti-Irish Prejudice in Victorian England* (Bridgeport, CT: Bridgeport University Press, 1968).

29 Bram Stoker, "The Censorship of Fiction," *Nineteenth Century and After* 64 (1908), 479–87.

30 Critics who do address the travel motifs in *Dracula* generally emphasize travel's connections to psychology rather than to politics. "Transylvania is Europe's unconscious," asserts Geoffrey Wall ("'Different from Writing': *Dracula* in 1897," *Literature and History* 10 [1984], 20). Alan Johnson quotes Wall approvingly, and argues that Harker's journey to Transylvania is a "symbolic journey into his own mind" ("Bent and Broken Necks: Signs of Design in Stoker's *Dracula*," *Victorian Newsletter* 72 [1987], 21, 23).

31 Gerard, *Land Beyond the Forest*, I, 30.

32 See, for example, the opening of Noyes's *Roumania* (1857). Noyes, an American surgeon living in Vienna, ascends "a lofty mountain" overlooking the city and gazes across the river at the "Orient": "There, looking into the purple distance eastward…I resolved to visit that mysterious Orient whose glowing portals seemed to open just beyond" (1).

33 Wolfgang Iser, *The Implied Reader: Patterns of Communication in Prose Fiction from Bunyan to Beckett* (Baltimore: Johns Hopkins University Press, 1974), 34.

34 Crosse, *Round About the Carpathians*, 342.

35 Gerard, *Land Beyond the Forest*, I, 211.

36 Williams, "Si(g)ns of the Fathers," 446.

37 Craft, "'Kiss Me with Those Red Lips,'" 107. Spencer concurs with this judgment, adding that late-Victorian Gothic was eminently suited both to articulate "the cultural crisis Britain experienced" at this moment and to "symbolically expel" frightening and disruptive elements ("Purity and Danger," 208, 218). Spencer persuasively argues for the existence of a genre she calls the "conservative fantastic" (209), into which she places *Dracula*.

38 David Seed, "The Narrative Method of *Dracula*," *Nineteenth-Century Fiction* 40 (June 1985), 73–74. See also Rosemary Jann, "Saved by Science? The Mixed Messages of Stoker's *Dracula*," *Texas Studies in Language and Literature* 31 (Summer 1989), 279: "The narrative repeatedly foregrounds the technology of information management in such a way as to reinforce the implicit equation of recorded fact with a 'truth' that defines and eventually yields control over reality."

39 Moretti, "Dialectic of Fear," 77–78.

40 See Howes, "Mediation of the Feminine," 106–07, for a discussion of Harker's missing diary entries.

41 Aside from Moretti's essay, little has been written on Morris. Hatlen gives the majority view when he says that Morris's function is to become "an honorary Englishman," whose "reward" is "the privilege of dying to protect England" ("Return of the Repressed/Oppressed," 83).

42 Moretti extends these speculations by asking why "Lucy dies – and then turns into a vampire – immediately after receiving a blood transfusion from Morris" ("Dialectic of Fear," 76). I am indebted to his essay for pointing out that Morris is the first to mention the word "vampire."

43 Seed further points out that in Stoker's working notes for the novel Morris goes for an extended visit to Transylvania, though he suggests only that the proposed section "would have awkwardly complicated" the novel ("Narrative Method of *Dracula*," 63).

44 Stoker's ambivalence about America is more visible in his earlier *A Glimpse of America* (London: Sampson Low, Marston, 1886). Stoker claims a kinship between the two countries, since their citizens spring from the same racial stock, but he also sees America becoming racially different, and he suggests that the countries may become antagonistic in the future.

45 Mark Hennelly, "The Gnostic Quest and the Victorian Wasteland," *English Literature in Transition* 20 (1977), 23.

46 Quoted in Howes, "Mediation of the Feminine," 116.

6 SHERLOCK HOLMES AND THE PATHOLOGY OF EVERYDAY LIFE

1 Fredric Jameson, "On Raymond Chandler," in *The Poetics of Murder: Detective Fiction and Literary Theory*, ed. Glenn W. Most and William W. Stowe (San Diego: Harcourt, Brace, Jovanovich, 1983), 124.

2 See Percival Spear, ed., *The Oxford History of India*, 4th ed. (Delhi: Oxford University Press, 1981), 539–47.

3 *Letters from Charles Dickens to Angela Burdett-Coutts, 1841–1865*, ed. Edgar Johnson (London: Jonathan Cape, 1953), 350. The letter is dated 4 October 1857. Useful accounts of the uprising are Christopher Hibbert, *The Great Mutiny: India 1857* (New York: Penguin, 1980) and Pratul Chandra Gupta, *Nana Sahib and the Rising at Cawnpore* (Oxford: Clarendon Press, 1963). Patrick Brantlinger surveys the literary responses to the Mutiny in *Rule of Darkness: British Literature and Imperialism 1830–1914* (Ithaca: Cornell University Press, 1988), 199–224. For a study of Dickens's response, see Lillian Nayder, "Class Consciousness and the Indian Mutiny in Dickens's 'The Perils of Certain English Prisoners,'" *Studies in English Literature* 32 (Autumn 1992), 689–705.

4 John Clark Marshman, *The History of India, from the Earliest Period to the Close of Lord Dalhousie's Administration*, 3 vols. (1869; rpt. London: Longmans, Green, Reader & Dyer, 1871), II, 92.

5 Wilkie Collins, *The Moonstone* (1868; rpt. Harmondsworth: Penguin, 1966), 36. Further references to this novel are included parenthetically in the text.

6 See John R. Reed, "English Imperialism and the Unacknowledged Crime of *The Moonstone*," *Clio* 2 (June 1973), 281–90, and Tamar Heller, *Dead Secrets: Wilkie Collins and Female Gothic* (New Haven: Yale University Press, 1992), 144–47. Heller notes the parody involved in Betteredge's attachment to "that classic imperialist text *Robinson Crusoe*" (145).

7 At Dickens's insistence, Collins collaborated with him on a short story, "The Perils of Certain English Prisoners," which appeared in *Household Words* in the wake of the Mutiny. Collins's contribution to the story, though racist, is decidedly muted in its condemnation of "native atrocities" next to Dickens's genocidal fantasies. Collins's only other public response to the Indian uprising is notable for its indirection: "A Sermon for Sepoys" (*Household Words* 27 [February 1858], 244–47) offers a parable of good government that only obliquely addresses contemporary events. Its tone, as Anthea Trodd notes in her introduction to the Oxford edition of *The Moonstone*, is "pointedly unexcited" (xviii), especially given the general atmosphere of hysteria in Britain at the time.

8 Sue Lonoff argues for Collins's largely sympathetic portrayal of the brahmins and suggests that he may have been influenced by the Governor Eyre controversy of 1865. See *Wilkie Collins and His Victorian Readers: A Study in the Rhetoric of Authorship* (New York: AMS Press, 1982), 176–79.

9 Albert D. Hutter draws on psychoanalytic theory to decode the theft in "Dreams, Transformations, and Literature: The Implications of Detective Fiction," *Victorian Studies* 19 (December 1975), 181–209.

10 Ronald R. Thomas, "Minding the Body Politic: The Romance of Science and the Revision of History in Victorian Detective Fiction," *Victorian Literature and Culture* 19 (1991), 239. In a slightly different vein, Heller argues that "by juxtaposing the plots of courtship and colonialism, Collins suggests an analogy between sexual and imperial domination" (*Dead Secrets*, 145).

11 Again, this does not prevent us from making such connections now. I argue only that the novel does not give us warrant to do so. That *The Moonstone* does

not offer itself as a critique of empire is suggested by contemporary reviews of the novel, none of which (to my knowledge) so much as mention the subject of imperialism. For a representative sampling of these reviews, see *Wilkie Collins: The Critical Heritage*, ed. Norman Page (London: Routledge & Kegan Paul, 1974), 169–81. By 1890, however, Andrew Lang was trying to annex Collins in general, and *The Moonstone* in particular, into the kingdom of late-Victorian romance. See his obituary essay, reprinted in *Critical Heritage*, ed. Page, 264–72.

12 For enlightening accounts of how female development is plotted in the nineteenth-century novel, see Susan Fraiman, *Unbecoming Women: British Women Writers and the Novel of Development* (New York: Columbia University Press, 1993) and Jean Kennard, *Victims of Convention* (Hamden, CT: Archon, 1978).

13 Nancy Armstrong, *Desire and Domestic Fiction: A Political History of the Novel* (New York: Oxford University Press, 1987).

14 Miller, *Novel and the Police*, 50–51.

15 Martin Green, *Dreams of Adventure, Deeds of Empire* (New York: Basic Books, 1979), 57.

16 Jon Thompson, *Fiction, Crime, and Empire: Clues to Modernity and Postmodernism* (Urbana: University of Illinois Press, 1993), 68.

17 *A Study in Scarlet* (1887; rpt. Harmondsworth: Penguin, 1981), 9. Subsequent page references to this text, abbreviated *SS*, are given parenthetically in the text.

18 In addition to *The Sign of Four*, see "The Boscombe Valley Mystery," "The Speckled Band," "The Gloria Scott," and "The Crooked Man."

19 Arthur Conan Doyle, *The Sign of Four* (1890; rpt. Harmondsworth: Penguin, 1982), 119. Subsequent page references to this text, abbreviated *SF*, are given parenthetically in the text.

20 For Doyle's pro-imperial stance, see his accounts of trips to war fronts in Egypt (1896) and South Africa (1900) in *Memories and Adventures* (Boston: Little, Brown, 1924), 121–29, 148–94.

21 The quoted phrase comes from Collins's early novel *Basil* (1852) and also forms the title of Jenny Bourne Taylor's fine study, *In the Secret Theatre of Home: Wilkie Collins, Sensation Narrative, and Nineteenth-Century Psychology* (London: Routledge, 1988).

22 For Doyle's uses of the Mormons, see Lydia Alix Fillingham, "'The Colorless Skein of Life': Threats to the Private Sphere in Conan Doyle's *A Study in Scarlet*," *ELH* 56 (Fall 1989), 667–88.

23 I thus take issue with Thompson's claim that "in Conan Doyle's fiction, political problems become decorations, part of a colorful background" (*Fiction, Crime, and Empire*, 73).

24 Franco Moretti argues that detective fiction "exists expressly to dispell the doubt that guilt might be impersonal, and therefore collective and social." See *Signs Taken for Wonders: Essays in the Sociology of Literary Form* (London: New Left Books, 1983), 135. Similarly, John G. Cawelti writes of "the special emphasis in the classical detective formula on domestic crime or crimes

within the family circle, as opposed to political or social crimes," arguing that this emphasis serves to affirm "the basic principle that crime was strictly a matter of individual motivations" and not an effect of wider social problems. See *Adventure, Crime, and Romance: Formula Stories as Art and Popular Culture* (Chicago: University of Chicago Press, 1976), 99, 105.

25 Lawrence Rothfield makes the best case for the similarities between Holmes's power and the power of Foucauldian "discipline" in *Vital Signs*, esp. 140–41.

26 Catherine Belsey, *Critical Practice* (London: Methuen, 1980), 111. Belsey goes on to show how the Holmes stories, "whose overt project is total explicitness," are nevertheless "haunted by shadowy, mysterious and often silent women" who transgress "the values of the text" (114–15).

27 "A Case of Identity," in *The Adventures of Sherlock Holmes* (1891; rpt. Harmondsworth: Penguin, 1981), 33. Subsequent page references to this text, abbreviated *A*, are given parenthetically in the text.

28 The quotation is from "The Red-Headed League," *A* 51–52. The other allusions are to "The Noble Bachelor," "A Case of Identity," "The Man with the Twisted Lip," "The Red-Headed League," "The Copper Beeches," and "The Blue Carbuncle." Pierre Nordon rightly says of the Holmes stories that they comprise "an epic of everyday events," though he finds the tales more optimistic than I do. See Nordon, *Conan Doyle: A Biography*, trans. Frances Partridge (New York: Holt, Rinehart, and Winston, 1967), 247.

29 Rothfield, *Vital Signs*, 145.

30 In his autobiography Doyle recalls fondly his first meeting with Wilde, when both were commissioned to write stories for *Lippincott's*. Doyle contributed *The Sign of Four*, Wilde *The Picture of Dorian Gray*. Shortly thereafter Kipling's *The Light that Failed* appeared in the same magazine. (See Chapter 7 below.) For Holmes as aesthete, see Paul Barolsky, "The Case of the Domesticated Aesthete," *Virginia Quarterly Review* 60 (Autumn 1984), 438–52. For an opposing view, see Dennis Porter, *The Pursuit of Crime: Art and Ideology in Detective Fiction* (New Haven: Yale University Press, 1981). Porter argues that Holmes unambiguously "embodies the heroic qualities of an ascendant middle class" (157).

31 Stephen Knight, in *Form and Ideology in Crime Fiction* (Bloomington: Indiana University Press, 1980), makes the strongest case for Holmes as a bourgeois *ubermensch* whose task is to "assuage the anxieties of a respectable, London-based, middle-class audience" (67). He notes in passing Holmes's frequent failures, especially in the *Adventures*, but argues that this fact "does not weaken the hero's authority" (76–77).

32 See Sedgwick, *Between Men*, esp. 1–27.

33 Indeed, the disruption caused to Holmes's "Bohemian soul" (9) by Irene Adler is the very point of the story in Watson's view. For his part, the doctor says that he "never felt more heartily ashamed" than when he conspires with Holmes against "the beautiful creature" whose "grace and kindliness" they abuse (27). Yet significantly Watson's shame immediately turns into self-

reproach for contemplating what he calls "the blackest treachery to Holmes" (27).

34 Bertrand Russell, "Descriptions," in A. P. Martinich, ed., *The Philosophy of Language* (New York: Oxford University Press, 1985). The essays by Sebeok, Ginzburg, and Hintikka can be found in *The Sign of Three: Dupin, Holmes, Peirce*, ed. Umberto Eco and Thomas A. Sebeok (Bloomington: Indiana University Press, 1983). For a persuasive critique of such approaches to the Holmes canon, see Rothfield, *Vital Signs*, 130–47. There is irony to be found in such dismissals of "history" from readings of Holmes, since it is also conventional to praise the stories for their evocation of late-Victorian London's distinctive "atmosphere." For readings that attempt to give more texture to that historical atmosphere, see Knight, *Form and Ideology*; Derek Longhurst, "Sherlock Holmes: Adventures of an English Gentleman 1887–1894," in *Gender, Genre, and Narrative Pleasure* (London: Unwin Hyman, 1989), 51–66; and Christopher Clausen, "Sherlock Holmes, Order, and the Late-Victorian Mind," in *Critical Essays on Sir Arthur Conan Doyle*, ed. Harold Orel (New York: G. K. Hall, 1992), 66–91. Finally, in this context can also be mentioned the many works by devoted Sherlockians which attempt to apply Holmes's own mode of "curious analytical reasoning" in order to fill in gaps in the "biographies" of Holmes and Watson, rationalize contradictions in the canon, and so on. Ronald De Waal's *The World Bibliography of Sherlock Holmes* (Greenwich: New York Graphic Society, 1972), for instance, lists twenty-five periodicals concerned at least in part with Sherlockiana of this sort. The foremost example of the genre probably is William S. Baring-Gould, *The Annotated Sherlock Holmes*, 2 vols. (New York: Clarkson N. Potter, 1967). For those interested in pursuing these matters further, Baring-Gould offers an exhaustive bibliography.

35 Rothfield, *Vital Signs*, 135–45.

36 Foucault, *The History of Sexuality*, 1, 45.

7 KIPLING, RACE, AND THE GREAT TRADITION

For Kipling's works published before 1895, I have used *The Writings in Prose and Verse of Rudyard Kipling* (New York: Charles Scribner's Sons, 1899), which is based on Macmillan's Uniform Edition of 1895. Page references to these works are given parenthetically in the body of the text, keyed to the following abbreviations: *BW*: *In Black and White*; *DW*: *The Day's Work*; *LF*: *The Light that Failed*; *PR*: *The Phantom Rickshaw*; *PT*: *Plain Tales from the Hills*; *ST*: *Soldiers Three*; *UD*: *Under the Deodars*

1 T. S. Eliot, ed., *A Choice of Kipling's Verse* (London: Faber and Faber, 1941), 5–36. While Eliot is more concerned with Kipling's poetry, his remarks also apply to the prose fiction (my primary interest in what follows) since, in Eliot's view, the two are "inseparable" (5) and cannot be considered in isolation from each other.

2 Andrew Rutherford, "General Preface" (1987) to the Oxford World's Classics Reprints of Kipling's works.

3 *Rudyard Kipling to Rider Haggard: The Record of a Friendship*, ed. Morton Cohen (London: Hutchison, 1965), 51. The drama critic Brander Matthews recalls Kipling saying in 1891: "Well, I'm not an Englishman, you know." See *Kipling: Interviews and Recollections*, 2 vols., ed. Harold Orel (London: Macmillan, 1983), I, 140.

4 Edmund Gosse called Kipling "a new star" in *Century Magazine* 42 (October 1891), 901–10; his essay is reprinted in *Kipling: The Critical Heritage*, ed. Roger Lancelyn Green (London: Routledge & Kegan Paul, 1971), 105–24. For the Henry James quote, see his letter of 21 March 1890 to Robert Louis Stevenson, reprinted in *Critical Heritage*, ed. Green, 67.

5 Quoted in Charles Carrington, *Rudyard Kipling: His Life and Art* (1955; rpt. Harmondsworth: Penguin, 1970), 178.

6 This is my own count, from the information in J. McG. Stewart, *Rudyard Kipling: A Bibliographical Catalogue*, ed. A. W. Yeats (Toronto: Dalhousie University Press, 1959).

7 Rudyard Kipling, *Something of Myself: For My Friends Known and Unknown* (1936; rpt. Cambridge: Cambridge University Press, 1990), 53.

8 Cyril Falls, *Rudyard Kipling: A Critical Study* (London: Mitchell Kennerley, 1915), 16.

9 "Kipling," *Bookman* I (October 1891), 28–30; reprinted in *Critical Heritage*, ed. Green, 125–28.

10 *Critical Heritage*, ed. Green, 107.

11 See George Gissing, *Charles Dickens* (1898; rpt. Port Washington, NY: Kennikat, 1966), 28, 53–64; and G. K. Chesterton, *Charles Dickens* (1902; rpt. New York: Schocken, 1965), 181, 296. In *Essays in Little*, Andrew Lang named *Nicholas Nickleby* and *Martin Chuzzlewit* as Dickens's two best works and argued that the novelist's weakest period encompassed the decade stretching from *Dombey and Son* to *Little Dorrit* (125–27). I call attention to these evaluations not to ridicule them, but to underscore my point that the widespread preference for the earlier, more genial, more "English" Dickens (like Chesterton and Gissing, Lang sees the early novels as embodying a characteristically English sensibility) tells us more about the fin de siècle than about Dickens; the same of course can be said of our preference for the troubling later works.

12 Alan Sandison, "A Matter of Vision: Rudyard Kipling and Rider Haggard," in John Gross, ed., *The Age of Kipling*, ed. Gross, 128.

13 James Harrison rightly calls the *Plain Tales* Kipling's "tribal stories." Kipling's early stories of Anglo-India are marked by an intense group consciousness which distinguishes sharply between members and aliens. See Harrison, *Rudyard Kipling* (Boston: Twayne, 1982), 26. For a concise, informative account of the development of a self-conscious Anglo-Indian sensibility in the nineteenth century, see B. J. Moore-Gilbert, *Kipling and Orientalism* (London: Croom Helm, 1986), 1–30. The growth of this sensibility was reflected in the publication of the first Anglo-Indian dictionaries (Hobson-Jobson's and G. C. Gilbert's) in 1886. Moore-Gilbert also usefully places Kipling's early tales in a tradition of Anglo-Indian fiction.

14 Andrew Lang, "An Indian Storyteller," in the *Daily News* (2 November 1889); reprinted in *Critical Heritage*, ed. Green, 47–50.

15 Dilke, *Greater Britain*, ix. Subsequent page references are given parenthetically in the text.

16 In what follows I am of course condensing an extraordinarily diverse and contradictory body of material. In sorting out the complexities of Victorian race theory, I am most indebted to the following works: George Stocking, *Race, Culture, and Evolution: Essays in the History of Evolution* (New York: Free Press, 1968), and *Victorian Anthropology* (New York: Free Press, 1987); Nancy Stepan, *The Idea of Race in Science: Great Britain 1800–1960* (Hamden, CT: Archon, 1982); Christine Bolt, *Victorian Attitudes to Race* (London: Routledge & Kegan Paul, 1971); Michael Banton, *The Idea of Race* (London: Tavistock, 1977) and *Racial Theories* (Cambridge: Cambridge University Press, 1987); and V. G. Kiernan, *The Lords of Human Kind: Black Man, Yellow Man, and White Man in an Age of Empire* (Boston: Little, Brown, 1969).

17 For the coexistence of typological and evolutionary paradigms in Victorian race theory, see Stepan, *Idea of Race*, 83–110, and Stocking, *Race, Culture, and Evolution*, 42–68.

18 See Robert Knox's notorious *The Races of Men* (1850), particularly lectures I and II, for an extreme version of the argument that races are immutable and cannot adapt to new environments.

19 Sir Richard Burton, "Terminal Essay," in *A Plain and Literal Translation of the Arabian Nights' Entertainments* (London: Burton Club, 1886), 207.

20 Carl Vogt, *Lectures on Man: His Place in Creation, and in the History of the Earth* (London: Longman, Green, Longman, and Roberts, 1864), 402–30. William Z. Ripley, *The Races of Europe: A Sociological Study* (New York and London: D. Appleton, 1899), 584. Herbert Spencer is quoted in Dijkstra, *Idols of Perversity*, 161. There were distinct ideological reasons for taking the position that Teutonic peoples were unsuited to the tropics. It often served as the basis for polygenist typologies of race which denied the common ancestry of man. Even for monogenists, the unadaptability of races to altered environments reconfirmed the vast physical and psychological gulfs that separated Westerners from "natives" in the present day. See Stepan, *Idea of Race*, 88–93. See also her "Biological Degeneration: Races and Proper Places," in *Degeneration*, ed. Gilman and Chamberlin, 97–120.

21 For a good overview of late-century thinking on race and climate, see Alfred Russel Wallace's entry on "Acclimitisation" in the ninth edition of the *Encyclopedia Britannica* (1875–89).

22 Ripley, *Races of Europe*, 584.

23 "The Function of Criticism at the Present Time" (1864), in Matthew Arnold, *Poetry and Criticism*, ed. A. Dwight Culler (Boston: Riverside, 1961), 248.

24 Edward Carpenter, *Civilisation: Its Cause and Cure, and Other Essays*, 2nd ed. (London: Swan Sonnenschein, 1891), 37. The quotation in the next sentence can be found on 8. For a discussion of the relation between Carpenter's dis-

affection with British society and his vision of India as a realm of psychological, cultural, and sexual renewal, see Parminder Kaur Bakshi, "Homosexuality and Orientalism: Edward Carpenter's Journey to the East," in *Edward Carpenter and Late-Victorian Radicalism*, ed. Tony Brown (London: Frank Cass, 1990), 151–77.

25 According to Darwin, new varieties and even new species arose from the "crossing and blending" of existing varieties, making the borders between species fluid rather than fixed. Darwin had argued that a species continued to thrive only by taking in new blood. Such interbreeding combined with "slight changes in the conditions of life are apparently favourable to the vigor and fertility of all organic beings." See *On the Origin of Species* (1859; rpt. Cambridge: Harvard University Press, 1964), 276–77.

26 James Anthony Froude, *Oceana, or England and Her Colonies* (New York: Charles Scribner's Sons, 1886), 10, 17, 386.

27 George Curzon, Marquess of Kedleston, *Frontiers* (Oxford: Oxford University Press, 1907), 58.

28 *Critical Heritage*, ed. Green, 48.

29 Carpenter, *Civilisation*, 14; Lionel Johnson, review of *The Light that Failed* in the *Academy* 39 (4 April 1891): 319–20, reprinted in *Critical Heritage*, ed. Green, 88–92.

30 John Strachey, *India* (London: Kegan, Paul, Trench, 1888), 358.

31 Lewis D. Wurgaft, *The Imperial Imagination: Magic and Myth in Kipling's India* (Middletown, CT: Wesleyan University Press, 1983), 10. As Francis Hutchins points out, this sense of group identity was strengthened by the fact that Anglo-India's civil and military elite was drawn from a relatively narrow band of British middle-class society. See Hutchins, *The Illusion of Permanence* (Princeton: Princeton University Press, 1967), esp. 101–18.

32 See Rao, *Rudyard Kipling's India* (Norman: University of Oklahoma Press, 1967), 49.

33 See James Urry, "Englishmen, Celts, and Iberians: The Ethnographic Survey of the United Kingdom, 1892–1899," in *Functionalism Historicized: Essays on British Social Anthropology*, ed. George W. Stocking (Madison: University of Wisconsin Press, 1984), 83–105; and Hannah Arendt, *The Origins of Totalitarianism* (New York: Harcourt, Brace, Jovanovich, 1973), 158–84.

34 Havelock Ellis, "The Ancestry of Genius," in *Views and Reviews: A Selection of Uncollected Articles 1884–1932*, 2 vols. (Boston, Houghton Mifflin, 1932), I, 84. Ellis found "that among twelve eminent British imaginative writers no less than ten show marked traces of more or less foreign blood."

35 Arthur Balfour, *Decadence* (Cambridge: Cambridge University Press, 1908), 42.

36 "School-days with Kipling," in *Interviews and Recollections*, ed. Orel, I, 36. The full connotations of Beresford's description are worth unpacking. In noting how Kipling's forehead slopes backward from jaw to brow, Beresford invokes Petrus Camper's taxonomy of "facial angles," a taxonomy well

known in the late nineteenth century. Writing at the close of the eighteenth century, Camper established a hierarchy of head types, with the forward-sloping classical Greek profile at one end and the ape at the other. Though Camper did not equate a backward slope with an innately primitive character, later writers routinely made precisely that connection. Beresford is thus grouping his friend Kipling with the "lesser" African races. By calling Kipling's face "Mongolian," Beresford invokes a second hierarchy of head types, in this case the one offered by John Langdon Haydon Down. Down sought to establish, as the title of his 1866 paper puts it, "an ethnic classification of idiots." He argued that different forms of idiocy had their corollaries in different head shapes; the most hopeless cases had African heads, the next Malaysian, and so on. Only one of Down's classifications passed into common usage, "Mongolian idiocy," or what is now called Down's syndrome. One final note: as late as 1942 George Orwell was still suggesting that "one necessary circumstance" of Kipling's success "was that he himself was only half-civilised." See Orwell, "Rudyard Kipling," in *Kipling and the Critics*, ed. Elliot L. Gilbert (New York: New York University Press, 1965), 83.

37 See Kermode, "Secrets and Narrative Sequence," in *The Art of Telling: Essays on Fiction* (Cambridge: Harvard University Press, 1983), 133–55.

38 *Something of Myself*, 33.

39 "Rudyard Kipling as Journalist," in *Interviews and Recollections*, ed. Orel, I, 82.

40 In *Kipling and Conrad: The Imperial Fiction* (Cambridge: Harvard University Press, 1981), John McClure also notes that "Kipling assumes the same relation to the Indian community that he celebrates in his hero Strickland" (55). I concur with McClure's further suggestion that this identification arises from Kipling's fear that too intimate a knowledge of the racial Other may "threaten his identity as an Englishman" (53). Yet McClure finally sees Kipling becoming increasingly bound to Strickland's perspective, whereas, as I argue below, I believe the identification with Strickland to be troubled throughout the early fiction.

41 *Critical Heritage*, ed. Green, 169–72.

42 *Interviews and Recollections*, ed. Orel, I, 82.

43 Falls, *Rudyard Kipling*, 44.

44 James wrote an admiring introduction to the American edition of Kipling's *Mine Own People* (1891), rpt. in *Essays on Literature*, ed. Edel and Wilson, 1122–31.

45 The very moniker "City of Dreadful Night," carefully placed in quotation marks by Kipling himself, alludes to James Thomson's long poem of the same title (1873), which Kipling much admired. Thomson's London prowlings are themselves later versions of Dickens's.

46 *Something of Myself*, 13.

47 The most forceful recent rearticulation of this myth is Mark Paffard's in *Kipling's Indian Fiction* (New York: St. Martin's, 1989).

48 For the importance of philology in the nineteenth century, see Edward Said, *Orientalism* (New York: Vintage, 1978), esp. 130–234; and Dowling, *Language and Decadence*.

49 The first reference to the manuscript comes in a diary entry of 7 March 1885. The last known reference to it by Kipling occurs in an August 1904 letter to Robert McClure. Kipling's 1885 diary has been published as an appendix to the 1991 Cambridge edition of *Something of Myself.* Other connections between Kipling and Jellaludin are equally visible. Both favor the poetry of Browning and of the Pre-Raphaelites: Jellaludin quotes "Soliloquy of the Spanish Cloister" and recites *Atalanta in Calydon* in full, in addition to singing the Rossetti poem. Kipling, related to Sir Edward Burne-Jones through his mother's family, professed an early love, later renounced, for the Pre-Raphaelites. Browning remained a passion; Kipling liked to compare himself to Fra Lippo Lippi (see *Something of Myself,* 22). Jellaludin also twice mentions his "seven years' damnation." Seven years was the length of Kipling's stay in India.

50 *The Letters of Rudyard Kipling. Vol. I: 1872–1889,* ed. Thomas Pinney (London: Macmillan, 1990), 83, 85.

51 Cohen, "Writing Gone Wilde," 801–13.

52 Quoted in J. I. M. Stewart, *Rudyard Kipling* (New York: Dodd, Mead, 1966), 78.

53 Johnson, "The Light that Failed," *Academy* 39 (4 April 1891), 319–20; rpt. in *Critical Heritage,* ed. Green, 88–92. Vestiges of this position remain in many critical accounts of Kipling's work. J. M. S. Tompkins begins her much-praised study of Kipling by taking up the topic of "Kipling and the Novel" and claiming that it was one of his great "disappointments that he did not prove a novelist." See Tompkins, *The Art of Rudyard Kipling* (London: Methuen, 1959), 1. A lone dissenting voice was that of Henry James, who, in his Introduction to *Mine Own People,* designated Kipling's talent as one "eminently in harmony with the short story" and urged him to eschew the novel. James found *The Light that Failed* nearly unreadable, and by the late 1890s he had dismissed Kipling from the ranks of serious artists.

54 For a while he thought that *Mother Maturin* might be that work. "Heaven send that she may grow into a full blown novel" (*Letters,* ed. Pinney, 1, 99). Kipling was from the first intensely conscious of his works as physical objects, objects whose "meanings" were inseparable from their material forms and their modes of circulation. He thus involved himself in the design and publication of his works. See his posthumously published essay, "My First Book" (1941), in which Kipling recounts the different values that accrued to the verses in *Departmental Ditties* as the book itself changed form through successive editions, from "a lean oblong docket, wire-stitched" in its initial India publication to its final version "with a gilt top and a stiff back" and advertised in the "poetry department" of London booksellers. See *Interviews and Recollections,* ed. Orel, 1, 59–60.

55 Angus Wilson, for instance, in his otherwise sympathetic biography of Kipling, calls *The Light that Failed* "a farrago of misogyny and false heroics and self-pity," a comment that can be taken as representative of the critical

consensus. See Wilson, *The Strange Ride of Rudyard Kipling: His Life and Works* (London: Secker & Warburg, 1977), 155. Recently, Robert L. Caserio has attempted to recuperate the novel as a meditation on loss, death, creative jealousy, and "the failure and mortality of all picturings of the world." His stimulating discussion can be found in "Kipling in the Light of Failure," in *Rudyard Kipling*, ed. Harold Bloom (New York: Chelsea House, 1987), 117–43.

56 It is also, as many critics have pointed out, thinly disguised autobiography. Stewart calls Heldar "a kind of dream-Kipling" (*Rudyard Kipling*, 92). For the novel's autobiographical elements, see Carrington, *Rudyard Kipling*, 47, 189–91, 212–18; Wilson, *Strange Ride*, 140–43, 155–58; Carrington, "*The Light that Failed*: A Problem," in *The Reader's Guide to Rudyard Kipling's Works*, ed. R. E. Harbord, 8 vols. (London: Kipling Society, 1970), IV, 2231–42; and Pierre Coustillas, "*The Light that Failed* or Artistic Bohemia as Self-Revelation," *English Literature in Transition*, 29:2 (1986), 127–39.

57 Alice Macdonald Fleming, "My Brother, Rudyard Kipling," *Kipling Journal* 14 (December 1947), 3–5.

58 See Wilson, *Rudyard Kipling*, 140; *Letters*, ed. Pinney, I, 94.

59 Stewart voices the critical consensus when he argues that "the supposed necessity of proving himself capable of being a real 'novelist' had got the better of [Kipling's] judgement... [and] he arrived finally at a state in which he could be persuaded to make the most vulgar of concessions to meet the taste of both an English and an American magazine public" (*Rudyard Kipling*, 90). Blame for the *Lippincott's* conclusion has also been accorded to Kipling's mother and to his friend Wolcott Balestier; see Wilson, *Strange Ride*, 160–62.

60 See *Critical Heritage*, ed. Green, 106.

CONCLUSION MODERNIST EMPIRES AND THE RISE OF ENGLISH

1 T. S. Eliot, "Kipling Redivivus," *The Athenaeum* (9 May 1919), 297–98.

2 See David Trotter, "Modernism and Empire: Reading *The Waste Land*," *Critical Quarterly* 28 (Summer 1986), 152. Trotter's entire essay is apposite to my discussion here. See also Hugh Kenner, "The Urban Apocalypse," in *Eliot in His Time*, ed. A. Walton Litz (Princeton: Princeton University Press, 1973), 23–49.

3 See Frank Kermode, *The Classic* (London: Faber and Faber, 1975), esp. 13–80. Eliot's letter to Ford is quoted on 15.

4 *Ibid.*, 21.

5 C. F. G. Masterman, *The Condition of England* (1909; rpt. London: Methuen, 1960), 110.

6 John Carey, *The Intellectuals and the Masses: Pride and Prejudice among the Literary Intelligentsia 1880–1939* (London: Faber and Faber, 1992), 21.

7 See Daniel Pick, *Faces of Degeneration*, 222–40; and Greenslade, *Degeneration, Culture, and the Novel*, esp. 234–63. As Greenslade puts it, "If the diagnostic

value of the concept was shrinking in the eyes of specialists, it stubbornly refused to surrender its value as generalizing shorthand currency" (128).

8 On eugenics and national efficiency, see Kevles, *In the Name of Eugenics*; and Searle, *The Quest for National Efficiency.*

9 To give one reasonably straightforward example, the narrator of Isherwood's *Goodbye to Berlin* (1939) encounters a lively and self-amused doctor who has taken an interest in Christopher's friend Peter.

> "My work in the clinic has taught me that it's no use trying to help this type of boy. Your friend Peter is very generous and very well meaning, but he makes a great mistake. This type of boy always reverts. From a scientific point of view, I find him exceedingly interesting."
>
> As though he were about to say something specially momentous, the doctor suddenly stood still in the middle of the path, paused a moment to engage my attention, and smilingly announced:
>
> "He has a criminal head!"
>
> "And you think that people with criminal heads should be left to become criminals?"
>
> "Certainly not. I believe in discipline. These boys ought to be put into labour-camps."
>
> "And what are you going to do when you've got them there? You say that they can't be altered, anyhow, so I suppose you'd keep them locked up for the rest of their lives?"
>
> The doctor laughed delightedly, as though this were a joke against himself which he could, nevertheless, appreciate. [The doctor informs Christopher that he is being "idealistic" and "unscientific," then continues:]
>
> "Every week, one or two such boys come to my clinic, and I must operate on them for adenoids, or mastoid, or poisoned tonsils. So, you see, I know them through and through!"
>
> "I should have thought it would be more accurate to say you knew their throats and ears."
>
> Perhaps my German wasn't quite equal to rendering the sense of this last remark. At all events, the doctor ignored it completely. "I know this type of boy very well," he repeated. "It's a bad degenerate type. You cannot make anything out of these boys. Their tonsils are almost invariably diseased."

See Christopher Isherwood, *The Berlin Stories* (New York: New Directions, 1945), 89–90.

10 Brian Doyle, "The Invention of English," in *Englishness: Politics and Culture 1880–1920*, ed. Robert Colls and Philip Dodd (London: Croom Helm, 1986), 89–115, at 106. See also his *English and Englishness* (London: Routledge, 1989); as well as Chris Baldick, *The Social Mission of English Criticism 1848–1932* (Oxford: Clarendon Press, 1983); and Ian Small, *Conditions for Criticism: Authority, Knowledge, and Literature in the Late Nineteenth Century* (Oxford: Clarendon Press, 1991).

11 Peter Brooker and Peter Widdowson, "A Literature for England," in *Englishness*, ed. Colls and Dodd, 116–63, at 118–20.

12 See William Archer and Harley Granville-Barker, *A National Theatre: Scheme and Estimates* (1907; rpt. Port Washington: Kennikat Press, 1970); and Granville-Barker, *A National Theatre* (London: Sidgwick and Jackson, 1930).

13 See Eric J. Hobsbawm and Terence O. Ranger, eds., *The Invention of Tradition* (Cambridge: Cambridge University Press, 1983).
14 Quoted in Doyle, "Invention of English," 98.
15 *Ibid.*
16 *The Teaching of English in England* (London: His Majesty's Stationer's Office, 1921), 259.
17 See Gross, *Rise and Fall of the Man of Letters*, esp. 139–50, 158–63, 179–89.
18 On Churton Collins's attacks on belletrism, see Gross, *Man of Letters*, 159–60, 174–80; and Small, *Conditions for Criticism*, 59–61. A more comprehensive treatment of his professional life is given in Anthony Kearney, *John Churton Collins: The Louse on the Locks of Literature* (Edinburgh: Edinburgh University Press, 1986).
19 See Doyle, "English as a Masculine Profession," in *English and Englishness*, 68–93.

Index

A Rebours (Huysmans), 65
Adderley, Sir Charles, 157
All Sorts and Conditions of Men (Besant), 50
"Ancestry of Genius, The" (Ellis), 160
Archer, William, 43, 51
Arendt, Hannah, 160
Armstrong, Nancy, 138
Arnold, Matthew, 30, 71, 89, 94, 157
"Art of Fiction, The" (Besant), 43–45, 73
"Art of Fiction, The" (James), 44–45
atavism, 33–35, 111

Baden-Powell, Robert, 94, 208n54
Bagehot, Walter, 23–25, 29; anticipates degenerationists, 23, 25; historicizes character, 23; on imitation, 24; on style, 24–25; theorizes national character, 23–25; on progress, 25
Balfour, Arthur, 93, 160
Barber, Agnes, 99
Battle of Dorking, The (Chesney), 110
Belsey, Catherine, 144, 219n26
Beresford, George Charles, 160, 224n36
Besant, Walter, 49, 50, 73, 74, 90; and professionalization of writing, 44–46; on sympathy, 73–74
Boner, Charles, 114
Booth, Catherine, 57
Bourget, Paul, 191n58
Bowen, Elizabeth, 96, 97
Bowlby, Rachel, 60
Boy Scouts, 94, 208n54
Brantlinger, Patrick, 111
Bristow, Joseph, 71, 94, 209n55
Brooker, Peter, 182
Buchanan, Robert, 11–18, 26, 179; attacks Kipling as hooligan, 11–14; attacks Rossetti as fleshly, 11–14; and degeneration theory, 13–16
Burke, Edmund, 24, 25
Burke, Kenneth, 6, 7
Burton, Richard, 157
Butler, Josephine, 57

Caine, Hall, 89
Camper, Petrus, 223n36
Carey, John, 181
Carmilla (Le Fanu), 113, 114, 116
Carpenter, Edward, 158, 159
Carson, Edward, 55–60, 65–67, 200n14
Case of Wagner, The (Nietzsche), 30
Caserio, Robert L., 226n55
Cawelti, John G., 218n24
Chamberlin, J. E., 25, 91, 188n15
"Chapter on Dreams, A" (Stevenson), 47–50
character: *see* identity
Chesney, Sir George, 110
Chesterton, G. K., 154, 193n10
Chrisman, Laura, 100
Christie, Agatha, 132
Clarke, I. F., 110, 212n10
Clifford, W. K., 62, 201nn28, 32
Cohen, Ed, 55, 56, 85, 169, 203n44
Cohen, William, 70
Colles, William Morris, 44
Collins, John Churton, 183
Collins, Wilkie, 133–142; response to 1857 Mutiny, 135, 217n7
common sense, 3, 13, 74; as folklore of philosophy, 16–17; Wilde's critique of, 59, 74
Conrad, Joseph, 110, 177
Cook, E. T., 51
Crackenthorpe, B. A., 191n60
Craft, Christopher, 126, 128
Criminal Law Amendment Act (1885), 54, 56, 57, 60
Criminal, The (Ellis), 34
"Critic As Artist, The" (Wilde), 61, 65, 67, 75
Cross, Sir Richard, 57
Crowd, The (Le Bon), 25
Curzon, Lord, 80, 158
Cuvier, Georges, 157

Dakyns, Graham, 83, 204nn11, 13
Darwin, Charles, 3, 156–158, 160, 223n25
decadence, 5, 13; as form of degeneration, 6;

and homosexuality, 86–87, 198n2; and Modernism, 179; relation to masculinist adventure, 6
"Decadent Movement in Literature, The" (Symons), 18
Degeneracy: Its Causes, Signs, and Results (Talbot), 20
Degeneration (Nordau), 18, 27–32, 74; cited during Wilde's trials, 3, 54–55; as literary criticism, 27, 30–31; popularity of, 27, 32, reviews of, 27–28, 30, 191nn53, 60, 192n63
degeneration theory: and aestheticism, 35; and atavism, 33–34; and the body, 12, 14, 18–22, 60; and character, 22–23, 55–59; as class discourse, 2, 16–17, 31–32, 34–38, 180–81, 189n33; and common sense, 3, 13–14, 16–17, 58; and criminal deviance, 33–35, 55–56; as cultural criticism, 3, 14, 16–17; and English studies, 181–84; and the "faker," 20–21; and homosexuality, 55–59, 71–73; and hooliganism, 11–14; and hysteria, 29; ideological fluidity of, 17; and imitation, 29, 71; and imperialism, 79–80; interdisciplinarity of, 3, 14–15, 18, 30–31; and interpretation, 4, 19–22, 29–31, 36, 58–59, 64–65, 71–73; and literary criticism, 18–19, 27, 30–31; and literary writing, 12, 14, 18, 22, 26–28, 30–31, 72–73, 189n37; and morbid deviations, 13–15; and modernity, 12, 14, 25–28, 91; and multivalence of signs, 20–21, 29, 31; and older paradigms of decline, 3, 15, 34; pervasiveness of in fin de siècle, 3, 15; and physiognomy, 20, 31; and phrenology, 20,31; and popular fiction, 4–5; as professional discourse, 3–4, 18, 31–32, 33; and progress, 2, 25–26; and psychological illness, 21, 189n33; and sensuality, 11–13; and stigmata, 19–21, 28; and strong representations, 21–23; and style, 27, 29; in the twentieth century, 180–81; used to account for national and racial decay, 2, 14–15, 27–30, 180–81
Derozio, Henry, 165
detective fiction, 132, 138; and aestheticsm, 144–45; and deviance, 143–44; and erotics of interpretation, 145–50; generic conventions of, 143–45; Holmes stories as examples of, 143–50; ideology of, 143–44; *The Moonstone* as, 137–38
Dickens, Charles, 90, 93; and Kipling, 152–54, 160, 171–73, 175, 177; late-Victorian views on, 153–54, 221n11; response to 1857 Mutiny, 133–34, 217n7
Dijkstra, Bram, 188n22
Dilke, Charles, 107, 156–58
Dollimore, Jonathan, 70
Dowling, Linda, 85, 86
Down, John Langdon Haydon, 224n36
Doyle, Brian, 182, 183
Doyle, Sir Arthur Conan, 4, 5, 47, 80, 88, 89, 132–34, 137, 139–48; as apologist for empire, 139–40; defends Wilde, 144–45; and erotics of interpretation, 145–50; and male romance, 133, 145–47
Works: *The Adventures of Sherlock Holmes*, 143–50; *The Lost World*, 133; *The Memoirs of Sherlock Holmes*, 143–50; *Micah Clarke*, 133; *The Posion Belt*, 133; *The Sign of Four*, 137, 140–42, 147, 148; *Sir Nigel*, 133; *A Study in Scarlet*, 139–40, 142, 143; *The White Company*, 133
Dracula (Stoker), 4, 7, 111–32, 189n31; composition of, 113, 122, 214n19, 216n43; and the Eastern Question, 113; and empire, 113–16, 123–26, 128–29, 213n17; fears of racial decline in, 112–18, 125–26; as Gothic novel, 111–13, 126, 129–32, 212n14; misogyny in, 118–19, 215n27; Morris's functions in, 128–29, 216n43; narrative construction of, 126–29; "Occidentalism" in, 120–24; Orientalism in, 122–23; and racial identity, 116–17, 124–25; relation to earlier vampire fiction, 113–14; Renfield's functions in, 127–28; as travel narrative, 112, 121–23, 130–32, 215n30; vampirism and degeneracy in, 20; vampirism and race in, 113–18; and writing, 126–32
dynamite novels, 110

Edison's Conquest of Mars (Serviss), 212n9
Eighteen Nineties, The (Jackson), 5
Eliot, George, 22, 73, 74, 89, 93, 104
Eliot, T. S., 178–81, 183; on Kipling, 151–52, 176, 178–79
Ellis, Havelock, 18, 81, 191n58; collaborates on *Sexual Inversion*, 160; popularizes Lombroso's work, 34
empire: fears of decline of, 79–80, 94–95, 101–02; and Modernism, 178–80
English studies, 181–84
Eugenics, 98, 110, 181
Evans, Sir John, 99
Expansion of England, The (Seeley), 158

"Fall of Fiction, The" (Watson), 89–90
Falls, Cyril, 153, 164
"Fleshly School of Poetry, The" (Buchanan), 11–13
Ford, Ford Madox, 180
Forster, E. M., 181
Foster, Milton P., 191n53

Foucault, Michel, 17, 57, 64, 143, 149, 185n6, 187n12
Freedman, Jonathan, 46, 47
Freud, Sigmund, 3, 4, 19, 47, 48, 82, 148; on *She*, 95–97
Froude, J. A., 7, 158

Gagnier, Regenia, 59, 71
Galton, Francis, 18, 23, 98
Garnett, Edward, 192n63
Garrett, Peter, 198n57
Gerard, Emily, 116, 117, 121, 125
Gibbons, Tom, 186n13, 188n18, 191n58
Gilbert, Sandra M., 98
Gill, Charles Frederick, 55, 60, 205n19
Gilman, Sander, 2, 25, 91, 188n15
Ginzburg, Carlo, 148
Gissing, George, 154, 177
Godding, W. W., 21
Goode, John, 209n62
Gosse, Edmund, 32, 43, 45, 49, 153, 177, 183, 206n28, 221n4
Gramsci, Antonio, 3, 16
Grand, Sarah, 189n38
Greater Britain, 155–58
Greater Britain (Dilke), 156–57
Green, Martin, 95, 138
Greenslade, William, 2, 13, 17, 19, 185n7, 186n10
Gross, John, 183
Gubar, Susan, 98

Haddon, Alfred, 157
Haggard, Ella, 103, 210n72
Haggard, H. Rider, 5, 6, 13, 47, 51, 79, 80, 88, 95–104, 108, 111, 132, 147, 151; anti-intellectualism of, 93; belief in reincarnation of, 201n69; criticized by Watson, 89–90; influence of mother on, 103; on male romance, 92–93, 95; and the Sherd of Amenartas, 99
Works: "About Fiction," 92–93, 95; *Allan Quartermain*, 210n70; *King Solomon's Mines*, 99, 210n67; *She*, 95–104, 107–08
Harrison, Frederic, 93
Hatlen, Burton, 112, 216n41
Heavenly Twins, The (Grand), 189n38
Heller, Tamar, 217n10
Hennelly, Mark, 129
Henty, G. A., 139
Herbert, Christopher, 25
Herford, C. H., 182
heroic masculinity, 84–87
Hichens, Robert, 203n45
Hintikaa, Jaakko, 148
Hirsch, Gordon, 193n10
History of India, A (Marshman), 135
Hobsbawm, Eric, 182
Hobson, J. A., 94
Hodgkin, Thomas, 208n54
Hogarth, Janet, 27, 191n60
Holden, Hubert, 99
homosexuality: and class, 206n26; construction of in fin de siècle, 56–58, 81; and Criminal Law Amendment Act, 55–59; and decadence, 198n2; as form of character, 55–58, 81–83; and gentlemanliness, 86–87; as ground of civic virtue, 86; as paradigmatic form of deviance, 56; and "posing," 58, 200nn14, 16; and prostitution, 199n13; and "social purity," 57; and "spiritual procreancy," 85–87; Symonds on, 80–88; and transmission of culture, 87–88; and Western history, 84–85; Wilde condemned for, 55–59; in Wilde's works, 65–68, 202n44; and writing, 82–83
homosocial bonding, 74, 79–80, 208n52; in *Jekyll and Hyde*, 38–41; in "Portrait of Mr. W. H.," 68–72; in *She*, 97; in Sherlock Holmes tales, 145–47, 219n33
hooliganism, 11–14, 26–27, 186n2
Howells, William Dean, 48
Hutchins, Francis, 223n31
Huxley, Aldous, 181
Huxley, T. H., 23, 26
Huysmans, J.-A., 65

identity: and art, 63–64; and degeneration, 21–23, 54–56, 59–60; historicizing of, 22–23, 189n38; humanist ideologies of, 59–60, 62–63; and individualism, 61–63; in *Dracula*, 116–17; in *Jekyll and Hyde*, 51–52; and "posing," 58; and the tribal self, 62; and the unconscious, 48–50; and writing, 50–52, 55–57, 63, 65, 80–83
imperialism: compensatory functions of, 94–95, 157–59, 207n51; and domestic ideology, 138–39; and "Greater Britain," 156–57; and India, 134–36; and Ireland, 119–20, 211n2; as response to domestic crises, 79–80, 207n51; and Victorian race theory, 156–58
Indian Mutiny (1857), 134–35, 217n3
Inge, W. R., 181
Interdepartmental Committee on Physical Deterioration (1904), 17, 188n21, 208n52
interpretation: as decoding, 66–67, 71–72, 204n13; and detective fiction, 145–50; and degeneration theory, 4, 19; erotics of, 69–75, 145–50; therapeutic value of, 4, 19, 147–49, 183–84; in *Jekyll and Hyde*, 34–36; in "Portrait of Mr. W. H.," 68–72; and sympathy, 73–75
Interpretation of Dreams, The (Freud), 95–97

invasion scare novels, 110, 212n10
Irving, Henry, 120
Iser, Wolfgang, 122
Isherwood, Christopher, 181, 227n9

Jackson, Holbrook, 5, 6
James, Henry, 31, 74, 89, 110, 177; critiques Besant, 45–46; on Kipling, 152, 164, 225n53
Jameson, Fredric, 4, 133, 148, 186n16
Jeyes, Samuel Henry, 202n40
jingoism, 5, 11; as form of degeneration, 6; as response to decadence, 6
Johnson, Lionel, 159, 171
Jowett, Benjamin, 80, 81, 85–87

Keane, A. H., 157
Keating, Peter, 44
Kermode, Frank, 1, 161, 180
Kidd, Benjamin, 25
Kipling, Alice, 173
Kipling, Lockwood, 166
Kipling, Rudyard, 5, 6, 16, 18, 26, 80, 88, 92, 147, 151–81; adopts Dickensian models, 172–73; alienation from English culture, 151–52, 172, 175; and Anglo-India, 153–55, 163–66, 221n13, 223n31; attacked as hooligan, 11–14, 26–27; Eliot on, 151–52, 176, 178–79; as journalist, 163–64; influence of Browning on, 225n49; narrative strategies of, 161–71; as novelist, 171–72, 225n53, 226n59; and Orientalism, 165–67; prose style of, 153–54, 164–65; racial anxieties of, 161–62, 167–71, 174–75; "racial" identity of, 158–60, 223n36; reception of, in England, 152–55, 171–72, 176–77; seen as heir to Dickens, 152–54, 171–73, 175, 177
Works: "Baa Baa Black Sheep," 173; "Beyond the Pale," 162, 165, 169; *The Book of Mother Maturin*, 168, 225nn49, 54; "'The City of Dreadful Night,'" 163–64, 165, 224n45; "The Conversion of Aurelian McGoggin," 159, 165, 169; *Departmental Ditties*, 225n54; "His Chance in Life," 161–62, 165; "In the House of Suddho," 164, 165; "The Islanders," 177; *The Jungle Books*, 177; *Kim*, 155, 177; "The Last of the Tales," 173; *The Light that Failed*, 171–77, 225n53; "The Man Who Would be King," 162; "The Mark of the Beast," 169–71, 177; "Miss Youghal's Sais," 162–63; "Namgay Doola," 169; "The Phantom Rickshaw," 169; "Recessional," 177; "The Three Musketeers," 155; "Thrown Away," 165, 168, 169; "To Be Filed for Reference," 166–68; "Wee Willie Winkie," 161; "William the Conqueror," 164; "Without Benefit of Clergy," 162
Knox, Robert, 222n18
Koestenbaum, Wayne, 83, 103
Krafft-Ebing, Richard von, 81, 87

Lacan, Jacques, 60
Lamarckianism: in the fin de siècle, 23–26, 28
Lang, Andrew, 36, 47, 89–94, 133, 155, 158, 159, 169, 172, 211n2; on contemporary fiction, 89–90; defends Haggard, 90; on Dickens, 221n11; influence of Tylor on, 91; on Kipling, 153, 155, 158–59; on male romance, 92–93, 95, 218n11; on modern overrefinement, 90–92; rejects "Mark of the Beast," 169; reviews *Jekyll and Hyde*, 33
Lankester, Edwin Ray, 25–26, 91
Le Bon, Gustave, 25, 191n57
Le Fanu, Sheridan, 113, 114, 116
Lectures on Man (Vogt), 157
Lenin, V. I., 16, 207n51
Lepps, Marie-Christine, 194n17
Light that Failed, The (Kipling), 6, 171–76
Lippincott's Monthly Magazine, 175
literature: and national character, 1–2, 55, 181–84; as expression of individual character, 58–59, 65–66; as expression of degenerative tendencies, 12, 18–19, 27–28, 55–59; social functions of, 18, 63, 73–74, 181–84; and sympathy, 72–74
Lockwood, Sir Frank, 55, 60
Lombroso, Cesare, 3, 17, 18, 20, 58, 81, 82, 87, 91, 181; and atavism, 33–35
Lonoff, Sue, 217n8
Low, Sidney, 152
Lukács, Georg, 1

McClure, John, 224n40
McClure, Robert, 225n49
McKelvy, William, 194n15
"Maiden Tribute of Modern Babylon, The" (Stead), 57
Maitland, Thomas: *see* Buchanan, Robert
male romance, 79–80, 89–95, 139; compensatory functions of, 94; and cultural renewal, 80; in Doyle's work, 133, 145–50; as expression of male anxiety, 89, 92–95; and imperial ideology, 79, 94–95; in Kipling's work, 154–55
"Mark of the Beast, The" (Kipling), 169–71, 177
Marshman, John Clark, 135
masculinity: fin-de-siècle crisis in, 89, 92–95; and homoeroticism, 84–87; and male romance, 79–80, 89–95
Masterman, C. F. G., 180
Maudsley, Henry, 17, 18, 20, 25, 91; on degener-

ate writing, 26; historicizes character, 22–23; links degeneracy and modernity, 26
Miller, D. A., 138, 202n41
Miller, Henry, 97
Moonstone, The (Collins), 133–36, 138, 140, 141; as critique of imperialism, 134–36; and domestic realism, 136–38
Moore, George, 51, 207n45
Moorman, F. W., 182
Morel, Benedict-Augustin, 2, 3, 17–19, 21, 31 187n12
Moretti, Franco, 126, 216nn41, 42, 218n24
Mosse, George, 73
Myers, F. W. H., 51; suggests improvements for *Jekyll and Hyde*, 36–39

Nabokov, Vladimir, 47
national identity: and English studies, 181–84; and fictional narrative, 1, 185n1; theorized by Bagehot, 23–25; theorized by Renan, 24; theorized by Nordau, 28–29
Nietzsche, Friedrich, 27; on decadent style, 30
Nisbet, J. F., 18
Noble, James Ashcroft, 27
Nordau, Max, 3, 5, 17, 18, 20, 23, 25, 27–32, 35, 38, 71–74, 82, 181; called degenerate, 30, 191n60; catholicity of interests of, 27; critiques modernity, 27; on dangers of reading, 72–73; links writing with degeneracy, 28–29, 71–72; and realism, 44; as spokesman for bourgeoisie, 32, 73–74; uses scientific paradigms, 27–28, 31; on sympathy, 73–74; on value of critical reason, 30–31; on Wilde, 54–56, 72–73, 198n2
Nye, Robert, 15, 17

Oceana (Froude), 7, 158
Osbourne, Lloyd, 197n46
Ortega y Gasset, José, 181
Orwell, George, 224n36

Pater, Walter, 46, 47, 86, 89
Physics and Politics (Bagehot), 23–25
Pick, Daniel, 2, 15, 17, 110, 186n10
Picture of Dorian Gray, The (Wilde), 55, 59–68, 71, 75, 79, 88, 111; acting in, 61–62; cited during Wilde's trials, 57–60; and the Cleveland Street Scandal, 199n13; Dorian as aesthetic artifact, 60; as "fatal book," 65, 202n39; as "fragile text," 202n41; homoeroticism in, 65–66, 202n41; notions of character in, 60–62; taken as Wilde's autobiography, 64
Plato, 71, 80–81, 85, 86
Polidori, John, 114, 116
popular fiction, 1; as cultural criticism, 4–5; and degeneration, 4; and ideology, 132
Porter, Bernard, 94
"Portrait of Mr. W. H., The" (Wilde), 65, 68–72, 74
"Present State of the English Novel, The" (Saintsbury), 90–91
Prest, Thomas, 116
professionalism, 3–4, 19; and English studies, 181–84; and Freud, 96–97; and literary writing, 44–49, 93; and literary criticism, 19, 31–32; as prostitution, 49–50; and women writers, 93, 207n44
professional men, 4, 19, 31–32; in *Jekyll and Hyde*, 33–34, 38–43
Proust, Marcel, 47
Punter, David, 111

Queensberry, Marquess of, 54, 55, 57, 58, 200nn14, 16
Quiller-Couch, Arthur, 183

Rabinowitz, Peter, 202n41
race: and narrative authority, 161–71
race theory, 156–58, 222n16; and miscegenation, 159–60
Races of Europe, The (Ripley), 157
racial decline: and climate, 156–58, 222nn20–21; in *Dracula*, 112–18; fear of, 1, 90–94, 158–59, 208nn52, 54; and hybrid races, 159–61, 223n55; and miscegenation, 166–68, 170–71; in *She*, 101–02; in *War of the Worlds*, 109–10
Raleigh, Walter, 183
Ranger, Terence, 182
Rao, K. Bhaskara, 159
Renan, Ernest, 24
Rentoul, Robert Reid, 21
"Reticence in Literature" (Waugh), 12
reverse colonization, 107–11; in *Dracula*, 113–19; in *She*, 107–08; in *War of the Worlds*, 109–110
Rhodes, Cecil, 207n51, 208n52
Ripley, William Z., 157
Robertson, Graham, 67
Robinson, E. Kay, 163, 164
Rossetti, Dante Gabriel, 18, 167, 205n17; attacked as fleshly, 11–14
Rothfield, Lawrence, 144, 148, 189n37, 219n25
Russell, Bertrand, 148

Said, Edward, 161
Saintsbury, George, 32, 89–92, 183, 207n47
Sandison, Alan, 154
Scott, Walter, 111
Sebeok, Thomas, 148

Sedgwick, Eve, 74, 79, 88, 146, 206n26
Seed, David, 126, 128, 216n43
Seeley, J. R., 158
Senf, Carol, 112
Serviss, Garrett P., 212n9
Shaw, George Bernard, 177; critiques Nordau, 28, 30
She (Haggard), 6, 95–104, 107–08, 211n2; as allegory for psychoanalysis, 96; Ayesha's functions in, 96, 98, 101–03; composition of, 99, 211n2; and fatal woman tradition, 97; Freud on, 95–96; and late-Victorian science, 98; and "magic femininity," 96; male self-generation in, 98–101; misogyny in, 98, 102–03; and the New Woman, 98; power of writing in, 97, 103; racial decline in, 101–02, 210n71; and reverse colonization, 107–08; Sherd of Amenartas in, 98–101, 210n66
Shelley, Percy Bysshe, 24, 178
Shewan, Rodney, 62, 201n28
Showalter, Elaine, 92, 93, 104, 193n9
Sidgwick, Henry, 83, 205n17
Siegel, Sandra, 92
Sign of Four, The (Doyle), 137, 140–42, 147, 148; indebtedness to *The Moonstone*, 133–34
Sinfield, Alan, 203n45, 208n52
Society of Authors, The, 44–45, 93, 196n36
"Soul of Man Under Socialism, The" (Wilde), 62, 74
Spackman, Barbara, 12, 17
Spencer, Herbert, 23, 25, 61, 157
Spencer, Katherine, 216n37
Stead, W. T., 57
Stevenson, John Allen, 116
Stevenson, Fanny, 44, 195n29; criticizes first draft of *Jekyll and Hyde*, 197n46
Stevenson, Robert Louis, 5, 33–53, 74, 83, 84, 90, 93, 146; and his Brownies, 47–50; and composition of *Jekyll and Hyde*, 47–48, 197n46; critiques Besant, 45–46; disdain for bourgeoisie, 43–45; and male romance, 47; and the literary marketplace, 48–50; opinion of reading public, 43; as professional author, 43–44, 48–49; and socialism, 45, 196n36; and style, 44, 46–47, 51; writes Myers about *Jekyll and Hyde*, 36–37
  Works: "Books Which Have Influenced Me," 46; "A Chapter on Dreams," 47–50; "A Humble Remonstrance," 45–46; "The Morality of the Profession of Letters," 46; "On Some Technical Elements of Style in Literature," 46; *The Strange Case of Dr. Jekyll and Mr. Hyde*, 33–45, 49–53, 83, 111, 143; *Treasure Island*, 44, 195n28
Stevenson, Thomas, 44–45, 195n29
Stoker, Bram, 4, 7, 20, 80, 108, 111–31; conservativism of, 119–20; national allegiances of, 119–20, relations with Irving, 120; views on America, 216n44
  Works: "The Censorship of Fiction," 119; *A Glimpse of America*, 216n44; *Dracula*, 111–32; *The Jewel of Seven Stars*, 214n17; *The Lady of the Shroud*, 214n17; *The Lair of the White Worm*, 214n17; *The Man*, 213n17; *The Mystery of the Sea*, 213n17; *The Snake's Pass*, 213n17; "Under the Sunset," 213n17
Stokes, John, 2, 5, 32, 188n13
Strachey, John, 159
Strange Case of Dr. Jekyll and Mr. Hyde, The (Stevenson), 33–45, 49–53, 83, 111, 143; aestheticism in, 35, 37–38; atavism in, 33–34, 38–39; class discourse in, 33–35, 37–38, 43–44, 193n9; composition of, 47–48, 197nn46–47; as critique of bourgeoisie, 36, 43–45; decorum in, 40–41; and domesticity, 42–43; functions of Hyde in, 34–43; homosocial bonding in, 38, 40–41; and professional men, 33, 36, 38–43, 50; Lang's review of, 33; status of writing in, 50–52
Study in Scarlet, A, (Doyle), 139–40, 142, 143
Stutfield, Hugh E. M., 12, 13, 27, 30, 191n56, 191n60
Swinburne, Algernon, 27, 32, 167, 178, 179
Symonds, John Addington, 5, 79, 80–88, 98; criticizes Wilde, 88; critiques contemporary theories of homosexuality, 81–82, 87; on heroic masculinity, 84–87; on history of homosexuality, 84–86; influence of Jowett on, 85–86; influence of Whitman on, 204n10; influence on Wilde, 85; reads *Jekyll and Hyde*, 83; reads Plato, 80–81; relation to male romancers, 88; on vulgar homoeroticism, 86–87; on writing and sexual identity, 82–83, 204n11
  Works: *Memoirs*, 80–84, 86–88; *New and Old*, 83; *A Problem in Greek Ethics*, 82–83, 84–86; *A Problem in Modern Ethics*, 81, 83, 84, 87; *The Renaissance in Italy*, 83; *Sexual Inversion*, 81, 85; *Studies in the Greek Poets*, 86; *Vagabunduli Libelles*, 204n13
Symons, Arthur, 18, 191n58
sympathy, 73–75

Talbot, Eugene, 20, 22
"Teaching of English in England, The" (Newbolt Report), 183
Thomas, Ronald, 51, 136
Thompson, Jon, 139
"Tommyrotics" (Stutfield), 13, 27
Tompkins, J. M. S., 225n53

Transylvania (Boner), 114
Trevelyan, G. W., 166
Trollope, Anthony, 46
Trotter, David, 80
Tylor, E. B., 91

Ulrichs, Karl Heinrich, 87

Veeder, William, 193n10, 194nn16, 18, 195n19
Virgil, 180
Vogt, Carl, 157

Wagner, Richard, 30
Walkowitz, Judith, 193n6
War of the Worlds, The (Wells), 26, 108–10, 211n7, 212n9
Waste Land, The (Eliot), 179–80
Watson, William, 13, 89–91
Watt, A. P., 44
Waugh, Arthur, 12, 13
Waverly (Scott), 111
Weeks, Jeffrey, 199nn10, 13
Wells, Frank, 108
Wells, H. G., 26, 80, 108–11, 132, 160
  Works: *The Time Machine*, 26; *The War of the Worlds*, 26, 108–10, 211n7, 212n9
Welsh, Alexander, 21–22
Whibley, Charles, 199n13
White, Allon, 19
White, Arnold, 25, 180
White, Gleeson, 164
Widdowson, Peter, 182
Wilde, Oscar, 1, 3, 5, 6, 29, 38, 46–47, 54–75, 79–81, 84, 85, 88, 144, 177; on acting, 61–63; on authenticity, 62, 65; on character, 59–62; critiques common sense, 59; on "healthy" art, 63, 65; as homosexual "type," 55–56; and humanism, 59–63; on individualism, 62–63, 65; on interpretation, 65–75; and melodrama, 62; and morbidity, 63, 188n13; on personality, 60–63; and pornographic puns, 50, 203n50; rewrites Spencer, 61; as socialist, 62–63; on sympathy, 74–75; trials of, 54–59, 65, 68–69, 71, 75
  Works: "The Critic as Artist," 61, 65, 67, 75; "The Decay of Lying," 65; *The Importance of Being Earnest*, 66; *Lady Windermere's Fan*, 67, 71; "Lord Arthur Savile's Crime," 67–68; "Pen Pencil and Poison, " 65; *The Picture of Dorian Gray*, 57–65, 67, 75, 79, 88, 111; "The Portrait of Mr. W. H.," 65, 68–72, 74; "The Soul of Man Under Socialism," 62–63, 65, 74; "The Sphinx without a Secret," 67–68
Williams, Ann, 126
Wilson, Edmund, 132
Wilt, Judith, 112
Woolf, Leonard, 51
Wurgaft, Lewis, 159

Yeats, William Butler, 181

Printed in Great Britain
by Amazon

34875067R00142